# GOLF
# *Widow*

**A MEMOIR**

# KIM JULIAN

AUTHORS NOTE: This story is drawn from memories of real events that took place several years ago. Most names, except for those of my immediate family, have been changed. In telling our story I have tried to be truthful, and where possible, to verify my recollections against those of others.

ISBN: 0615469256
ISBN-13: 9780615469256
Library of Congress Control Number: 2011926916

"The human conflicts, which inevitably occur when death is certain, combine to make this account of Jeff Julian's life and those he touched an emotional spiral of human interaction."

-Tom Watson Hall of Fame golfer

"No story has touched me more in nearly 20 years of covering golf than that of the Julians. This book is a wonderful, emotional showcase of true love, unimaginable pain and inspirational resolve."

-Mercer Baggs
Award Winning Writer and Managing
Editor at GolfChannel.com

"Kim Julian's story is one very much worth telling and very much worth knowing. Any of us who have thought we had adversity in our lives can learn a lot about dealing with true adversity and finding a way, somehow, to come out at the other end of the tunnel."

-John Feinstein
NY Times Best Selling Author

# Dedication

To caregivers of the past, the present, and the future.
And FOR MY FAMILY

# *Acknowledgments*

Father James Woods, S.J.: Thank you for your wisdom, your guidance, your support, and your infectious laughter. Terri Giuliano Long: Thank you for so graciously giving your time, your energy, and your expertise to this project and thank you for helping me grow as a writer. Tom Zonay: Thank you for your wisdom and helping me through the aftermath. Tom & Hilary Watson: Thank you for your gracious support and encouragement, and for all you've contributed to ALS.

# *"Dream Chaser"*

I chased a dream one day. It seemed so distant so far away. Outside my human being grasp some said to me but with patience and persistence it was always mine to be.

At times my personal faith was all I had to see me through and then one by one others gathered around me to see what I could do.

I reached out beyond the heavens it seemed with expectations and places I shouldn't try to go then quietly my dreams became a reality with loved ones surrounding to help them grow.

Allusive and haunting, always dancing like ballerinas on floating clouds just on the edge of our mind's eye they soar and once you've chased and caught the first one you will and you should always be chasing more.

—J.R. Youngblood

# *One*

The Wednesday pro-am was long over and the sun was getting low. The course was beautiful, so quiet, and at peace. Nature seemed to be relishing in its own tranquility, in anticipation of the four days of abuse ahead: ball marks and divots inflicted by the best golfers in the world and a herd of fans trampling the lush green grass behind the ropes.

Jeff suggested we start on eighteen and play the holes in reverse. He was teaching me how to measure yardage with a pin sheet while my eight-year-old was lagging fifty yards behind us, trying to be quiet by preoccupying himself with nature, occasionally tossing a handful of grass into the air and watching with intent as the ocean breeze consumed the scattering blades. Every now and then, Jeff would turn and look back to check on him. When Tyler caught him looking, he would smile and give Jeff a thumbs up, signaling, "I'm OK, Dad."

Tyler had called and referred to Jeff as "Dad" from the moment we became engaged. He longed for a father figure, someone to look up to and emulate—a role my ex-husband had neglected to play.

Watching the speechless interaction between my son and my soon-to-be husband filled my heart and warmed my soul. However, the anticipation regarding the task at hand was trying to ruin the moment. I knew enough about golf after growing up with a golf-crazed father flaunting a five handicap, but I was no caddy. When my dad wasn't on the golf course, he was watching golf on television. Sometimes, if I begged long enough, he would take me with him, but he had very strict rules: Be as quiet as a mouse; don't ask to drive the cart, because the answer will always be *no*; when you're on the green, don't walk in a golfer's line; and never, ever repeat any four-letter words you overhear. These were the only skills I had been equipped with to help me survive the next two to four days as a caddy on the PGA Tour.

The field of roughly 140 was full that week, and Jeff was on the alternate list, which is made up of players who, because of their position on the money list, don't have first dibs on playing in the best tournaments. The money list is a player's nemesis, because to keep your PGA Tour card (and playing privileges) for the next season, you must be within the top 125 players in winnings, and you are competing with 230 other guys to be in that top 125.

The Sony Open in Hawaii is a favorite. Any event at a place as desirable as this with a high purse always fills up the quickest. The only way to get a spot in the field is to take someone else's. Unfortunately, if you're on the alternate list, you subconsciously wish injury or illness on another player. We knew Jeff's chance of actually getting into the event was slim, but we went anyway and accepted the fact that we might have to spend the entire week at the beach. We had been in Tucson the week before, where Tyler realized he was absolutely not a lover of the desert. This made the ocean even more enticing.

We had arrived in Honolulu late on Sunday night so that Jeff could play in the Monday pro-amateur event. A pro-am is open to any tour player who wants to spend five hours with a foursome of amateurs. Although a lot of work, they are a great opportunity to practice on the tournament course and at the same time make a little extra cash. The PGA Tour professionals are compensated for participating in these events, usually around $1,500.

This particular week Sony coaxed the players with a free Sony PS2 in addition to their regular compensation. The Sony PlayStation 2 had just been released and was selling like hotcakes for more than $300. When Tyler became privy to this information, he insisted Jeff play so he could bring one back for Tyler and his soon-to-be stepbrother, Keegan. Jeff's son was a year older than Tyler and lived with his mom in Vermont. Our two boys had been chumming it up fairly well during our weeks back home in Vermont, when Keegan would come stay with us.

Jeff played in that pro-am and returned with a PS2 in hand. His group that day had consisted of four Japanese men who didn't speak a lick of English. This made it impossible for Jeff to really engage them, a part of his job that he took very seriously—he loved teaching, talking, and laughing. From then on, during our weeks at home, Jeff had the pleasure of constantly reminding the boys of the pain and suffering he endured to obtain that PlayStation. "Five hours of charades, just for you mutts," he would say anytime he found the boys in the playroom with joysticks in hand. Jeff loved teasing them.

This was only our second event on the PGA Tour, and the glamour had already worn off. In and out of airports, the lugging, the laundry, the layovers, and traveling from one hotel to another was exhausting. It was especially exhausting for Tyler, who would have to spend the majority of his day being quiet, or whispering. His fourth-grade teacher had generously agreed to provide us with class work when we traveled. Three weeks of class work and assignments would keep Tyler up to speed when he returned to the classroom during our off weeks. To avoid boredom for Tyler, my strategy was to alternate an hour of class work in the clubhouse with an hour following Jeff's group, until the round was over.

Each week the tour would provide golfers a packet of information, including a list of hotels it recommended. We would be picked up at the airport by a driver, someone who had volunteered to shuttle players for the week, and delivered to the host course, where Jeff would register and pick up our courtesy car, almost always a Buick, but it depended on who the title sponsor was that week. Then, it was off to our hotel to check in, unpack, and acclimate to our new surroundings. Unbeknownst to me Jeff had taken the liberty of choosing a hotel that was not on the list that week. He thought it sounded perfect because it was right across the street from the beach and had a kitchenette that would give us the option of cooking in, because eating out got old quick. When we arrived it didn't seem so appealing. The lobby looked more like a counter at a small convenience store. We were exhausted so we resisted the urge to turn around and walk out.

When the clerk handed Jeff a large brass key with "666" engraved on it, we knew things would only get worse, and they did. Our suite was at the end of the hallway. Wood paneling lined the narrow entryway, so narrow that Jeff's shoulders practically brushed the walls as we walked from the front door to the living room. The bedrooms were so small that the beds took up all the floor space. It was very strange. We walked in, turned around, and immediately walked out. Jeff called his buddy Olin to ask where he and his wife Pam were staying, and a minute later we were headed to the Hyatt, which ended up being our home for that week.

On Tuesday we went to the beach, which was within walking distance from the hotel, and waited to hear if anyone had withdrawn. On the walk back to the hotel, Tyler spied a surfboard rental. Noticing that Tyler was intrigued, and assuming he wasn't going to get a spot in the field, Jeff told Tyler he'd always wanted to try surfing and asked him if he'd try it with him. Jeff had been so good about engaging him in anything and everything, treating him like his own son. Tyler's eyes lit up at the offer. "Wait till I tell my class when I get back!" he crowed.

Tim Clark withdrew on Wednesday afternoon due to a wrist injury. Jeff had just enough time to get in a practice round. We were all psyched—and a little bummed. Jeff promised Tyler they would go surfing even if it meant staying an extra day.

Caddies don't typically make the trip to Hawaii unless they have a player committed in advance. Jeff's caddy chose to stay behind, knowing the odds were against us. At any other event, several caddies would be hanging around hoping to snag a player whose caddy had fallen ill or who had made it off the alternate list. Hawaii was different: it was too expensive to go without having a firm commitment.

Tim Clark's caddy was nowhere to be found. My guess was he was already soaking up the surf and sun or on a flight home. Once this realization struck, Jeff looked at me and grinned, "Well, my beloved, will you be my caddy?"

I stood there, brow furrowed, biting my lower lip. "Do I have a choice in the matter?"

"Nope," Jeff replied, as an even bigger grin appeared. "I'll compensate you," he said, pausing to watch my reaction, "with a trip to the mall afterwards?" He knew I loved to shop, but he also knew I was no girlie girl and required more intellectual stimulation than a trip to the mall can offer. I gave him a shove. "You have a lot to teach me by tomorrow morning. Let's get out there."

We rushed to the pro shop and purchased a small golf bag, referred to as a "Sunday bag," which weighed several pounds less than Jeff's enormous staff bag. The sun was already getting low in the sky by the time we made it out for what would be a very short practice round, so Jeff decided we should just walk the course so he could take a look at all eighteen holes. Otherwise we'd be racing the sunset to play only four or five.

As we approached the apron of the eighteenth green, a golfer appeared. I let go of Jeff's hand, turned, and walked back toward Tyler, a finger to my lips warning him that a player was within earshot. The golfer was moving about the green slowly, gracefully tapping putts and carefully investigating the undulations of the green. As Jeff grew closer, the lone golfer looked up, abandoned his practice, and walked toward Jeff, smiling. They met in the middle with a handshake. An old friend, I thought. Slowly walking with Tyler to keep some distance, I watched them. I felt so light, so content, Tyler at my side. Jeff was so completely in his element. He belonged there on the golf course. It was clearly his sanctuary. Another handshake and then Jeff turned and walked back toward Ty and me, still standing at a good distance. He smiled as he came closer. "Sorry about that," he apologized.

"No worries. An old friend?" I asked.

"Zinger," Jeff said, referring to Paul Azinger, as he moved between Tyler and me, placing his arms around us, one hand resting on my shoulder, the other fatherlike on the nape of Tyler's tiny neck. "He told me it was nice to see me out here again. That was nice of him. Paul's one of the good guys out here, a true class act." Jeff was quiet for a moment. "He and Payne were good friends."

"Payne" was a name I recognized immediately, having heard it growing up. "Payne Stewart, right?" I asked, looking over at Jeff, who was suddenly sober. Payne had died in a plane crash in 1999. He was a PGA Tour champion from Springfield, Missouri, a town not far from my hometown of Branson. Coincidentally, Jeff and I had met in Springfield only five months before, when he was playing on the Buy.com Tour at the Ozarks Open.

"Yep, Payne Stewart. Tragic," Jeff answered. We continued on our walk, appreciating life and suddenly reminded to live it to the fullest.

Looking through the registration packet, I found that day care was being offered free of charge that week for players' kids. Oh, thank you, thank you, thank you, I thought. I was already stressed out enough about caddying. I hadn't yet met any of the players' wives, and pushing my kid on someone would not have been a good way of introducing myself. Later I would find that the few amazing women I would befriend wouldn't have given it a second thought.

My first "loop" the following day was relatively uneventful, but I did make a few mistakes. On the first hole, I was standing at the edge of the green; Jeff was waiting to putt for a birdie, while his playing partner, Paul Gow, was lining up his shot, a forty-footer for a birdie. When Paul finally hit the ball, it seemed to roll forever. The small gallery of fans gasped in anticipation of the outcome. Forgetting I was a caddy, not a spectator, I was getting caught up in the moment. Following the ball, I made a little knee-bending, breath-holding gesture in anticipation of the outcome. I topped it off with a smile of relief when, to my surprise, the ball dropped in the hole. My body language overall indicated that I might have been elated to see Paul make the putt. One couldn't deny that it was a great putt.

Jeff missed his birdie putt and made par. As we walked off the green to the next hole, he calmly but firmly said, "Kimberly, you may want to reserve your enthusiasm for my good putts." He was clearly pissed off—and rightfully so. I'd never seen him angry. I felt horrible. I had basically cost him a birdie on the first hole. Not a good way to start the round. I wanted to run to the Porta-Potty to cry like a girl. But I was a caddy, so I sucked it up.

After my faux pas on No. 1, I managed fairly well. Jeff actually enjoyed my being out there with him. It must have been my insightful comments, like, "It's an easy uphill putt," or, "What hole are we on?" Critical when you're calculating yardage with the pin sheet. I was wearing capri pants, which were not allowed: Caddy rules state that all caddies must wear pants no shorter than two inches above the knee or have the hem touching the top of their shoes, in stone, khaki, or navy blue. How can a girl be fashionable being held to these standards? Of course, my shirt had to be a golf polo and under no circumstances be sleeveless.

Jeff recorded a 4-over-par 74 that day, not great, but not horrible considering his caddy had no professional advice on the lay of the land and started the round by cheering for the competition. From that point on, we laughed about my blunder and wrote it off as the "Gow-wow incident."

Meanwhile, back at the tour day care, Tyler was going on six hours. I left Jeff practicing at the range and rushed to get him. They had set the day care up at a local middle school. I was greeted at the door by a policeman who asked for my credentials, more commonly known as my bitch pin in PGA Tour lingo. Just inside the door, a woman sat behind a table while another law enforcement official paced the hall. I wondered if they'd be taking me to a room where I would be allowed to talk to Tyler on a phone while separated by Plexiglas. "Yes, she's my mother," he would confirm before they released him to me.

The woman at the table asked for my credentials and license and asked me to sign something. I was led to the gymnasium, where I was greeted by an angry babysitter and Tyler, holding a white square of what looked like ceramic tile. On the front he had painted a yellow dog resembling the one we had back home. Next to the picture it read, "Max the Wonder Dog."

We referred to our yellow Lab, Max, as the wonder dog because he was rotten—the *Marley & Me* level of rotten. Assuming we'd live happily ever after, my ex-boyfriend, John, more commonly known as "Goober," and I had adopted Max when Tyler was five. John had moved to Branson from Los Angeles after we'd survived a long-distance relationship for a year. His mother, Janet, was the youngest of Lawrence Welk's Lennon Sisters. All four sisters were living and performing for the Welk Theater in Branson. There were probably more than thirty members of the Lennon family living in Branson by the time John made the move. I loved him to death and loved his family too. We were certain we'd be together forever, so adding a puppy to the family was kind of like adding a child John had fathered to go with the one he had not.

Well, Max ended up being a neurotic pain in the ass. I had him neutered at six months old. When I picked him up after the surgery, he jumped up on me several times before I could get him settled down. "I don't think this guy is going to calm down for a long, long time," the vet stated, knowing I'd hoped the surgery would somehow remedy his rambunctiousness. John and I broke up not long after he gave me a Crock-Pot for our third Christmas. Not that I expected anything more; I actually loved the slow cooker. We were simply in different places. He was going back to college and I was a single parent. Anyway, I was awarded full custody of Max after the breakup.

Standing there in the gymnasium, still out of breath from rushing, the unhappy sitter informed me that the day care was not a child-care facility but rather a place for players' wives to drop their children off for a few hours, providing them a break. A break? In Hawaii? I thought. I apologized to the warden and explained that I really needed help for at least one more day. Considering how Jeff was playing, we'd be at the beach on Saturday and Sunday. She sympathized and agreed, with reluctance. Tyler thanked her for helping him make the tile, and we were set free.

Jeff missed the cut after shooting a 72 on Friday. Paul Gow missed it too, thank goodness. The weekend was spent on the beach, of course. The boys rented surfboards, just as Jeff had promised. I sat on the beach with my camera at the ready and watched them wrestle with those surfboards for over an hour. Finally, Jeff held on to Tyler's board while Tyler climbed up for a photo. He couldn't possibly return to Vermont without proof of his newfound surfing prowess. They decided to lie on the boards while letting the tide bring them closer to the shoreline.

As I watched the two of them laughing and being typical boys, I wondered what I had done to deserve such contentment. I felt truly blessed.

# Two

My best friend, Honey, and I both worked for Comrade Entertainment, also known as the "Yakov Smirnoff Show" (famous Russian comedian before the wall came down; mid-eighties; Miller Lite commercials; jokes about the KGB). I had been working for Mr. Smirnoff for about three years as a performer, portraying the Statue of Liberty. During my number Yakov would tell the story of his first days in America. This story would culminate in a very emotional song, at which point the main curtain would open, exposing a screen referred to as a scrim. The scrim is a translucent screen, but when lights are shining directly on it, no one can see what is behind it.

I, however, could see everything from where I stood on the other side, like a statue, high on my perch overlooking Ellis Island. Once Yakov reached the first chorus, "Sweet Lady, Liberty," the scrim would be yanked from the floor to the rigging above, revealing me standing completely still and statuesque for the remainder of the song. I would spend a little over a minute in this position, trying not to give away the fact that I was a real girl in green paint.

While patriotism consumed the audience, Yakov would walk off stage to greet and touch the entire front row. The famous Russian comedian would then return to the stage, climb the steps of my prop to join me where I stood in my green costume and painted skin, and bring me to life. The audience would gasp, and then Yakov would walk me down to the stage, where we would waltz, Viennese style, before he returned me to my perch in the harbor, and I would go back to my statuesque form as fireworks spewed from both sides of me. I'm not sure why, but the crowd absolutely loved it.

The day I had interviewed for the role, I wasn't at all expecting what took place. The busy carpeting of red, gold, black, and green made my head spin when I walked into the theater. An elderly woman with a kind smile sat in an enclosed counter at the center of the lobby. She wore a black and gold vest resembling the carpet, a neatly pressed tuxedo shirt, and a black bowtie around her neck. I informed her I was there to interview for the role of Lady Liberty.

"What's your name, hon?" she asked, so nice it seemed unnatural.

"Kim. Kim Youngblood," I replied.

"OK, dear, have a seat and I'll let them know you're here," she said, smiling.

The lobby was suddenly flooded with people, mostly older folks who looked as though they frequented the all-you-can-eat buffet at Golden Corral. This explained why Yakov had no evening shows, only morning and afternoon: the majority of his target market was in bed by eight.

The gaudiness of the inside and outside of the theater somehow matched the clientele. The crowd stirred as Yakov emerged, still in costume, and made his way to the autograph-hungry crowd.

Bored, I returned to my inspection of the place and spotted one wall covered with several framed photos that were all the same in size. All the photos were of Yakov with a celebrity, a Miss America, a famous athlete, or a president. There was one of him with Nancy Kerrigan. He was wearing the same cheesy grin in all of them. As the midday sunlight seeped in the large windows at the entrance, the light revealed black marks on Yakov's head and beard. I moved in for a closer inspection, squinting, wondering if I was seeing what I thought I was seeing. Oh my, his grey is being concealed by a Sharpie! I thought. Giggling as I entertained myself with this discovery, I realized someone was standing behind me.

"Keeem?"

"Oh, yes, hi, hello." I quickly stood up straight, abandoning the wall of fame, and struggled to keep a straight face.

"I'm Yakov Smirnoff."

As if I didn't know. The mink Cossack hat on his head was exaggeratedly big. He couldn't be more than five foot eight without it. He had very good posture, disguising the natural droop of his shoulders.

"Nice to meet you, Mr. Smirnoff."

"Call me Yakov. So, you want to paint yourself greeeeen?" he asked with that cheesy grin. The role of Lady Liberty involved an hour of painting exposed skin with theatrical makeup before every performance.

"Of course, who doesn't?" I replied, trying not to be condescending.

"Can you dance?" he asked.

"Uh, yes, I can dance."

"Well, let's dance."

"Um, here?"

"Why not?" he replied nonchalantly.

I looked around me to find people still gathered in the lobby looking our way. Is this how an audition is supposed to be conducted? I wondered.

"Waltz, right?" I inquired, feeling it would be best to confirm which steps I would be taking. Minor details.

"Yup, that's what the number requires," he replied, as if I were supposed to know.

He stepped in too close to me, lifted his left hand to meet my right, and wrapped his right arm around my waist to the point that our form was totally incorrect. After ten seconds I concluded that he was insecure, had no rhythm, and following his lead would be a challenge.

Once we stopped abruptly, the audience members still lingering applauded. I wondered why in the hell they were clapping. We must have looked like a clumsy mess.

"Tomorrow, come to the morning performance and watch. That way you'll know what to do, and we'll give you a trial run in the afternoon show. Let's see how it goes," he said, in a bossy Russian tone.

"A trial run? You mean a rehearsal?"

"Yup, on stage, in front of the afternoon audience," he was obviously proud of his ability to terrify me, and I despised him for it.

"By the way, how many counts?" The waltz has a basic one-two-three count, but knowing how many steps we'd be taking was vital.

"Just follow my lead."

What a jackass, I thought. But I wanted the job. The money was great and would require only around thirteen hours per week once I became efficient at applying the makeup. I had recently resigned from my job as a manager for J. Crew, because it didn't provide a flexible enough schedule that would allow me to be home with Tyler in the evenings and on weekends. I came to the realization that as a single mother the only way to obtain this would be to work for myself. I had started cleaning houses and in no time had a full clientele, which gave me the idea of hiring a staff and building a real business. Now, working for the theater would allow me to do just that while making extra cushion money.

Watching the morning show was not at all helpful and only made me more nervous about the afternoon. My predecessor, Theodora, was a professional dancer and choreographer. Her husband, Mark, was the only American in the Russian dance troupe. John and I had taken ballroom lessons together when we were dating, but I was no professional. I was clearly out of my league. Thankfully, the actual dance number was very short and looked as though it would be the easy part. I watched Theodora's feet closely. It wasn't easy to see her feet under her long green costume, but I came up with six counts. I thought I would for sure be a disgrace up there, even with a very short dance number.

During my first performance, the main curtain went up, and I could clearly see the audience. I thought my heart was going to pop out of my chest. Having seen the show only once, I had forgotten that it was impossible to see Lady Liberty behind the scrim when the main curtain opened. Standing as still as I could, looking down at the floor, I felt my body moving with my heartbeat. I was certain everyone could see that I wasn't a statue and I was blowing the entire finale.

At once the scrim lifted dramatically; "Sweet...Lady...Liberty, You are the face of freedom for me," Yakov sang. My heart started beating even faster. I thought the song would never end. My arm began to ache so badly that I didn't think I was going to be able to hold the torch up until he came to relieve me. At last he climbed the steps to the prop and touched my arm. I looked up, moving quickly, as if he had surprised me, and the crowd gasped and applauded as Yakov led me to the dance floor. Even though we were completely out of synch for the short six counts we danced, it gave me a rush I'd never felt before.

I was hired for the role of Lady Liberty, and after the first few nerve-wracking shows, I convinced my dance partner to take private lessons with me. A wonderful instructor named Don started coming to the theater to teach my partner how to lead, making my job of following much easier.

Dick and Terry were the backstage hands who worked diligently helping Yakov with quick changes, controlling the main curtain and scrim, and handling any emergency. Like the time my friend David, also known as Slim Chance, the other comedian in the show, had difficulty lighting his finale on fire. Dick's arm suddenly came out from behind the curtain with a lighter in his hand. The crowd thought it was part of the act. Dick took me under his wing, always making sure I had what I needed and helping me find my way to the top of my prop in the pitch black, until I was comfortable doing it on my own.

I got to know Yakov and acquired the ability to see beyond his quirkiness. Chatting backstage daily I realized he wasn't so bad. After I'd been performing for four months, he approached me one day and suggested there was a better use of my time than cleaning houses.

"Well, sir, I know that, actually; but spending time with Tyler is the absolute best use of my time, and cleaning houses makes that possible. Besides, I'm a neat freak and love to clean. I honestly like doing it," I explained.

"How about you clean your own house and be my theater ambassador? You'll work on marketing me; you know, schmoozing the public. I know you'll be very good at it," Yakov replied, encouraging me to accept the position.

I agreed to give it a try. During the hours I wasn't on stage, I worked with our outsourced marketing agent to create campaigns, find billboards with good visibility, and promote Yakov within the local community. It was fun, and, as Yakov had predicted, I was good at it.

Honey was Yakov's executive assistant. She also fulfilled the duties of a personal assistant, even though this chore was not on her job description. He drove her completely insane with his idiosyncrasies and proclivities. If she started one task, he'd either change it midway or have her stop what she was doing and begin something completely different. He'd be out gallivanting around somewhere and end up in a cow field. We didn't have GPS in the late nineties, so Honey was always the one he called.

"Yakov, look around you, what do you see around you?"

"I see cows, lots and lots of cows."

Even with the negatives, Honey and I shared the same love for working at the theater and the people we worked with, even that crazy Russian.

We had a post-lunch ritual that consisted of making laps around the theater while discussing current issues. I had just turned thirty and hadn't dated anyone since my breakup with John, the first man that I'd opened our lives to since I divorced Ty's dad. John had a profound effect on Ty. John's nickname, Goober, combined with being a video game savant was enough to enamor an eight-year-old.

I married young, at twenty, to a man six years older. I had Tyler at twenty-two and divorced by age twenty-four. The complexity of a six-year age gap, the maturation of my frontal lobe, and having nothing in common were minor compared to his denial of a drinking problem. Not the kind of drinking that occurs daily; rather, the kind that just won't stop once it begins and then ends up on the floor for someone to clean up.

He once told me he was tired of raising me. I was so young and naïve when we were together. Well, I grew up, and he just stayed where he was, holding me back with himself.

When Tyler was a year old, I gave his dad an ultimatum, and he called my bluff—but it wasn't a bluff. He refused to get help with his drinking issue. I insisted we sell the home my parents had helped us purchase in Atlanta a year earlier and move back home to Branson. I was almost hoping Tyler's dad wouldn't come with us, but he did. He quit his job with hopes of starting his own business in Branson with the profit we made on the house, which was essentially my parents' money.

The first thing my father said was, "You're not moving back home," with a grin. I understood and agreed with him. Then he suggested a mobile home park that he owned. I cringed, but accepted the reality of our situation.

I knew my marriage was ending, because I knew Tyler's dad would never get help. I had lost all respect for him. I had every intention of divorcing him and began preparing myself to be a single parent. The loan payment for a new mobile home costing under $300 per month along with the free space rental dad offered would ease the financial burden I was about to endure. I was surprised to find that the home we'd be living in was brand new, 16 feet wide and 80 feet long, had a huge living room, two bedrooms, each with a full bathroom, and central air. The best feature of all, my grandfather. Ever present in my life as I grew up, he lived at the bottom of the hill within walking distance and would now be close to Tyler.

I came to the conclusion that there were worse places to live. The majority of tenants were older couples who migrated to Florida every winter. The grounds were kept pristine, and strict rules my father had put in place prevented the park from becoming the stereotypical trailer park; mullet haircuts (business in the front, party in the back), grimy Hanes undershirts more commonly known as wife beaters, and cars on blocks surrounded by overgrown grass.

Our lot was at the end, on a cul-de-sac. The tiny, private backyard was shaded with big trees, and a big wooden fence separated the park from the property next door, which happened to be a funeral home. My uncle built steps leading to a deck at the front door big enough to have a table and two chairs out there.

I found a great daycare for Tyler and went back to work. I filed for a legal separation, and the divorce was final within a few months. Tyler's dad promised me he wouldn't drink when Tyler was in his care. I don't know why I believed him. I guess I simply wanted to. I didn't want Tyler's life to be completely disrupted. He needed a father.

Here I was six years later, still a single, divorced, thirty-something single mom whose life revolved around her child. When you're a single parent, you're always in a different place than those who aren't. It's inevitable. After my relationship with John failed, I became keenly aware that I needed to be with someone in the same situation that I was in, or with no one at all.

During one of our post-lunch walks around the theater, Honey suggested we create—verbally create, that is—a man who possessed every characteristic I saw as a must-have.

"What?" I said, not sure she was serious, but the look on her face told me she was dead serious. "OK, fine, let's make a man," I said grudgingly, rolling my eyes.

"He's six feet tall and has dark hair. I know you love dark hair," Honey said, as we briskly tended to our first lap.

"Yes, dark hair is good, but the height thing. You know I'm naturally attracted to men who aren't what one would consider tall," I replied.

"Yes, but we're changing that. You stand at five feet and nine inches! You need a tall one." Honey knew me well, even better than I knew myself. "Now, does he have a scar or facial hair?" she wondered out loud in a completely serious tone.

"Yes, I love scars, but no facial hair, please," I replied, playing along without enthusiasm.

"When you're on stage, he'll sneak into the office and leave poems on your desktop. You'll be delighted when you return to your desk!" Honey exclaimed, getting way too much enjoyment out of this.

"His name is Finnegan," I insisted. Giving him a name was fun, like naming a new puppy.

Honey looked at me. "Finn will have broad shoulders, won't he?" she questioned glibly, nodding.

"Yes, Finn has broad shoulders. A must with the amount of baggage he will be toting around," I replied. My smirk turned into a smile, and we both laughed out loud.

"Does he wear a suit or some kind of uniform to work?" she asked.

"I don't care, but after a long day of work, he throws on a pair of chinos and we prepare dinner together while sipping on a nice red." I knew she wouldn't quit until I was playing an active role in the conversation. It was silly, but it did get me to thinking. How many of us actually know what we want, and moreover, how many of us stick to what we want without settling? It's important that you still have enough in common with your mate to stick with him or her after the new wears off and you realize every relationship has the same struggles.

A few weeks later, I was having dinner with a friend, Will, who was a writer, a yogi—you know, your modern-day hippie. Will was in town co-writing a book with Yakov. Will was very spiritual, new age, and always full of frou-frou advice, albeit enlightening. His longish, wispy gray locks and the way he sat with his legs crossed made him look so wise you almost felt obligated to listen to him. During dinner I was moving from one topic to the next, telling Will about my fear of being thirty and about the man-of-my-dreams Honey and I had created, while he tried to cajole me into thinking that life as a thirty-something was going to be full of wonderful experiences. Having been thrown into what felt like a premature midlife crisis, I wasn't convinced.

"Your thirties will be the most amazing years of your life!" Will said, wide-eyed and smiling. I resisted and changed the subject to the new car I had bought that week.

Will was quite intrigued by the story of Finnegan. "Did you write this down?" he asked. Expecting him to give me a mantra or yoga pose that would manifest this man of my dreams, I couldn't help but giggle. "Of course not."

"Write it all down, then take the paper outside on a clear night and burn it. Release it into the universe, give it to God," Will said, lifting his hands toward the ceiling.

I leaned forward, "You're not serious, are you? Are you and Honey in cahoots?"

"No, Honey is not my co-conspirator. Just do it," Will said with confidence. "You'll be amazed; just wait and see."

So I did.

I wrote it all down on a piece of notebook paper, and on the next clear night, I did it. The air was crisp but not cold that night, and the sky was so clear it danced with even the tiniest of stars. I held a lit match in one hand and the piece of paper with my scribbled must-haves in the other and began to pray out loud, "Find me where you know I need to be," over and over again. I lit the paper and watched the edges curl up slowly, burning every word I had written on it. I let go and stood watching as the cindered pieces floated gently upward and disappeared into the darkness. I couldn't deny it; there was something spiritual about it.

The month of May came and went.

In June, Tyler turned eight. He requested an extraterrestrial theme and a party with horseback riding. I didn't know why he decided aliens and horses together. The kids had a blast. I took photos of all of them on their horses, and Tyler handed them out later as party gifts.

July came and went. Still no sign of Finn, my fictitious significant other whom I had attempted to conjure by burning him on a piece of notebook paper.

Now, here we were in August, and I was beginning to have doubts as to the validity of Will's suggestion. About to feel sorry for myself, I suddenly remembered how lucky I was. Tyler was happy, and I was happy. Life was good.

# Three

That August, the twelfth to be exact, my friend Diane called to ask me if I would go out with her that night to a barbecue/post-tournament party in Springfield at the Buy.com Ozarks Open. Diane had a thing for golfers and wanted to go, but I was returning from a yoga class and was looking forward to curling up with a good book.

"Sorry, I'm just not up for it tonight," I replied, cringing because I find it difficult to say no to friends. "Tyler will be back from his dad's early tomorrow, and I want to be well rested," I continued, feeling I needed to explain myself. "Max has been cooped up all day too, so I need to dedicate some time to him. If I don't, there will be hell to pay."

"Are you sure? Come on, a lot of cute golfers will be there." Diane was persistent.

"I'm sure there will be, but I have to pass tonight. I'm sorry." I had no intention of giving in this time. I knew how I wanted to spend my evening, and it wasn't mingling with golfers, regardless of how cute they were.

Tyler had been with his dad for two months of his summer vacation. I couldn't wait to have him back and was also looking forward to one last night of peace. Just as I was thinking that saying no to Diane was beginning to feel kind of good, I said, "OK, why not, I'll go." Why, I thought, did I just say that?

"Great!" Diane was thrilled to have a wingman. I was wondering what evil spirit was taking over my body, making poor decisions.

Diane and I decided to meet at a commuter lot just off Highway 65 northbound around eight p.m. I continued on my way home, dreading the evening to come.

At home my Labrador, Max, greeted me and forced his way out before I could close the door. I ignored him and chose to check my voicemail before chasing after him. Tyler had called around eleven o'clock that morning when I was in yoga. My mother had called, too. Even if we had nothing in particular to discuss, speaking on a daily basis was the norm.

I spotted Max in the backyard, anxiously sniffing around and stopping to scratch occasionally, like a coke addict needing a fix. "Want a cookie, Max? Maxie? Come on, good boy," I pleaded. He stopped and turned to look at me. "Good boy, Max! Come to Mommy." I thought I had him, but he turned and ran farther up the hill, along the fence line. A few times before, he had run out of the park to the funeral home next door, behind which sat a reservoir—for what, God only knows—and Max enjoyed swimming in it. Frustrated at Max and at the plans that I had made for that night, I went inside the house. "I hope that idiot dog drowns," I mumbled, slamming the door behind me. But I didn't really want him to drown. I loved the little bastard.

Thirty minutes later he was sitting at the back door. I opened the door, grabbed him by the collar, and yanked him through the kitchen and living room toward Tyler's bathroom, cursing him the whole way.

After bathing Max and wiping Tyler's tub down, I escaped to my bathroom, where I ran a hot bath and soaked until the water was almost cold. I dried my hair and got dressed while Max gave me the stink eye, knowing I must be getting ready to leave him again. It was the middle of August but still hotter than hell, so I slipped on a simple white halter top that tied behind my neck, black summer-weight jeans to dress the halter up just enough, and strappy sandals. My smile grew until I eventually laughed out loud.

When we arrived at the party, the tent was full. Live music played loudly, and for a moment I no longer regretted going. We had no sooner found a table to call our own and were on our first round of drinks when a short, enthusiastic gentleman sneaked up behind Diane. His name was Dwayne. He was a local married man of the unfaithful type and continuously hit on Diane. How she even knew this joker and why he was there was beyond me. She finally just came out and asked Dwayne to leave her alone and then accused him of keeping the single men from approaching her. She was getting nowhere with him hovering. He started name-dropping, claiming to know most of the players, and asked Diane which golfer she'd like to meet. Hoping to get rid of him, she quickly picked some random man with his back to her, because he happened to be the tallest in the crowd. Dwayne walked off, on a mission.

I had been listening to them banter for thirty minutes, with no desire to get involved in the conversation. All I could think about was seeing my little boy walk through the front door the next morning. "Mommy, I'm home," he would announce. Memories of my mother saying, "You kids are growing up so fast," haunted me. I was trying to slow down and cherish every moment. I knew Tyler would soon be calling me "Mom" instead of "Mommy." He would soon be a young man.

Less than two minutes passed before Dwayne called Diane's bluff and returned with the tall guy she had pointed out. I was a little surprised. Did she know he would actually go and get this guy? I thought. Was she really interested in him?

"Diane, Kim, this is my friend Jeff." Dwayne glanced from Diane, to me, then to Jeff. He was so proud of himself. "Jeff is a pro on the Buy.com tour. We actually went to high school together."

Liar, I thought, looking up at them standing there like two frat boys. "Did you really?" I finally spoke up, directing the question at the golfer. He nodded. I rolled my eyes and looked away, annoyed. Diane got herself into this, she can get herself out, I thought.

At that moment the golfer named Jeff pulled a chair over so close to mine that it was on the verge of an intrusion into my personal space. I found him attractive, albeit pathetic, and tried everything to divert his focus to Diane. Jeff showed no interest in the fact that she was a songwriter and singer. Her surgically enhanced breasts didn't even faze him. Nope, this golfer had his eye on one thing and one thing only: my toes.

Jeff kept staring at my feet and at one point reached down and brushed an index finger across my toenails. I found this odd almost to the point of disturbing. "I like your toes. They're so...pretty," he said, looking at me with an innocent awkwardness. Trying to come up with a logical explanation as to what kind of a man would notice a girl's feet instead of her breasts, I began to see him differently. This one had something genuine about him.

His face had a fresh glow—I assumed from being in the sun all day. His dark, olive skin exaggerated his teeth, which were so white I pictured him wearing bleaching trays at night. His hair was jet black and his sideburns were sprinkled with gray. His bluish-green eyes had pain in them, but his big grin disguised it well. His scraggly eyebrows needed attention, but he was definitely handsome.

The party was packed with golfers. Some had been on the PGA Tour, a.k.a. the "big tour," but had lost their card (their eligibility to compete) and were working to get back there, and some were rookies just starting out. Regardless of their status, they needed to be preparing for the final day of competition, not drinking and socializing like the man sitting next to me admiring my feet.

Jeff asked me to dance, and I quickly declined. Then suddenly the demon that had possessed me earlier that day spoke again. "OK, let's dance," it said, and I stood up and moved toward the makeshift dance floor, and Jeff the golfer joined me there. Dwayne and Diane were suddenly dancing next to us. I hadn't noticed, but they had already been on the dance floor for one or two songs.

Jeff looked like a groupie at a Grateful Dead concert, dancing with a Dixie cup of gin and tonic in each hand. After a few moments, he had spilled both of them, forming a circle around his feet, and I was back at home in my mind, curled up with a book. This was not where I wanted to be. Once the gin splattered far enough to hit my feet, I left the dance floor, irritated. I stormed off to the only available facility, which was a sun-faded turquoise Porta-Potty at the edge of the tent, and dried my feet with toilet paper. When I reclaimed my seat, Diane and Dwayne had also returned from the floor. Jeff the golfer was still out there bopping around in one spot, oblivious to the fact that I had abandoned him. Once he regained consciousness, he stood there in the middle of the crowd with his arms stretched out, as if to say, "Why on earth would she go?"

A few minutes had passed since I'd sat down. I was sitting there minding my own business, wishing I could click my heels, thinking, *there's no place like home,* when I spotted a man walking in my direction, smiling. He was puffed up like a blowfish and had to be pushing forty-five. Steroids were definitely at work. I looked away quickly, hoping he wasn't smiling at me. Then he did it. He sat down in the chair once occupied by Jeff. I noticed an O'Doul's in his hand and felt somewhat relieved that he was at least sober and wouldn't be spilling his drink on my open-toed shoes.

He introduced himself, first name and last. Maintaining the cheesy smile, he said that he had noticed I was dancing with his friend Jeff. "Yes?" I was trying not to be a bitch, but I really wasn't interested in anything he had to say. Then he proceeded to give me some sob story about how his friend Jeff was having a rough day and had missed the cut the day before. Then the O'Doul's guy proceeded to give me the reason behind all of it, the rough day, the drinking more than usual: Jeff's mother had been found dead that morning of an apparent heart attack. Oh, Christ, I thought.

I returned to the dance floor and rescued him, resisting the motherly instinct to wrap my arms around him, pat his back, and tell him everything would be all right. I invited him to sit down next to me, and let my defenses down enough to find that I actually liked him.

We sat and talked about several things, the conversation moving from one topic to the next with ease. A year ago Jeff had moved into his late grandparents' farmhouse after separating from his son's mother, whom he had never actually married but had built a life with for ten years. He proudly pointed out the bracelet made of embroidery floss on his wrist that his son had made for him.

"Keegan made it for me. It brings me good luck," he said, grinning.

He spoke of Keegan with so much love. Not the bragging you usually hear from the majority of parents, but just the simple things. He was proudest of the simple things. It was obvious that he wanted to share him.

I caught myself looking down at his shoes, an indication that I was now checking him out for potential dating material. A man's shoes are a window to his style. He was wearing brown oxfords, untied. For some strange reason, I loved that they were untied.

"So, can I call you Jeffrey, assuming that's your real name?" I asked, wanting him to have a name other than that of my ex-husband, whose name was just Jeff. Not Jeffrey or Geoffrey, just plain old Jeff.

"Sure. My sisters call me Jeffrey. Everyone else pretty much calls me Jeff, but you can call me whatever your heart desires."

"Great." I smiled, feeling relieved. Then the realization struck that I somehow knew I'd be saying his name again, many times.

"How many siblings do you have? I asked. "Too many, he replied," and changed the subject.

Midnight approached and the party was winding down. Diane had been fighting Puffy the O'Doul's guy off with a stick since Dwayne went home to his wife. I felt badly that she had come hoping to meet someone, and here I was handing out a business card.

As I was saying goodbye, Jeff stopped me. "Hey, so, uh, I have a tournament in Fort Smith, Arkansas, in a week, so I might be coming through Missouri again, and…um…"

As he stumbled around for the words, I finally put him out of his misery, "And you would like to take me out for dinner on your way through?" Visibly relieved, with an "aw shucks" look about him, he replied, "No."

I was speechless, one eyebrow rising in suspicion, not knowing whether to play dumb and giggle or turn and walk away. He was looking especially mischievous. "I wouldn't like to take you to dinner. I would love to take you to dinner."

Trying to hide my relief, I accepted with a straight face. He leaned down and hurriedly gave me a peck, one of those half-on-the-cheek-half-on-the-lips kisses, as though he feared I would resist if given the chance. Overwhelmed, I stood there, wondering what in the hell I was getting myself into.

# Four

Jeff called on Tuesday night from Vermont, where he was handling his mother's funeral arrangements, to discuss our Saturday night dinner plans. It was like talking to an old friend, which I found almost unsettling. Like when you suddenly get goose bumps, but you're not cold. I could hear voices in the background. I pictured him surrounded by family and friends and wondered what the scene looked like there. I had so many questions about him, about his family. I told him I had made our reservations for 8:30; since the theater was closer to the restaurant, he should just pick me up from work.

I was reluctant to give my home address to a complete stranger, not only for obvious reasons, but also because I was embarrassed to be living in a mobile home.

I made reservations for us at my favorite place to dine, a restaurant called Top of the Rock. Top of the Rock was essentially the only venue within a twenty-mile radius that was capable of satisfying even the slightest of sophisticated palates. Situated on a hill overlooking a magnificent view of the Ozark Mountains and Tablerock Lake sprawling below, the restaurant was adjacent to a nine-hole course Jack Nicklaus had designed. I was overly proud of my venue selection and anticipated that my date would be too.

The day of the big date, I stood backstage and tried to convince my friend and mentor, Mark, also a performer in the show, to assist me in sabotaging the whole thing.

"I should probably just cancel, right? I don't normally date men who come without recommendations."

Mark, being Mark, didn't let me suck him in.

"You could have a horrible time. Or you could find that he's your Prince Charming. One thing is for sure: if you don't go, you'll never know, and you may always wonder, what if? Think about it; what have you got to lose?"

Knowing I couldn't deny the logic in it, I surrendered, "OK, fine, I'll go," I said, giving Mark a look of disgust as I walked out of his dressing room and into mine.

After the show I showered, making certain no smidgen of green paint remained behind my ears, pulled my hair back, put on mascara—not part of my normal routine—and got dressed. I traded the jeans I'd worn that day for a long black skirt, the mate to the top I was wearing, which I had strategically planned that morning, and still had some time before he would arrive at eight o'clock.

The theater gradually became quiet as the backstage crew finished preparing the stage and sets for the next day. I sat in my dressing room reading and lost track of time. It was twenty past eight by the time I made my way outside to greet him. The theater was pitch-black. I walked down the steps from my dressing room, the exit sign lighting my way, then down the ramp backstage and out the backdoor. Peeping around the side of the building, I spotted him walking down the hill from the Olive Garden that is perched at the top of the hill in the theater parking lot. Taking a deep breath, I walked out from behind the building so he could see me.

As he slowly approached, I scanned his attire, starting with his shoes: the same brown oxfords, the laces still untied, stone-colored chinos, and a casual button down, untucked. After one good look at him, I felt at ease. I didn't even consider the fact that he could be a psychopath and take me into the woods behind the theater to strangle me. Something was guiding me toward him, and I knew I was safe. I knew I was supposed to be with him, which calmed me and freaked me out all at the same time.

We walked in and stood waiting for a moment until the hostess returned to her post. I'd requested a table for two on the veranda, next to the fire. A bubble of warmth encapsulated us as we walked past the brick oven. The smell of garlic, rosemary, sage, and thyme made my mouth water. Breathing it all in, along with the low hum of people chatting, glasses clanking, and flatware serving its purpose, was comforting somehow, like home. Warm and soothing.

We walked through the door leading to the veranda. Our hostess showed us to a table for two and placed the dinner menus and wine list in front of us. Jeff was overwhelmed by the view. We could see for miles. The sun had already set, but the fire pit was burning strong, providing us with the perfect subtle light and just enough warmth for an August evening.

While examining the wine list, Jeff was surprised to find a cabernet from a California vineyard named "Julian" on the list, and he ordered it. He'd never heard of this vineyard bearing his last name. When it arrived at our table, we laughed when we saw that the label read "Joullian." Jeff took a sip and accepted it anyway, and we enjoyed every drop. We'd found a new favorite wine on our first date. We were already making memories.

I was overwhelmed by how easy it was to tell Jeff almost anything, as if I'd known him forever. I didn't yet know enough about him and wanted to know more. If I tried to pry, he'd be vague and turn the focus of the conversation back to me. Finally, I called him on it.

"The night we met you mentioned that your sisters call you Jeffrey. I'm interested in knowing more about your family and, more importantly, how you're dealing with your mother's death. If you want to share it with me, that is."

Just then three couples, all friends of mine, came walking up the steps to the veranda. The hostess seated them at a large table on the opposite side of the fire.

"You're not off the hook on this topic, but I want to introduce you to these guys. Come with me," I insisted.

Jeff hopped up, grateful for the diversion from the current topic, and followed me over to their table. The guys all stood to shake Jeff's hand, and my friend Nancy gave me the "you go, girl" look. We went back to our table after a few minutes of small talk. I became very aware of how good and natural it felt to be introducing him to my friends.

For the remainder of dinner we talked about our boys, and Jeff spoke of various friends he'd grown up with that were still in touch and of a couple of golf buddies, one of whom he told me he referred to as Choppy. And Jumbo, who was also a professional golfer on the Buy.com tour. His real name was John, and I failed to ask how he had earned the nickname Jumbo. Jumbo preferred to drive his Cadillac Eldorado to each tour stop, and Jeff would often ride with him, which provided him with many, many good stories to tell.

He then confessed that his trip through Branson wasn't actually necessary or convenient. Getting here had actually taken a lot of effort and would require even more. After the Springfield event where Jeff had met me, he'd devised a plan in which Jumbo would drive to the next event in Fort Smith, Arkansas, and Jeff would fly home to take care of family matters in Vermont. Following the tournament in Fort Smith, Jumbo would leave his car at the airport and fly home to Florida, skipping the next event, in Odessa, Texas. Jeff would then fly into Fort Smith, pick up the car at the airport with Jumbo's golf clubs in the trunk, and drive to Branson to meet me. Jeff would fly from Springfield to Odessa and back for the tournament, hoping he would have the opportunity for another date with me. Jumbo would fly to the tournament following Odessa, which happened to be in Salt Lake City, Utah, and Jeff would be responsible for getting Jumbo's car and his golf clubs, which were still in the trunk, to Salt Lake City. I couldn't decide if this was romantic or just plain asinine.

I was busy in my heart stacking bricks as fast as I could, smearing mortar between each one, building a wall to protect everything I'd worked so hard to create for my child and me. I had become independent, with a career that I loved, raising my son on my own and even considering a move to a larger city with more opportunity, more diversity. I was thinking about going back to college, something I felt was doable now that Tyler was becoming more independent. I had no boundaries, and for the first time in my life, everything was going according to my plan, not someone else's.

Here was this disheveled pro golfer who didn't even have a place to call home and nothing to put inside a home. He wasn't making any money because he was missing cuts and just seemed down on his luck. Did I need the hassle? Sure, I wanted someone in my life, someone to help fill up the empty space, someone to give to; but I wanted this someone to make things easier, if anything, not more difficult. I was determined I would not attract another project.

We left the veranda and headed to the parking lot. Walking across the grassy area to the car, he stopped and turned to face me.

"Can I kiss you?" he asked, so sweetly I melted slightly.

No one had ever asked for permission. All the blood in my body rushed to my cheeks. I was relieved that we were standing in only the glow of the moon, where my beet-red face couldn't be detected. I looked down at my feet, resisting the urge to shuffle them while wringing my hands. I took a deep breath, looked right at him, and, teasing him to lighten the moment, said, "Well, since you asked so nicely, why not?"

It wasn't awkward, like first kisses can be. The doubts and fears reinforcing the wall suddenly gave way, and a heap of rubble was all that remained. Jeff later told me that he knew he could get through to me and win my heart if he could just kiss me once.

Before dropping me off at my car—still parked at the theater—we made a lunch date for the next day.

"I need to practice; is there a range nearby? Maybe we can go hit a few balls after lunch? Work on your game a little?"

Earlier at dinner, I had told Jeff how important it had suddenly become to me to have something in common with my parents. Something we could do as a family other than gather for Sunday supper. The simplest solution was golf, since they both played, so I had made a birthday resolution to go back to learning to play and promised myself I would not quit like I had numerous times before. I was determined to gain the ability to get through at least nine holes without completely embarrassing myself.

"Yep, there is a new course not far from where we just dined," I answered.

I had heard my father speak of a new development with a great course and range and figured it would be a good place to take him. I agreed to lunch and the driving range but warned we must fit all of this in before my three o'clock show. He waited until he was certain that my car had started before pulling out of sight. I was still being cautious, but I was experiencing a feeling I'd never felt before, and I couldn't stop smiling.

# Five

My cell phone rang the next morning around nine o'clock just as I was leaving for my morning hike. I glanced at the number calling and it was Jeff's. I believe I let out a little squeak like a high school girl beaming with excitement, as I understood this to mean he couldn't wait another moment to call me. Some stomping of feet may have occurred as well.

Two hours later I was patiently waiting outside the theater when I saw the silver Cadillac enter the parking lot. I was standing against my car in a parking spot on the west side of the theater reserved for performers. Jeff drove into the restricted area, pulled into Yakov's paved space as if he belonged there, turned the engine off, and got out of the car nonchalantly. It was funny. I couldn't decide if he was oblivious that he had just parked in the boss's space or if he did know and didn't care. I walked over to greet him, this time with a hug.

In Nike sneakers, untied, another pair of chinos, and a pale yellow golf shirt with "Callaway Golf" embroidered over his heart, he was the epitome of a golfer. His tanned face was clean shaven. I had not paid as much attention to his appearance the night before; or perhaps I was just looking closer now. His hair was neatly parted on the side and conservatively combed. I had a sudden urge to tousle his hair into a boyish mess and untuck his shirt but refrained.

After a quick lunch, we headed to the driving range. The Counting Crows CD we had listened to on our drive to dinner the night before was still playing.

Situated on hundreds of acres near the Arkansas border, the newly constructed golf course and soon-to-be-gated community called Branson Creek was breathtaking. Once we arrived I stayed in the car and changed my shoes while Jeff went into the makeshift pro shop. The development was still so new that construction on the clubhouse had not started. It was rather windy there on top of the hill that overlooked the hitting area of the driving range. After several minutes Jeff emerged and returned to the car with a golf cart: our chariot. Jeff opened the trunk of the car and in one motion gracefully lifted his clubs out and strapped them to the back of the cart. The only equipment I had was a pair of golf shoes.

I climbed in the cart, and down the hill we went to the driving range. He lifted his massive black leather golf bag from the cart and carried it to the hitting area. On each side large white lettering read "Callaway Golf." Ah, how cute, I thought, his big golf bag matches his shirt. One side had a strap, and toward the middle on the opposite side, "Jeff Julian" was embroidered in white block letters. A neatly dressed young man in khakis and a collared shirt came down the hill in a cart, stopped, and looked our way. "Hello, Mr. Julian, welcome to Branson Creek. Just let us know if you need anything."

"Thank you," Jeff yelled back at the lad, holding a pitching wedge in one hand and giving a kind, casual wave with the other.

"Mr. Julian? Where are we, the Ritz?" I said, teasing, but curious as to why they were making a fuss. Grinning, Jeff looked my way but didn't offer a reply.

We had the entire range to ourselves. Jeff hit ball after ball far and straight, with a rhythm to his swing that was so smooth and soft it seemed effortless. With every stroke the club head would scoop up a piece of the earth, send it soaring into the sky and gracefully back to the ground, landing several feet in front of him. The sound that was produced when the clubface made contact with the ball was crisp and clean. I had never heard anything like it, nor had I ever seen anything like it, and I was no stranger to golf. This guy was good. Mind-bogglingly good. I wondered how anyone who hit a ball in this fashion could ever miss a so-called cut.

I stood there in awe, my linen pants billowing in the wind while I held tight to the sides of the straw hat that was shading my face from the sun. Jeff turned around and summoned me to take a swing. I reluctantly grabbed the tee he was offering me. I was saying a silent prayer—Please, God, don't let me miss the ball entirely—when a golf cart came up over the hill and stopped. I turned to find my father sitting there in a cart with his friend Jack.

My parents live fifteen minutes from Branson Creek on another golf course that was built several years ago. My father had been playing Branson Creek and was contemplating a move to the new development.

"Hi, Daddy," I said, walking toward the cart path, not surprised to see him there but uneasy seeing him while on my second date with Jeff.

"Hi, Sissy," he replied. My brother dubbed me "Sissy" when I was born, and it had stuck.

I had approached my father a week or so earlier and asked if he knew of a tour golfer named Jeff Julian. My father knows everything there is to know about golf. "Name doesn't sound familiar," he had replied, "but there are so many guys out there trying to make it."

I proceeded to tell my dad that I had been introduced to this Jeff Julian and would be going to dinner with him in the near future. I expected to be treated like a child and forbidden to go out with a total stranger. Instead, without diverting his attention from what he was doing, he said, "It's pretty grueling out there. So many try to make it on the big tour, but very few do. It's not the life most people think it is." Translation: "Don't get involved, Kim. You'll have the life of a gypsy."

At the range I was about to explain that the man with the intimidating golf bag was the one I had mentioned to him when I realized Jeff was standing directly behind me.

"Oh, um, Dad, this is my friend, Jeff. Jeff Julian," I said, looking at my father, then Jeff, and feeling very awkward. "Jeff, this is my father, Jim Youngblood, and our dear friend Jack Smith." I studied my father closely as he extended his hand and gave Jeff a smile.

"It's nice to meet you, Jeff."

"Nice to meet you, sir," Jeff replied.

Jeff made a little small talk by asking about their round and telling them how he was going to help me with my birthday resolution. A stranger within earshot would have thought Jeff was talking to a couple of lifelong golf buddies. My dad and Jack had just finished their second eighteen and were heading in. It's not unusual for my father and his cronies to play thirty-six holes before noon; they're golf addicts.

"See you later, Sis. Jeff, nice meeting you," my dad said finally, and continued up the hill. That's it? No interrogation? No request for a background check or credit report? My mind was reeling with amazement on so many levels.

I later learned that when my father and Jack proceeded to the pro shop that day, Jack asked my father who Jeff was, and Dad replied, "I don't know him, but I do know he's my future son-in-law." My dad could see something that Jeff and I were only on the verge of.

"Don't think you're off the hook, I still want to see that swing of yours," Jeff reminded me as he pulled a club from his bag and holding it by the head handed it to me.

Without hesitating, I stepped up to the ball that Jeff had so politely prepared for me, took a swing, and just like I feared, missed the ball. "That was a practice swing," I fibbed with a smile.

"You've got potential Miss Youngblood. Your swing is good, with a few adjustments you'll be hitting it every time."

"Really?" I replied, shocked but hopeful.

"Really," Jeff answered, as he walked up behind me, placed his hands on my hips and gently nudged me to the left.

"First of all, do you know what club you're holding?" he asked, sounding like a teacher.

"Of course I do," I replied, sheepishly, but I had no idea. "It's an iron," I said laughing, as I peeked at the club head.

"Well, we have to know which iron we're holding to know where the ball needs to be in our stance, don't we?"

"It's an eight! An eight iron," I blurted. Jeff made his point.

"OK, the larger the number, the farther forward the ball should be in your stance. So, when you're holding a wedge or a nine iron, the inside of your right foot should be almost parallel to the ball. As you decrease the number, you move the ball back in your stance." I immediately knew he had a love for this game that he played, and the patience required to teach others to love it.

"OK, I got it. Thanks," I said, looking at him with admiration, "You're a much better teacher than my dad is, but don't you dare tell him I said that."

"Well, sometimes we learn better if a parent isn't the one that is teaching us," Jeff replied, "Now, take a few more swats at that ball."

Two minutes later I was making contact with the ball every time I took a swing.

"That's what I'm talking about!" Jeff remarked, gloating a bit, "Finish that bucket and I'll let you take a break." Even in his teaching mode he was as charming as can be. I wondered how many girls he'd taught, and charmed. Too many to count, I thought.

As three o'clock approached, we left the range and headed back to the theater. I had plans to go to a company barbecue that evening following the show. I thought about asking Jeff to go with me but didn't because I wanted to give all of my attention to Tyler, and introducing him to a guy I'd been on two dates with was against parenting policy. So we said goodbye. I would go to work, and he would leave for Odessa the following day.

Like his graceful swing, our time together had been so effortless that it scared me. I didn't even kiss him on the cheek when I got out of the car. In fact, I practically jumped out before we came to a complete stop. Jeff later told me that at that moment he thought he might never see me again. My abrupt departure made him think I just wasn't interested. It was a crossroads for both of us. I was on the brink of running away, and he was on the brink of letting me. In my heart I knew I would fall in love with him, if I hadn't already. My son was my priority. A man in my life at this point would take too much time, time I wanted to dedicate to Tyler.

That night I had just put Tyler to bed when the phone rang. I saw the number and hesitated for a moment but couldn't resist picking up. "Hello?"

"Hi there. How was the barbecue?"

"It was good. How was your night?" I could feel myself pushing him away and I didn't know why.

"What are you doing now?" he asked, ignoring my question.

"I just tucked my little guy in. I'm turning in too, but I'll probably read for a while."

"I'd really like to see you again," Jeff said suddenly, with confidence, not arrogance.

"Jeff, listen, I really like you, I do…it's just…" I began.

"I can be there in thirty minutes," he interrupted me.

"What? Right now?" He had to be nuts.

"Yes, now." Again, confident but genuine.

"Now? It's after nine o'clock!" I said, with a smile big enough to be heard.

"Yes! My flight leaves early in the morning, but I don't care. I just…I just need to see you, just for a minute."

"Well. OK, I guess," I said and gave him directions before hanging up. "I live at State Highway 248, the house number is 30. As soon as you turn off of 65, the entrance isn't far, on the right-hand side." I was opening myself up now, no turning back. "It's called Northwoods Mobile Park… you'll see the sign," I added, shrinking in my chair.

"I'm looking for a trailer park?" he asked.

"Yeah, so if you need some meth, you know, I can hook you up," I joked.

In a half hour, I'd be giving Jeff a tour of my home on wheels. I ran to my bedroom, my mind reeling, contemplating a shower and thinking about what to change into, when I suddenly stopped, sat down on the edge of my bed, looked into my dresser mirror, and let out a sigh. Deciding I was fine the way I was, I closed my eyes, fell backwards onto my bed, and surrendered.

Jeff showed up an hour later, having been delayed by a state trooper. He was driving 90 mph in a 65 mph zone when he was pulled over. The trooper informed Jeff that he could, and should, take him to the slammer. Jeff charmed him, of course, and replied, "Officer, I met this girl and I've gotta see her again before I leave town in the morning."

The trooper didn't arrest him but did come back to his window with a violation. Jeff signed it, handed it back, and thanked him, several times.

"You're welcome. Now take it slow," the trooper said as he turned, then hesitated, and turned back to Jeff. "And, uh, I hope you get the girl."

I offered him a drink and we sat down on the couch. "So, this is not your ordinary trailer park; it's pretty swank," he commented.

"Yes, well, I am quite proud to be living in the only upscale trailer park in the state of Missouri," I replied, joking.

"I'm serious, it's nice. I could see the well-manicured landscape under the street lights. It's like daylight out there!"

"Thanks. Yes, well, the owner is obsessive compulsive and doesn't skimp on esthetics," I teased my father behind his back.

We sat there until almost two o'clock in the morning. He finally opened up about his mom's death and helped me understand the family dynamics he has endured over the years, which is why he'd evaded my questions. "I have a very feuding family, consisting mostly of women. This has always caused problems in regard to the woman in my life. I know they'll like you, so don't worry." I wasn't sure how to react to this. I couldn't imagine fighting with family members. Disagreements yes, but in my family we just respect each other's opinion and move on.

"Don't worry, I'm a big girl. I can take care of myself. We'll get along just fine." I wasn't worried, just somewhat perplexed.

He changed the subject, moving the focus to us. "I gotta go to Utah next week, so if I miss the cut this week, I can see you Saturday, if that's all right with you,"

"It's all right with me. I'd really like that, actually," I replied, blushing slightly.

"You've got me hoping for missed cuts!" he laughed. I walked him to the door. He leaned down and gave me a long, still kiss and then hugged me tight. "Good night." He smoothed the back of my head with his hand.

"Good night. Drive safely this time!" I called after him.

"I will." He climbed into the silver El Dorado and slowly drove away.

Back inside I checked on Tyler, who was sleeping soundly while Max lay sprawled out next to him. I headed to bed hoping to get at least five hours of sleep while dreaming about this Prince Charming who had suddenly dropped into my simple little life.

# Six

Tyler's dad pulled into the drive just before six o'clock to pick Ty up for the weekend. He said they would be staying in Branson at Ty's paternal grandpa's place. I thought it was odd that he came down so soon after their summer visit but figured he must just really miss Tyler after having had him for an extended amount of time.

Jeff called not even ten minutes after they left to tell me he missed the cut in Odessa. He was getting a flight into Springfield that would arrive at eight p.m. and wondered if it would be all right if he came to Branson to see me. I already knew he had missed the cut because I had watched the live scoring online that day; but I had assumed I wouldn't see him until Saturday.

"Tonight?" I was beside myself like a lovesick teenager. "I love your spontaneity, Mr. Julian. I'll gladly clear my Friday night dance card for you."

"I'm a lucky man. I'll call you when I'm on my way, sound good?"

"Sounds perfect. See you soon."

I changed from my work clothes to jeans and headed to the Springfield airport, which is almost an hour from Branson. Jeff had been so thoughtful from the beginning that I had the urge to surprise him for a change. One of my favorite restaurants was located in downtown Springfield and I thought he'd love it too.

The dinky airport in Springfield at that time had only three gates. Standing there waiting I began doubting myself, wondering if it was too presumptuous of me to show up at the airport. Was I just being a stupid girl? I wondered. Right about then Jeff came around the corner. My heart fluttered at the sight of him, and as I was rolling my eyes at myself, he looked up and saw me there. After dropping his computer bag that very second, he ran to me, picked me up like a rag doll, spun me around and hugged me tight for a moment. He let go and looked at me. "You're a sight for sore eyes." Nope, not presumptuous, I thought. We went to dinner looking so happy I'm certain passersby were either elated at the sight of us or sickened.

Jeff enjoyed Bijan's. We both had the pecan-crusted Chilean sea bass: my favorite. Three hours later I dropped him off at his friend's house in Springfield and said good night. I found myself running to the idea of him, then stopping halfway. One moment I would surrender, the next, push away. My life was just fine the way it was. No commitments other than work and my little guy. Getting over John had been difficult for both Tyler and me. Why complicate things yet again? I kept asking myself.

I had two performances the following day, on Saturday, so I invited Jeff to the afternoon show. He arrived early enough for me to give him a backstage tour. Instead of sitting out in the audience, he wanted to stay in my dressing room with me until a few minutes before I went on stage, at which point he found his seat in the auditorium in the front row. I was taken aback by his confidence and his ability to just feel comfortable jumping right into my surroundings.

Jeff was scheduled to leave for Utah on Sunday and would be on the road for three to five weeks to play in events on the West Coast. He mentioned the tour qualifying school, which was coming up in November, and said he needed to play as much as possible. This meant I probably wouldn't be seeing him for a while, maybe a long while.

Jeff appeared backstage as soon as the curtain closed, before I could even ask one of the crew to go fetch him. Yakov's dressing area was located next to the steps leading backstage. A long velvet curtain could be drawn to conceal the small, mirrored room. Yakov, preparing to go sign autographs, popped his head out from behind the curtain to see who was coming backstage, assuming it was Dick. He looked at me standing there, a bit surprised, then at Jeff, then back at me, eyebrows raised as if to say, Who's the new suitor?

"Yakov, this is my friend Jeff," I quickly introduced them.
"For a moment I thought Dick had grown a foot taller during the last act," he joked at Jeff's height and Dick's lack thereof.

"It's nice to meet you," Jeff said, extending his hand.

"Likewise," Yakov replied and gave Jeff a firm handshake before disappearing behind the curtain.

Jeff waited just outside of my dressing room while I slipped my costume off over my head and put on my robe. I invited him in to have a seat before I headed downstairs to the shower. When I returned he was leaning up against the vanity, flipping through *If the Buddha Dated: A Handbook for Finding Love on a Spiritual Path,* a book that Yakov had recommended.

I walked in with a towel on my head. "Engrossing, isn't it?"

"Too enlightening for me. You need to read some fiction," he replied.

I invited him to dinner at my place. He accepted on one condition; he would do the cooking. I suggested we compromise and make dinner together. He agreed but reserved the right to decide what we'd make and insisted that he buy all of the ingredients. We stopped at Country Mart, our local market not even a minute from my place.

"OK, we need angel hair, shrimp, heavy cream, garlic, parmesan cheese, mushrooms, and asparagus." Jeff rattled off the list as I listened carefully.

"I have angel hair and garlic at home," I informed him. After gathering the other ingredients at the grocery store, we visited the wine store right next door. Jeff picked a nice Italian dolcetto. It was during this visit that we discovered we both preferred a red, regardless of the entrée. "I never drink white. What's the point?" Jeff said.

"I have been strictly red since my ex-boyfriend, John, claimed that I turned into the devil one night when my friend Denette and I decided to get trashy and drink white zinfandel. We downed two bottles in two hours. It wasn't pretty."

"The devil? Really? Maybe I should buy a bottle for tonight." Again, he was trying to be cute, and he was succeeding.

"Don't be deceived," I replied, "No one mentioned pleasure. John says my head spun around several times and we went to bed angry. We were at a party and, as the story goes, John, being the nice guy he is, was cordial to this trampy girl who had forever wanted him in the worst way. She approached him, he gave her the time of day, and later I, as John described it, went into a fit of jealous rage. I haven't had a drink of white wine since."

We were still joking about white zinfandel and jealously when we pulled up to the trailer and carried the groceries inside.

Jeff opened the bottle of red, poured two glasses, and set them aside. I pulled a stockpot and a sauté pan off the rack and handed them to Jeff. He filled the pot with water to boil and began preparing a light, garlicky sauce with shrimp. I was in charge of the side dishes, steamed zucchini and a garden salad.

"You first," he said, handing me a glass of the wine. I inhaled the aroma, took a sip, and was nodding with raised eyebrows by the time I'd handed it back to him. Jeff did the same. "Not bad," he said. "Not bad at all."

I lit a candle for the table and fetched the place mats and napkins before sitting down. Jeff filled our plates and set them on the table before reaching back to the counter for our wine, handing me a glass and sitting down with his.

We sat there for a moment to take a breath; then Jeff held his glass up and I followed his lead.

"Here's to discovering something new, something extraordinary," he said.

"Indeed. Cheers," I added as we lightly tapped our glasses, causing the crystal to sing for a second or two, and took a drink.

We set our glasses down to begin eating, but neither of us picked up a fork. Instead, we sat there in some kind of awe. We finally looked at each other, so caught up in the moment that we were both practically in tears. We were both utterly shocked at the idea of finding someone with whom we so easily connected.

I was impressed with Jeff's culinary capabilities. By the time we finished dinner, it was getting rather late. Jeff had been the perfect gentleman, having only attempted to kiss me a few times, to which I had showed no resistance. Another night of sleeping in each other's arms would most definitely end up under the covers, so we decided it would be best if he went back to Springfield. Jeff was playing golf up there the next morning and had an early tee time, giving good incentive for him to scram.

We were at least making an effort to resist the temptation of young lust, like two teenagers. We just couldn't bring ourselves to say goodnight. We had tea and dessert and kept talking as the minutes flew by.

I began struggling with the thoughts in my head. I'm a grown woman, why can't I act like one? I recalled the first time John and I made love. I'd succeeded at making him wait. I flashed back to the night he stayed over. I put sheets on the futon for him, and as I walked back to my room, I turned back to look at him, wishing I wasn't walking away. John was lying there on his stomach, watching me, also wishing I wasn't walking away. Lingering was also good. What's a girl to do?

When one o'clock in the morning came, I suggested he stay the night. "Thank goodness," Jeff said, rolling his eyes. "I thought I'd never get you into bed!" He grinned, and we laughed out loud, thinking how ridiculous the whole thing was. We hardly knew each other. The decision to succumb to either being a good girl or a sexually uninhibited tramp was a difficult one. His decision, however, would not affect him one way or another. Men have it so easy. How many men have felt the need to use the caveat, "I never do this."?

"I'm teasing you; I can sleep on the couch," he said, squinting at me, afraid I would agree and go fetch him a blanket. The battle in my head continued, with me weighing the pros and cons. I was opening myself up to be disappointed, hurt, or swept off my feet, whichever came first, so why couldn't I surrender to premature premarital sex? I'd only known him for what, two weeks? I thought, cringing.

"Any diseases of any kind ever?" I blurted out, and his jaw dropped. Uh oh, I'm choosing the tramp, I thought.

"No. Never. Ever," Jeff replied, now looking somewhat frightened.

"I'm on the pill. I'm not interested in making a baby, but if I were to get pregnant, I could not have an abortion. You in or out?" I said in all of five seconds.

"I had a vasectomy several years ago. I'm all in," he replied, thinking he was being cute.

"Not without a condom, you're not," I informed him.

"Wow, with three forms of birth control, I can bet there'll be no accidental babies," Jeff chuckled. I did too.

"I don't even know you!" I pushed him. "Would it be cliché for me to say, 'I never do this'?" I asked, biting my lower lip a little.

"Never do what? Meet your soul mate?" he asked, this time without his trademark grin. "Come on." He said, grabbing my hand and the candle that had been burning earlier at the dinner table. We walked into my bedroom, where he placed the candle on my bureau. I fumbled for the matches in my nightstand and handed them to him. He lit the candle while I slipped into the bathroom and reappeared a few moments later. I was probably fretting over this more than I would fret over some temporary fling. This one... this one was special, and I didn't want to do anything to screw it up.

Jeff was sitting on the edge of my bed. He reached for my hand and pulled me closer. Resting his head on my stomach, his arms were wrapped around my thighs. I stood there cradling his head tightly against my tummy while stroking his hair. Both of us sighed. We explored each other's bodies gracefully and clumsily, all at once. I felt so tiny in his arms. Removing my shirt and kissing my stomach, Jeff stopped and placed his hand sideways at my rib cage. "No way did a baby fit in here," he said, his strong hand covering my entire abdomen. It felt good to feel physically small. Jeff looked up at me. "We've got our two boys. That's enough?" he asked.

"You mean, enough children? Yes, one is plenty for me. You?" The last thing a single mom wants is to raise two kids alone; this was my mind-set.

"I'm good with one, but I reserve the right to change my mind."

It was somewhat strange discussing this. As if we were already planning a future together. "I'm good with that," I replied, handing him the condom I'd retrieved from the bathroom, suddenly wondering if I should have checked the expiration date. "Really?" he begged. "Really," I replied.

When we woke the next morning, both of us were smiling. Jeff called the course and pushed his tee time to eleven o'clock. I made French toast and we ate al fresco at my little black wrought-iron table for two on the front deck. The two of us sitting there on a deck attached to the side of a trailer was kind of ridiculous. We may as well have been in Paris, having breakfast al fresco. We were oblivious to the real environment around us.

"Wow, this really is an upscale mobile home park," Jeff said, grinning.

My mother called when we were cleaning up. "It's Mother," I said, glancing down at the phone.

"Get it. I'll do these," Jeff said, taking over the dishwashing.

"Good morning, Mama," I said cheerfully.

"Hi, Sis. When will T-Bug be home?" she asked. Once you have children, you take the back seat to all parental affection. Mom was trying to plan Sunday supper, a weekly occurrence she hosted that included my parents, my grandfather, also known as Popo Hugh, Tyler, and me.

"I assume by five," I replied. Tyler was usually dropped at my parents' house on Sunday unless his dad left town early. I would typically go to the theater around three in the afternoon and to Mom and Dad's immediately following my performance. "I'll confirm and call you back," I said, and rang Tyler's dad, who informed me he wasn't going back to St. Louis until the next morning and asked if I would give him permission to keep Tyler for another night so that he could take him to school in the morning. I agreed, reluctantly, but suggested Tyler's 8:30 p.m. bedtime be strictly enforced.

I called Mom back, and Jeff was still working on breakfast cleanup. "Hey, Mom. Tyler is going to stay with his dad tonight. He wants to take him to school. I couldn't say no."

"So it will just be you for supper?" She was clearly disappointed Ty wouldn't be there.

"Actually, Mom, would it be all right if I invite a friend?"

"Well, of course. Who?"

"My new friend, Jeff," I replied. "Daddy met him at Branson Creek last weekend. I don't know if he can make it, but I'll give him a call and let you know," I said, and looked at Jeff, who had turned from the sink full of suds to look at me as though I were a big fat liar.

I set the phone on its cradle. "Well, dinner with my parents? Or is that too much too fast?" I joked.

"What, you couldn't just ask me while your mother was on the phone? You mean you didn't want to tell her you welcomed a stranger into your bed last night?"

"I don't think so," I replied. "It would break her heart to know her daughter is a tramp. I've been on how many dates with you? *Two?* And we're already doing it?"

"I think we're up to three, if last night counts," Jeff said, quite proud of himself. "Yep, I believe that classifies you as a tramp."

My jaw dropped and I shot him a look. "Oh, really?" I said, walking closer. "I guess you fancy this tramp enough to hang around for dish duty," and gave him a firm shove. He grabbed me quickly and pulled me close. "I more than fancy you, Miss Youngblood."

"Get lost, don't you have a tee time?" I said, smiling at him.

"Yeah, but it's flexible. See, you're already interfering with my game," he replied.

"You are rotten!" I yelled. "Seriously, now. Will you come back down for dinner later?"

"Sure, that'll be great." Jeff replied.

"OK, can you meet me at the theater? I should be ready by five forty-five or six. My parents don't live far, so it makes more sense to meet there, and then we can drive over together."

Perhaps some would think it premature to be taking Jeff to dinner at my parents' this early in our courtship. It didn't feel premature. If anything it felt way overdue. Life is just too short.

Jeff left right away, so I cleaned the house and showered before running errands. I stopped by the house to drop off some groceries quickly before heading to the theater. I found the little red light on my machine blinking. Butterflies. It was Jeff. "I've been smiling all eighteen holes…my cheeks hurt. Thanks for that." Click. Sigh.

I walked offstage and found Jeff chatting with Terry and Dick while they tended to their backstage duties like clockwork.

"Hey, what a nice surprise," I greeted Jeff with a hug.

"The course was wide open today. Played eighteen in three hours." He looked refreshed, his cheeks rosy from the midday sun.

"Did you hit it straight?" I inquired.

"Middle of the fairway every time. Unusual for me, actually," Jeff replied, letting out a laugh.

"Doesn't playing on tour require hitting it straight?"

"Pretty much, unless you can get it up and down from anywhere, even the trash can behind the green. My nickname is the Trashman, for that very reason."

"Seriously?" I asked, amused.

"Yep. Off the tee, only God knows where it's going, but my short game rarely fails me."

"OK, Trashman, you stay here and talk to the boys while I get out of this green." I walked up the steps to my dressing room. "Terry, Dick, put Jeff to work, why don't you?" I suggested, turning to look back at Jeff, who had not taken his eyes off of me.

We pulled into the driveway and walked into the house as the garage door started to open. We turned around to find my father approaching in his golf cart. He pulled the cart into the garage and then reappeared.

"Mr. Youngblood, good to see you, sir. Been out hitting a few?" Jeff asked, genuinely interested.

"Yep, my nightly routine. I missed Ty tonight. He's my usual partner," my father replied as he walked up and greeted Jeff with a handshake. Since Tyler was two, every Sunday night Dad would take him out to play a few holes before dinner. He would also take him to the nineteenth hole for a chocolate bar, unbeknownst to me. Tyler was able to keep this secret, not one of his strengths.

"Must be nice to just get in the cart and go to the backyard." Jeff was talking to my father just like one of the guys.

"Number fourteen runs right behind us. It is a nice convenience, indeed. How about we get inside and eat quickly, then you and I will go hit a few before sunset?" Dad said, looking up at Jeff from where he sat removing his golf shoes.

"Sounds great, let's do it!" Jeff was winning my father over, a feat no man before him had accomplished.

Mother met us in the foyer and greeted Jeff with a smile.

Dinner went surprisingly well. As if Jeff were an old friend. Not that my parents aren't lovely people. They are very easygoing and friendly—but very protective. Dad and Jeff were eating as quickly as possible in hopes of getting out on the course before dark. In our house dessert is served immediately after dinner. That's the way it's always been. However, when Mom got up and headed into the kitchen, my father looked up at Jeff. "So, Jeff, how do New Englanders do it? Dessert now, or later?" This question was probably followed by a wink, or kick under the table.

"Well, sir, honestly, we always wait for a while before dessert." This was actually true, but Jeff would have said so even if it weren't. They were dying to get out on the course before dusk.

"Barbara, honey? Let's wait on dessert."

"Well, OK, sure," Mom replied, confused.

"Jeff and I are going to go hit a few before the sun goes down."

"Oh, I see. Now it makes sense," Mom said.

"It's true, Mrs. Youngblood, we typically wait for a good half hour before diving into dessert, but the important thing here is, well, I want to see if your husband has any game."

We all laughed and the boys headed into the garage.

While Mom and I were cleaning up and doing the dishes, I spotted Tyler's sneakers in the laundry room.

"Oh no, Mom, Tyler doesn't have shoes for school tomorrow. They were going to be at the lake most of the weekend, so he left wearing sandals." I was already dreading a drive to Tyler's grandpa's place because it was on the opposite side of town.

"You better call Ty's dad, and we'll run them over there before it gets too late." Mom dried her hands and went to fetch her handbag.

When I called Tyler's dad, I immediately knew something was wrong.

"Jeff, it's Kim. I just realized that Tyler doesn't have proper shoes for school tomorrow."

"Why can't he just wear sandals for one day?"

It often seemed as though his dad made an effort to be an idiot.

"Jeff, sandals aren't allowed. Not even for one day."

"Well, we're not at Dad's. We're still at a friend's house." He was being argumentative and difficult, a good indication he'd been drinking.

"Have you been drinking?"

"No," he replied with certainty.

"Jeff, it's almost Tyler's bedtime, why aren't you home yet?" I was no longer calm. He didn't answer. "I will meet you at your dad's in thirty minutes. You better be there." I hung up and looked at Mom. On the verge of tears, I grabbed my car keys off the counter.

"Mom, he had that tone, the one he gets when he's been drinking. I should have just asked where they were and gone to pick him up," I said, angry with myself.

Tyler's dad's dad, Chuck, lived on a dead-end street that was about five hundred yards from the main road. My ex's car was nowhere to be seen when I pulled up to the house. I called his cell. No answer. After we sat there for ten minutes, I went to the door.

Chuck appeared at the door and opened it as he greeted me. I didn't feel like chatting and wanted to get right to the point of my visit. "Jeff is supposed to be here. I need to give him Tyler's shoes."

"I just talked to him, Kim. They'll be here in about twenty minutes. You can just leave Ty's shoes; I'll make sure he gets them." Chuck was as trustworthy as his son and also had a problem with alcohol.

Chuck's wife, Lynn, came to the door. "Kim, don't worry, I'll see that Tyler is OK." She knew what my concerns were, because she had lived with the same concerns for years.

"Hi, Lynn. OK, thanks. Will you please call me if there is a problem? I'd appreciate it." I had no intention of leaving, but I wanted them to think I was. I handed her Tyler's little shoes and turned to go back to the car where my mother sat, listening, and watching like a hawk.

"I know he's been drinking. They're covering for him."

"Yes, and they're also enabling his problem." My mother had slipped into her *don't mess with me or my family* mode. "Drive back out to the main road and park in that vacant lot on the opposite side of the street," she commanded.

I followed her directions, parked the car, and turned the lights off. Sure enough, five minutes later, headlights appeared and turned down Chuck's road.

"See, there he is. He was waiting until he thought you were gone. I guarantee you he was parked somewhere like we are now, waiting for a call from his dad that you were gone." She was exactly right.

"You're right, Mom. Chuck said they'd be here in twenty minutes, not five."

When we pulled into the drive, both Tyler and his dad were still sitting in the car. Jeff's door was cracked open and the dome light was on. I parked quickly and walked up to the driver's side door and yanked it open. The smell of beer that escaped was so strong it made me nauseous.

"What are you doing here?" he slurred.

Not wanting to make a scene in front of Tyler, I held my tongue and went to the passenger side. I slowly opened the door, "Hi, T, I brought your sneakers for school tomorrow," I said, trying to sound chipper. As I reached in to unbuckle him, I spotted several beer cans on the floorboard at his little feet. Adrenaline pumped through my veins. "Tyler, honey, go inside and brush your teeth. I'll be right there, OK?" I said, kissing him on the forehead as he climbed out.

Chuck and Lynn had come to the front door. "Come on, Tyler," Lynn said, "Grandma Lynn will help you get ready for bed." Chuck remained in the doorway after Lynn walked inside with Tyler.

"You stay right there," I pointed my finger at him. "You created this. Now you'll be witness to it," I said, trying to refrain from yelling. Meanwhile, my mother, mad as a hornet, remained in the car watching every move. I marched back to Jeff's side of the car, where he had finally stood but was struggling to remain upright. It was sad.

"My God, you are totally shit-faced. You could have killed someone, not to mention your child." I didn't raise my voice; I was too disgusted at him.

Is this the example you want to set for Tyler?" I held back my tears.

He stuttered something about me being crazy, because he wasn't drunk, and then stumbled toward the front door and into the house.

Chuck stood at the door, holding it open for Jeff, who disappeared into the house. I was not about to leave him with Jeff in this condition. Lynn appeared at the door with Tyler. "Tyler wants to give you a hug good night."

"Maybe you should just come home with Mommy and get a good night's rest," I said, looking at Tyler. I didn't want to make a scene or bring attention to what had happened, but I was concerned about Tyler's safety. Tyler was probably well aware that his dad shouldn't have been driving after drinking, but it didn't change the fact that he was his dad, and Tyler loved him.

"But Dad's taking me to school in the morning, Mom. You said it was all right before." His response turned into a whine. It was obvious that Tyler was looking forward to his dad taking him to school.

Lynn stepped toward me from where she was standing in the doorway and quietly said, "Kim, I understand your concern, but Tyler is safe here. Let him stay. I promise I'll get him in bed right now. I'll also see that he gets to school on time in the morning."

Lynn was right. Tyler loved his dad, regardless of the poor decisions he made. I didn't want Tyler to feel as though he was abandoning him, and I knew Jeff wouldn't be a problem because if he had not passed out already, he soon would.

Lynn stepped aside and I peered into the house. "Ty, call Mommy on the way to school in the morning, OK?" He came running to the door. I hugged him tight and gave him kisses on his cute little cheeks.

"Thanks, Momma. I love you."

"I love you too, dear one. Remember, Nannie will be picking you up after school tomorrow."

My mother was still sitting in the car, resisting the urge to get out and wring Jeff's neck. "You did the right thing letting Ty stay, Sis. No need to get him upset." Mom was always right. Still, I questioned every decision I was making. "I called Daddy to let him know we had to bring Ty's shoes to him."

"Good," I replied, as my thoughts returned to the fact that I had a dinner guest.

When we returned Dad and Jeff were sitting at the kitchen table, laughing about something. They looked like old friends. I wasn't about to tell Jeff all that had just happened, but I also knew that if I had to, he'd deal with it. He was solid. He was as solid as they came.

Dad glanced up, took one look at me, and said, "Everything all right, Sissy?"

"Yes, Dad. Everything is all right, now."

I walked over to Jeff as he reached out toward me without even thinking, as if he'd done it a thousand times. I wanted to fall into him and hide there where it seemed so safe. "I better get back to Springfield. I have a long drive to Utah tomorrow," Jeff reminded me.

# Seven

I was content living in Branson near my family and friends, and I loved my job; however, I had for quite some time been feeling complacent. I longed for a change and for more culture than my hometown could offer. The larger cities in Missouri, St. Louis and Kansas City, were both only four hours from Branson, and I had seriously been considering a move to one or the other. A few weeks earlier, I had scheduled an interview with a photography studio in Kansas City and wasn't about to let Jeff Julian interfere with my momentum. Nor was I going to let the fact that he was the first man that had ever gained my father's immediate respect change my plans.

A job interview, a little shopping, and dinner with my friend Tammy, who lives in the Kansas City area, was all that was on my mind. I wasn't sure if I'd stay at Tammy's and drive back on Tuesday or make the drive late that night. Mom was planning to pick Tyler up from school and keep him overnight, regardless.

I left early on Monday and headed immediately for the police station where I filed a restraining order. I called my attorney and friend, Randy Anglen who reassured me he would make certain that Tyler would remain with me until Jeff completed a rehabilitation program. A half an hour later, heading north on Highway 65, I became conscious of the fact that I was picking up my cell phone and setting it back down. The fourth or fifth time I picked it up I gave in and dialed Jeff's cell.

Jeff answered on the third ring, and without even saying hello, he said, "You just made my day." *My God, where does he come up with this stuff?* I thought, while a smile broke out all over my face. Those words, and the way he spoke them, were the words that captured my heart. I made his day. My measly phone call made his day. How could any woman in her right mind turn that down?

"I'm glad I made your day," I replied, blushing. He was on the golf course, of all places, and still in Springfield. He had decided to postpone

53

his departure for Utah until the next day. I suddenly felt an urgency to get back in time to see him before he left. I told him I was in route to Kansas City and had planned to stay the night, but might be coming back after all. "If you do come back, I'd love to see you, even if for only one minute," he said, in the most sincere tone.

I called Tammy and confessed that it was a man that was behind my need to cancel our plans and asked if I could take her to lunch instead. She was not at all offended, but at lunch she insisted I tell her everything about Jeff. I made it to the interview on time, at a studio where I thought I might hone my skills by working as an assistant. I'd been taking pictures since I could walk. By the time I was eight, I was dressing our Schnauzer, Scrappy, in old baby clothes my mother had kept in a keepsake box from when my brother and I were tots. That poor dog continually allowed me to humiliate her, from a Gerber onesie to Oshkosh overalls; I dressed her in every outfit in that box. The overalls were a bit snug on her, but I did capture some stunning shots that our family will enjoy for years to come. Leaving the theater would not be easy, and I wasn't even confident I would be able to go through with it. I had been taking photography classes and, just like I did when I was little, felt something pulling me to pursue it. At the studio, after talking for only fifteen minutes, the interviewer told me I was overqualified. At that point I couldn't get out of there and on the road to Jeff fast enough. I stopped for gas and was driving south by 1:45 p.m.

Jeff had been staying with the O'Doul's guy again, who lived just off the highway between Springfield and Branson, so I rang him to let him know I was definitely coming back and my estimated time of arrival. He gave me directions to the house, and just before five o'clock, I pulled up to find Jeff standing in the middle of the road in his socks. He was wearing shorts and, yes, a golf shirt with a Callaway logo. His hair was messy for once, having been in a hat all day on the golf course. He looked lost standing there in the middle of the road. Lost, desperately hoping to be found. I parked and joined him there in the street. Standing there, embracing and surrendering, we both let out a sigh of relief. It felt like coming home after a long, arduous journey.

Jeff put his shoes on and we went out for sushi. When we returned two hours later, I intended to say goodbye and head home to surprise my little guy. Instead, Jeff talked me into staying, even though I knew I shouldn't. Even though I'd planned to stay overnight in Kansas City, I didn't, so not going home now was selfish of me. Mother's guilt made my heart ache. "He's with your mom; he doesn't know you didn't stay in Kansas City. Don't worry," Jeff said to console me. Here I was, thinking of my needs instead of what was best for Tyler. The bad mother won, and I stayed.

We slept on top of the covers all night, fully clothed, just holding on to each other. Jeff was so appreciative of just being there with me. It felt right being there with him.

The next morning I wriggled out of his arms quietly, hoping to retrieve my bag from the car and make myself presentable before he woke. I had packed a pair of sneakers, sweat pants, and a T-shirt for both sleeping in and driving home. Jeff was supposed to be departing for his long drive to Utah, but he talked me into first going to breakfast. We sat in a booth at the Golden Corral eating an absurd amount of food from the breakfast buffet, including scrambled eggs, biscuits and gravy, and pan-fried potatoes, while conversing over numerous topics. We talked a long time about the farm just up the road, where I had spent most of my childhood. My grandparents owned forty acres there, the Finley River bordering one end and a county road the other. I told him stories of my brother and me and our shenanigans. How my Popo Hugh taught me to drive on that farm when I was seven or eight, and how my Grandma Lottie taught me self-defense techniques and fostered my obsessive-compulsive tendencies by carrying a can of Lysol in her handbag at all times.

Jeff sat there listening and asking questions as if he were talking to a new species. When I tried to get information out of him about his family, he only spoke of Keegan. It was high noon before we knew it.

"Oh my gosh, shouldn't you get on the road?" I was concerned, knowing he had to be in Salt Lake for the pro-am. I was also thinking about Tyler getting out of school at 3:00 p.m. and all of the things I had planned on accomplishing before picking him up. The theater was dark on Mondays and Tuesdays in August and September, so I usually spent those days running errands and grocery shopping. I estimated I would arrive home around 12:45 p.m. and have two hours to spare before heading to school to pick up Tyler. I was missing him terribly and couldn't wait to see him.

Back at the house, I found myself in the middle of the street again. I stepped in close offering a hug good-bye. I wasn't sure when we would meet again and found myself hoping it would be soon.

"Go with me," Jeff suddenly blurted.

"How fun would that be, right?" I replied, grinning.

"Seriously," he said, with a straight face.

"Go to Utah? With you? Drive to Utah? Put the crack pipe down, Jeff."

He laughed. "I'm dead serious. Come with me. Please?"

"Um, no, I have this thing called a job and a little boy who I can't wait to see in a few hours."

"Can your mom pick him up?"

"No, she can't. Because I want to!" My hackles rose, but I let it go, realizing he was just being spontaneous, not thoughtlessly disregarding the most important person in my life. I don't do spontaneity well. I prefer a well-thought-out plan, a list, and a knapsack. "Listen. You're talking crazy. I don't even have clothes."

"We'll buy you clothes." He had an answer for everything. "We can buy you makeup. Wait. Do you even wear makeup?"

"No, only on stage, which is where I have to be tomorrow morning and Thursday afternoon!" It was almost exciting talking about it, but I was determined I would not get sucked into a world of improvisation, disorganization, irresponsibility, and chaos.

Taking time off from my PR and marketing duties at the theater usually wasn't problematic, but the show was a different story, and so was being a single parent. I couldn't just miss a show; nor could I suddenly abandon my child and run off to Utah with a man I hardly knew. I had not missed one show in the three years I had been performing with Yakov, nor had I ever left Tyler for impromptu escapades.

"We'll park your car at the airport on the way. It will be there for you when you get back. I'll get you a flight home early on Thursday, in plenty of time for you to make your afternoon show." This one had all the answers. I began to wonder what he would talk me into next. Robbing a bank, perhaps?

After several minutes of persisting, I caved, turned the ignition off in my car, and went inside to call Yakov while Jeff packed Jumbo's Cadillac.

"Yakov, it's not an emergency or anything, but I'd like to leave town for a few days. If I go I won't be on stage for our nine o'clock show tomorrow."

"If it is that important to you that you would miss a performance, you must do it. I will call Theodora. Don't worry, go. It's all right," Yakov said.

"Thank you so much, really. I'll see you at the three o'clock on Thursday," I promised.

Other than a light jacket in the car, I had the trousers and button down I had worn to my interview the day before, and the sweats and T-shirt I had put on that morning. I had none of the necessities a woman usually requires when going on an adventure with a new boyfriend. On one hand I did want to go, but on the other I missed Tyler so much. I just wanted to go pick him up and hug him tight.

Jeff came inside and hopped up on the kitchen counter, where I stood having second thoughts. "So, what did he say?" he asked. He patted the space on the counter next to him, gesturing me to sit beside him. I hopped up, keeping a little distance between us. Jeff immediately put his arm around me, grabbed the side of my left thigh with his enormous hand, and pulled me in, eliminating all of the space I had so carefully put there. Again, I felt petite. "He pardoned me for one show," I replied as I glanced down at his bare feet. They, too, were huge.

"That's great! Your mom?" he asked.

"I'm calling her next," I replied, then made fun of the unusually large gap between his big toe and second, "What big, prehensile feet you have."

"Why, thank you. You know what they say about guys with big feet?" he said, grinning with confidence.

"No, what do they say? Big feet, big ego?" I gave him an elbow in the chest, and rang my mother again.

"You're a thirty-year-old grown woman. If you want to go and feel safe going, I will make sure Tyler is taken care of," she said. This meant she would make sure Tyler was spoiled rotten. I honestly believe the only thing that prevented my father from sending law enforcement was the fact that he had met Jeff on two occasions and predicted he was my future husband.

And so it was, we were setting out on a journey to Salt Lake City, Utah.

The drive was 1,263 miles and would take us approximately nineteen hours. We would have to drive straight through the night to make it in time, which was how he sealed the deal. Driving so far alone without stopping to sleep was dangerous, so he earned my sympathy.

We stopped at the mall on the way to the airport. Jeff insisted on buying a change of clothes for me. It was kind of weird. I ran into the Gap and bought a pair of chinos and a simple white sleeveless top. We walked past Victoria's Secret, located right next to the Gap, when it dawned on me that the bra under my sweatshirt was black, the same bra I'd worn under my dark blouse the day before. Jeff was more than willing to stop there for a quick white bra purchase.

It was three in the afternoon by the time we dropped my car at the airport. We would gain one hour going from Central to Mountain Time, which would put us in Salt Lake around nine o'clock the next morning, just a few hours before they'd have to tee off.

The drive was long, but we didn't notice. Jeff drove the majority of the way. I took the wheel for a while somewhere between Colby, Kansas, and Golden, Colorado. Neither of us slept. We bought a Dixie Chicks CD at a truck stop in the middle of the night and snacked on nuts and chocolate. Our conversing about old boyfriends and girlfriends, mistakes we've made and learned from, and what we were looking for in a partner was interrupted with a brief silence every now and then. We learned a lot about each other spending so many hours in an enclosed space with no sleep. Still, I was wondering who this man was and where he came from.

When we arrived the infamous Jumbo Elliot greeted us. They had reserved a suite, thank goodness. "Jules! I didn't think you were gonna make it, buddy."

Jumbo was of average height, with blond hair and a profound Jay Leno chin. He looked like a golfer, with a rosy round face like Ted Kennedy. Maybe he drinks too much, I thought. I wanted to know more about the person with whom we would be sharing a room.

"The only things Johnny Mod is addicted to at the moment are sugar, caffeine, gambling, and dysfunctional women," Jeff answered when I asked.

"Johnny Mod?" I questioned.

"Johnny, Master of Disaster," Jeff replied with his big grin. "Jumbo is the master of disaster. If there's trouble to be found, he finds it. For example, this crazy chick he was seeing practically bit his chin off one night…

he had to get like five stitches." How did he explain that to the ER doc? I thought.

"And you practically live with Johnny Mod while traveling around to tournaments?" Teasing, I acted concerned. "Note to self, apprentice to the master of disaster. Beware."

"I don't find trouble, trouble finds me," Jeff replied. "You found me, didn't you?" he added with a smirk.

"If I remember correctly, you came over to my table and sat down— uninvited, I might add. So you, Trouble, found me," I replied, entertained with our bantering.

The suite had two bathrooms, thankfully, so both Jeff and I were able to take time for a shower before I accompanied him to the course. I called Tyler on the way. Mom picked up. As soon as she said, "Hi, Sis," she was handing me off to Tyler, who was eager to speak with me. "Momma, where have you gone?" he reprimanded me.

"I'm sorry, baby. Someone needed help with driving because the drive was very far away," I appeased.

"Why didn't they just take a plane if the drive was so far?" Tyler had to find the logic in everything—a trait that created havoc in his younger years but will serve him well as an adult.

"Well, they needed to take their car. I, however, will be taking a plane home early tomorrow. Be good for Nannie and go to bed on time tonight. I love you!" I quickly changed the subject. I didn't want Tyler to know about Jeff. Not yet.

"OK, Mom. I love you more. Be careful on that plane," he pleaded.

"I will, don't you worry. Ciao, dear one."

"Ciao, Mom."

Tyler and I had said "ciao" instead of "good-bye" from the moment he could talk. I never wanted to say good-bye to him, only hello. Since "ciao" translated to both, it just felt better so that was how we handled good-byes.

A rush of homesickness came over me as I turned the ringer on my phone to silent and slipped it into my pocket.

At the pro-am, I walked along watching Jeff's every move. This was the first time I had been to Utah. Looking up at the mountains from the vale that engulfed the course, I was amazed at what a magnificent sight it was. I strolled alongside my golfer, the autumn breeze gently blowing, wondering when I was going to wake from this crazy dream. It was strange being in a new place, wearing new clothes. It was as if I had stepped out of my life, into another. I didn't want the day to end; however, I was looking forward to dinner with Jeff.

I suggested that Jeff invite Jumbo, since I knew he probably wanted to anyway. I wanted to watch him converse with one of his buddies and learn more about him by the way he handled himself in a setting where I would be the third wheel. I knew I could find something I didn't like if I looked hard enough.

A nice, unhurried meal sounded so inviting after eating fast food in the car for twenty hours. We decided to have sushi again. Jumbo-Johnny-Mod Elliot agreed to dine with us.

I made another call home, knowing Ty would be asleep, so I could get a report from Mom.

"So, you made it?" My mother was always upbeat, but I could tell she was frazzled and glad to have Ty in bed.

"Yeah, Mom, all is well. You?"

"Yes, honey, everything is just fine here. T-bug had a good day at school and he and Papa played golf before dinner, as usual. He ate well and took a shower before bed." What would I do without my parents? I thought.

"So, we'll see you after your show tomorrow?" Mom asked.

"Yep, I have an early flight and will be back in Branson in plenty of time for my three o'clock. I'll be there to relieve you by six. Thanks, Mom. We're having a really nice time. I'll tell you all about it tomorrow night. I love you."

"I love you too, Sis, I'll plan on you and Ty eating dinner with us tomorrow, OK?" I agreed and hit the end button on my cell phone as I took the mother/daughter hat off and returned the "girl-gone-wild" hat to my head.

I found Jumbo to be a pleasant person and couldn't imagine him doing anything horrible enough to deserve having his chin bitten off. Jeff was great at making me feel included without making me feel awkward. We had a great time, eating, drinking, and laughing.

After dinner Jeff and I slipped back to the hotel and Jumbo stayed behind. We desperately needed a good night's rest. Exhausted, we cuddled up together and fell fast asleep in no time.

The next morning we were up early so that Jeff could deliver me to the airport and still make his tee time. When we left Jumbo was still unconscious, so I didn't get to say good-bye. Jeff cracked the door to his room open and said to me, "Check him out." Jumbo was on his back on top of the made bed in the clothes he had worn the night before. All around him on the bed were chocolate bar wrappers and diet Coke cans. He looked like a junkie. "It's how he gets to sleep. A sugar coma," Jeff whispered, and closed the door. We laughed quietly as we walked out of the room, our fifth date behind us.

The flight home was a nightmare. I was bumped on my connecting flight in Dallas, where I had to spend the night and take a flight early the next morning. I had to call Tyler and tell him I would be gone another night. Tyler wasn't pleased, of course, but my mom handled it well, almost as if she expected it.

I missed the three o'clock show on Thursday and the nine o'clock show on Friday morning. Yakov wasn't angry; he basically laughed at me, knowing I had to be gaga for this guy to miss work for him. Honey was the one pissed at me, because Yakov had added "Lady Liberty emergency substitute" to her already lengthy job description. Honey is an athlete, but other than the ever-so-popular-at-wedding-receptions shopping cart dance, Honey doesn't dance.

A visit to Vermont and a few weeks later, Jeff was on the alternate list for the Buy.com Boise Open, which was to be held on September 14 in Idaho. Jeff hadn't planned on going until he found out that I had that week off. The theater was always dark for a week or two in the fall, right after back-to-school time. He decided to go, but only if I agreed to join him.

# Eight

I was truly expanding my horizons with this Jeff Julian, as well as neglecting my son. I was accustomed to dealing with being apart from Ty while he visited his dad, but until meeting Jeff I had only left him once for leisure travel. Tyler was always in good hands with my parents; still, I hated being away from him and felt selfish for leaving him. I kept telling myself that I deserved to embrace the beginning of my relationship with Jeff—the beginning, when everything is new and good and no misunderstandings or resentment follow you.

I boarded a plane destined for Boise, Idaho, a place I'd never been. Jeff, flying from Hartford, Connecticut, while I was departing from Springfield, Missouri, strategically arranged our flights so we would both arrive within an hour of each other. Tyler was going to be with my parents for two days, and his dad would be picking him up for the weekend.

Jeff was excited to be taking me with him to an actual competitive round. Having spied my inline skates in my closet, he insisted I bring them along. Just in case I don't get in, he had said.

Boise was a college town, which probably played a part in its progressiveness. We arrived early in the afternoon, thanks to the change in time zone, and checked into our hotel. Actually, it was a motel. We had our own entrance, and, this time, one bed and one bathroom.

We arrived late in the afternoon at Hillcrest Country Club, where Jeff needed to register. I followed Jeff into the clubhouse. He walked up to a table where a woman sat on the opposite side with a list on a clipboard and stacks of what looked like a newsletter. Jeff wrote a check and filled out a document of some kind. I stood quietly, feeling out of place.

A young Oakley representative was milling around the registration area. He stopped Jeff as we were walking outside to the putting green.

"Hey, Jeff, check these out. I think you'll like them." He handed over a pair of silver-framed sunglasses with mirrored lenses that had an orange tint. Jeff took the glasses, put them on top of his head, and said, "Wow, those are pretty cool." He then reached out to shake the kid's hand. "I'll give 'em a try."

"Great, hope you like them," the rep said, then handed Jeff a hard case for carrying them.

I loved them. "Those are awesome," I said. "But if you're going to wear them, you'll have to lose that part in your hair," I teased. I had commented on Jeff's conservative look before, telling him he should loosen up a bit.

He took his hands and screwed his hair up, eliminating the part completely. "How about now?"

I laughed. "That's better, but you'll need some hair product to get the look you really want," I said. "So, if you don't like the sunglasses, do you give them back or pay for them anyway?" I reached up and moved a few hairs around on Jeff's head, perfecting the messy look he was going for.

"If I don't like them, I give them to someone who does. If I do like them, Oakley knows there's a good chance I'll wear them, and therefore a chance that Oakley will get some Golf Channel airtime," he explained.

I stepped back to take a look at his new do. "You're totally hot without that *Leave It to Beaver* part on the side. You look more intimidating too. I think you can pull it off—you should go with it." I smiled at him.

"We'll see about that," Jeff said as he tossed three brand-new Nike balls onto the green and proceeded to putt.

Being on the alternate list meant getting there and being ready to tee off. If no one withdrew during the morning tee times, you waited around for someone to withdraw before the afternoon tee time. We had to be at the course before seven the next morning, so we had a quick dinner, called our boys to say good night, and went to bed early.

In the morning, after a quick breakfast at the clubhouse, we went to the range to warm up. Several other guys were hitting. Some very pretty women, probably the wives and all around my age, were watching. One sat behind the player hitting next to Jeff. She had two very well-behaved toddlers. I sat in the manicured grass several feet behind Jeff and watched him hit ten balls with his pitching wedge, ten with his nine iron, ten with his seven iron, ten with his five iron, ten with his three iron, then ten or more with his driver. It was so peaceful and quiet, just the sound of clubs swinging and making pure contact with the balls, and the hushed dialogue between the young mom and her children sitting near me.

Jeff didn't get in, which was bittersweet. He was still third on the list, so he decided to throw in the towel. We left the course, changed out of our "country club" clothes, and played for the rest of the day. We had lunch downtown and inline skated along the Boise greenbelt until dusk.

During our skate I could hear what sounded like bagpipes in the distance. "Jeff, stop for a sec," I said, reaching across and touching his chest with my hand as we both came to a halt. "Do you hear that?" Jeff listened for a moment. "I do. Sounds like bagpipes," he said.

"That's exactly what I thought."

"Come on, let's follow it," Jeff said, being his adventurous self.

I followed him over a footbridge and down a path. We came upon a lovely courtyard. A canopy of huge trees covered the manicured grass. The brick building that was situated beyond it was hardly noticeable. Jeff took my hand and we continued to skate as the sound grew nearer and nearer. From under a huge canopy of tree limbs, the source of the music appeared. The gentleman, probably in his twenties, was standing in the middle of the courtyard alone, playing the bagpipes. He was even wearing a kilt.

Jeff and I looked at each other, both of us smiling in fascination. I looked around and didn't see a soul on the path in front or behind us. No stray student huddled under a tree with books. Just the three of us.

We stood there, only fifty feet from the man, holding hands, watching, and listening. The bagpiper looked in our direction, but he didn't move other than to play his pipes. It was really amazing, hearing the faint sound and then just stumbling upon him. After several minutes we quietly turned and followed the path back to where the bridge crossed over the water. I couldn't help feeling as though we were abandoning the lone bagpiper.

Thursday night, we dined at a restaurant downtown and ate like royalty. It was on the top floor of what seemed to be the tallest building in Boise, so the view was remarkable. The evening was perfect. Unbeknownst to me Jeff had been crafting a plan for our weekend. For the first time in my life, I had no plan and didn't care.

"So, Kimberly, I have a proposition."

"Uh oh, what? Fly to Paris tonight?" I replied, being playfully derisive.

"No, smart ass. I wasn't thinking Paris. I'm thinking New York City." Jeff leaned forward and whispered the last three words.

"Seriously? I've never been to New York," I stated, actually feeling spontaneous.

"What?" Jeff looked at me, shocked, "You've never been to New York City?"

"Nope, I'm just a hillbilly from Missouri, my love," I smiled, "We hillbillies, we don't go nowhere outside St. Louie," I said, speaking as hick as I possibly could.

"How about New England? You've been to New England, right?"

"Nope." Realizing how unworldly I was, I started to feel a little embarrassed. "Other than annual ski trips to Colorado, we stayed pretty close to home. I've been to a few places but mostly out West. As far as the East Coast goes, I have never been north of South Carolina."

"OK, well, it has been decided then. I'm taking you to the Big Apple, baby, and to New England!" Jeff said as he lifted his glass of wine toward me and then took a sip. "By the way I'm honored to be the one who gets to witness the first look you take at both," he said, with sweet sincerity.

I was thinking how wonderful, but I wanted to go home to my little guy, and Jeff read my mind.

"Don't worry, my beloved, you'll be home Sunday night when Ty's dad drops him off. This is going to be a quick adventure."

Early the next morning we headed to the airport while Jeff was on the phone with the agency that handles all the flight arrangements for the players. We'd be on standby for at least the first leg, but he assured me we'd have no problem thanks to Boise being a smaller airport.

"OK, here's our itinerary," Jeff said, moving the cell phone from his ear to his pocket. "We fly into Hartford, Connecticut, where my car is parked. We drive to New York City, a two-hour drive from Hartford, after a quick stop in Jersey. We spend the weekend, then I drive you back to Hartford on

Sunday to fly home to get Tyler, and I drive back to Vermont to see Keegan. Sound good?"

"Perfect! So, what's in New Jersey?"

"Some family members are there, cleaning out the house where my mother lived. I should probably make an appearance since I'll be close."

"Yes, you should definitely make an appearance." I was concerned with meeting Jeff's family at such a delicate time. Jeff and I had just met, and his mother had just passed away. My instincts told me this was not the right time. "Just one request. In Jersey I'd like you to drop me off somewhere while you go take care of family business, OK?"

"No, you are my guest, and you'll be treated as such."

"Jeff, I need you to do it this way. Trust me, I am a woman, and my womanly instincts tell me this is not the time."

"OK, I understand. You're probably right. All I ask is that you let me drive you by the house. I would like for you to at least see the neighborhood where I spent most of my youth. I'll run you over to Short Hills after, it's not far, while I go back and make an appearance."

"OK, I am good with that. Thank you for understanding and trusting me on this one." I gave him a hug and a kiss on the cheek and then looked at him with a smile. He pulled me back and gave me a tender peck on the mouth and said, "No, thank you."

"I'm so excited! New York City!" I could no longer contain myself. I was finally going to the Big Apple.

We arrived at Bradley International Airport by early afternoon. I waited by the curb with our luggage while Jeff fetched the car. It wasn't long before a lime green Volkswagen Beetle zoomed up in front of me. Stuffed animals lined the back window. I leaned down and peered inside to make sure the driver was indeed my travel companion and spotted a small bear sitting atop the gearshift. In the driver's seat sat Jeff, grinning. I opened the door and looked at him. "You do realize you look like a pedophile, right?"

"What? You don't like the stuffed animals?"

"I love the stuffed animals, and so do five-year-olds, which is exactly why you shouldn't have them decorating your car. It's weird. I don't even think I can get in." I started laughing.

"I admit that it's a little strange. I bought this car right after I left Keegan's mom. Keegan and I picked it up together in Massachusetts. It's kind of his car, and all of these are his animals."

"I see. Well, in that case, I can get in without worrying I'm going to be molested," I said, joking and trying to lighten the fact that I was making fun of something sentimental to him.

"I never said you wouldn't be molested. Frankly, you more than likely will be," Jeff said.

"Could a girl be so lucky?" I smarted back. "Now, get out and load our bags, Chester."

Three hours later, we were driving along a beautiful road in Bernardsville, New Jersey. Trees with falling leaves canopied little rolling hills lined with stone walls. Before I knew it, we were slowing down in front of a sprawling ranch-style home situated slightly up the hill. "That's it. That's my mom's house."

At Short Hills I found a Crate & Barrel, so I took the opportunity to spend a gift card my brother and his wife, Melissa, had given me for Christmas the year before. Crate & Barrels are hard to find in rural Missouri, so this was my big chance. I purchased fun dinnerware with daisies and had it shipped home. That daisy dinnerware would forever haunt me with memories of Jeff and of our weekend adventure in New York City.

Driving into the city, the traffic was still horrendous at seven o'clock. We checked in at the Omni Berkshire on Fifty-second and Madison Avenue. The city was fantastic. People were everywhere. The hustle and bustle gave me goose bumps. I couldn't believe how friendly people were, everywhere we went. By the time we settled in, we didn't want to go out, so we ordered room service and snuggled in for the night. We were in the most incredible place, and staying in was more appealing than going out.

On Saturday we walked around, taking in the sights. I could have walked around in awe all day, but Jeff insisted we go shopping. After I gave him a modeling show in Banana Republic and Donna Karan, Jeff insisted on buying everything he chose for me. It was very *Pretty Woman,* without the being-a-prostitute bit. We returned to the hotel barely able to carry all of the shopping bags.

Before showering for dinner, we made love, at which point the maid, attempting to provide turndown service, walked in on us. I think she was more mortified than we were. Once the shock wore off, we couldn't stop laughing. "If there is no mint on my pillow tonight when we return from dinner, all because of your selfish needs, you're going to be in big trouble," I joked.

"My selfish needs? You attacked me! I'll buy you a whole fucking box of mints, how's that sound?"

"You're catching on quickly, Mr. Julian."

On the way back from eating sushi, we stopped at a corner market, where Jeff found and purchased a box of Andes mints. "As promised," he said, handing the mints to me as we walked out of the store. We strolled down the sidewalk. Everything I'd ever heard about New York was an understatement. This has got to be one of the best places on Earth, I thought.

Sunday night I tucked Tyler into bed, and could no longer wait to tell him about Jeff.

"I've met someone, someone who is very special, and I want you to meet him," I said, looking into my little boy's big blue eyes.

"You did? When can I meet him?" Tyler was very interested.

"He'll be visiting soon, just to meet you," I replied.

Tyler was so articulate; he had been holding adult conversations from the moment he started talking. Precocious and sensitive, he often processed things as an adult would.

The next morning when we were driving to school, he sat quietly in the back seat of the car. I was worried that the news of a new man in my life had somehow upset him. He had been the only guy in my life until John, whom he loved and lost. I worried there would be some resistance.

"You OK back there?" I asked him.

"I cried last night, Mom." Concerned, I quickly turned and looked at him, trying to keep my eyes on the road at the same time.

"Why, sweetheart? What was the matter?"

"Nothing, Mom, everything's fine. It was just joy cries."

I smiled at him in the rearview mirror as I pulled up to the curb where the teachers were retrieving their students from cars. "Ciao, dear one. Have a great day!" I called after him. Then I proceeded to the theater, having a joy cry of my own.

After a week in Vermont, Jeff had flown into Kansas City and rented a car. The night he arrived, Tyler and I met him at a Steak-n-Shake in Springfield, the very town where Jeff and I had met. Ah, the power of food. A Frisco Melt and chocolate shake and they were forever bonded. Tyler was great. Not jealous of Jeff in any way, which one would expect from a nine-year-old child when his mom is falling for another man. He was just happy for me, and soon that happiness would be his own.

Jeff decided to stay in Branson for a while. He expressed a need to clear his head and focus on training and preparing for the upcoming PGA Tour qualifying school in November. Q-school is a grueling process consisting of four stages, all played like a regular tournament, with four days of competition; with the exception of the final stage, when six rounds are played. The stages are pre-qualifying, first, second, and final. Only a few advance from one stage to the next, and only the top twenty-five players from the final stage actually earn their tour cards (their eligibility to play on tour) during the upcoming year. Due to a tournament win in 1997, Jeff was granted an exemption for the following three years to automatically advance to the second stage. This was to be the final year he would be granted such an exemption. He was planning to use this last chance wisely.

For some reason, Jeff hadn't been able to focus in Vermont. I knew he missed Keegan terribly and figured he must have been desperate for sanctuary. It was as if he were running from something. I was curious, but I didn't force the issue. I knew whatever it was would reveal itself in time.

As part of his workout regimen, I suggested Jeff accompany me to a trail off of Fall Creek Road called Lakeside Forest. My friend Denette and I used to go there almost every day, but as our kids got older and our schedules became busier, we rarely made it at all. We'd promised each other we wouldn't go anywhere in the woods alone after an experience we'd had at nearby Stockstill Park one morning. The park was in a little valley surrounded by woods. Denette and I were making laps around the track early one morning when Denette spotted some derelict in an opening in the trees, about fifty yards from us, with his pants down around his ankles and whacking off. He was looking straight at us. Denette, being more sensitive than me, was visibly upset. It was most definitely disturbing; however, I did find a little humor in it. What kind of issues must a man have to do this sort of thing? I thought. *Deliverance* came to mind.

I called the cops to make them aware that a pervert was on the loose. From that point on, we both surrendered to the fact that there were a lot of weirdoes in the world, especially in rural Missouri, and the buddy system was best.

The Lakeside trails were so beautiful that it was difficult to stay away. It was the place I felt closest to God. A gentle, winding trail led about a half of a mile or so into the woods before reaching 312 man-made steps that descended to a level walkway; at the end of the walkway, if it had rained, you'd find a gushing waterfall. The peacefulness of the woods was addictive. Now I had a hiking partner who would always accompany me.

We went every single morning after driving Tyler to school. Unlike me Jeff would jog the whole way, going down and back up the steps twice by the time I had jogged down and quick stepped back up once. I felt I would hyperventilate just watching him. The quiet stroll through the woods as we walked back to the parking area afterwards was the best part. The morning sunbeams filtering through the leaves that were still clinging to the trees was such a beautiful sight and went nicely with the natural high we had from simply being in nature. God was so present there; each morning as we left, all I could think about was returning the next day.

# Nine

Jeff left for another visit back East on Sunday, October 22. Coincidentally, Yakov was on the road for most of that week so the theater was dark. Jeff asked me to join him, thinking it would be a good opportunity for me to meet Keegan. The end of the year was fast approaching, and I was swamped with Christmas promotions and preparations for launching the 2001 advertising campaign. Thinking two workdays wouldn't put me too far behind, I planned to fly out and meet them there on Thursday and then return early on Sunday. Again, I arranged for Tyler to stay with Mom and Dad.

Jeff and Keegan picked me up at the airport in Hartford. Keegan was a spitting image of his dad. He kept his distance, but smiled at me, revealing the braces on his teeth. "Hi," he offered.

"Hi there, it's very nice to meet you," I replied.

We stayed at the farmhouse that had once belonged to Jeff's grandparents, a massive, now decrepit old house that his mother had left to Jeff and his siblings. Jeff's grandfather had built it when Jeff's mom was a young girl, and Jeff had spent every summer of his childhood there.

The gravel drive from Waterman Hill Road to the attached two-car garage was probably fifty yards long. A short walkway led to a side door, which opened to a haphazard mudroom. Perhaps because I suddenly remembered Jeff's mother had just passed away and I would never meet her or see her when we walked in, the house wasn't at all what I had anticipated. Instead of walking into a warm home where a loving family resided, it felt vacant and cold.

The mudroom was filthy. Coats hanging from hooks lined the walls, and various shoes were strewn about. A flimsy door on spring hinges opened to the kitchen, a much smaller space than I would have imagined for such a big house. In front of the farm table that occupied most of the room was a

73

beautiful bay window covered with photos that had been affixed to the glass with Scotch tape. The edges of every photo curled from the sunlight. The photographer in me thought it was a shame; all of those memories would eventually be faded and lost. A television was perched in the corner at one end of the farm table and a small table in the corner on the other end. On the opposite side of the narrow room, a counter with a sink and cabinets above stretched from one end to the other, where an ancient yellow refrigerator stood, humming.

A hallway led through a dining room past the steps and into a sitting room. A laundry room was just beyond it, equipped with a washer, dryer, and full-sized bed. As we headed back toward the kitchen, I saw a door on the left. It led to a small, overgrown garden. Just beyond the entryway, a set of French doors led to what Jeff referred to as "the green room," because of the pale green paint that covered the walls. A woman came from out of nowhere and obnoxiously screamed, "Jeffreeeeyyy!" She had long, dark blonde hair, was of average height, and was wearing sweat pants and a ratty old T-shirt. She spoke quickly and ignored me while I stood there smiling until Jeff interrupted her to introduce me. After a quick "nice to meet you," she went back to talking. I immediately felt I couldn't trust her. I had had my first real dose of the Julian clan.

On Friday Jeff played golf in Hanover with his friend Scott while I spent the day exploring the little town of Norwich, Vermont, and the quaint college town of Hanover, New Hampshire, just across the Connecticut River. In Hanover I stumbled upon a boutique where one could buy fabulous designer jeans, a great bookstore, a Gap, several great restaurants, and a coffee shop called the Dirt Cowboy Café. I sat in the café for quite some time reading the newspaper and sipping a hot tea. The café happened to be right next door to Murphy's Pub, and I would later learn that Murphy's was where Jeff had been a bartender in the '90s. After he dropped out of Clemson University, he'd decided to return to the place where he spent his childhood summers and make the area his home. Working at night left his days wide open for golf.

I ventured as far as West Lebanon, New Hampshire, where I found a Pier 1 Imports. There, while browsing, I found beautiful bluish tinted wine glasses. I recalled the only stemware to be found in the cupboards at the farmhouse were white wine glasses painted with holly leaves and bells; it was Christmas year round at the Julian farm. I bought two of the glasses and headed back to the house, where Jeff would soon be arriving.

I was just washing the new wine glasses I'd purchased when Jeff rang to tell me he was on his way and would be making one stop for a bottle of wine. When he arrived twenty minutes later, daylight was almost gone. I told him about the adventure I went on that day and presented the glasses. He loved them and said something about me reading his mind.

"I was going to cook dinner but felt as though I'd be intruding if I did," I confessed.

"This house is now your home too, and you should treat it as such. But I'm glad you didn't make anything. I was thinking we might go out." Jeff was always thinking in a mischievous way. "Let's relax with a little wine and cheese; then we'll figure it out."

"OK. Sounds great!" I was always excited when the corkscrew appeared. I could live on wine with cheese and crackers alone.

"Hey, I just thought of something," Jeff said, working at pulling the cork out. "Why don't we run up to the barn and take those photos?" Jeff had been planning to transform the horse barn that was a few hundred yards from the main house into a home for Keegan and himself. Knowing I would be bringing my camera, he had asked if I would take some photos of it while I was there.

"What about our wine and cheese?" I asked, hoping he'd decide the photos could wait so we could just sit for a while.

"How 'bout we take our wine with us and have our snack when we get back?" Jeff replied, as he sliced off a chunk of Cabot cheddar. Famished from being on the golf course all day, he devoured it.

"Well, OK, but we'll have to hurry. The sun is going down soon," I said, my mouth watering as I watched him slice another piece off the block. I was a little perplexed at the sudden urgency to take the photos but didn't push the issue. I trusted Jeff so much, explanations simply weren't necessary. "How about you slice a piece for me, Piglet," I asked, as Jeff crammed another slice in his mouth and started laughing.

Jeff poured the red wine into our new glasses, and as I reached for one, he said, "Wait, don't drink it yet."

"What? Why not?" The aroma of the wine suddenly hit me. "Oh, wow, this is a good one."

"It needs to breathe," Jeff replied. "And I have a toast to make once we get up to the barn." He was up to something.

We trekked to the barn with wine glasses in hand and my camera strapped over my shoulder. I walked a few steps ahead of Jeff and turned to take a few pictures of him. "Look at you, one handed. Impressive," Jeff said as I stood there snapping photos while holding my wine glass.

"I'm on auto. Trust me, it's not impressive," I replied.

Jeff grabbed the handle of the big red door and slid it back.

The barn was two stories with horse stalls downstairs and a full loft upstairs. The stalls were cluttered with a hodgepodge including a few pieces of antique furniture. The absence of horses gave off a lonely energy. It felt abandoned. I took a few shots at angles Jeff instructed and then held his glass while he climbed the ladder leading up to the loft. He then reached down to grab both glasses from me while I climbed up to join him. The loft was spacious and empty except for a few old rickety chairs. I could picture a big family room, floors of wide pine boards, a big couch with puffy pillows, and bookshelves filled with books, old and new.

Jeff walked over to the loft door and pushed it open, exposing a beautiful sunset casting beams of light over the vast greenness of the mountains and the little barn where we stood. He pulled two chairs over to the front of the opening and placed them near the edge. We sat for a moment in a comfortable silence. The contentment we were feeling was pure, like a deep breath. Expanding and at the same time being pulled in, safe.

I imagined Jeff's grandparents below, having tea in the garden, children plodding around them, causing a ruckus while they smiled and sipped their tea. Jeff woke me from my daydream and asked me what I was thinking. "Just thinking about how much love must have once lived here," I replied.

Jeff, with a slight furrow in his brow, let out a long sigh. "Dad left Mom after all of their children had graduated high school."

"After that Mom lived in the Jersey house most of the time, but when she did come up here, she would spend the majority of her time mowing. Even at night she'd be out here, headlights gleaming on that John

Deere riding mower that's sitting in the garage." Jeff's eyes turned pink and glassy. "Something in her died right along with their marriage. You know, it didn't have to be that way." Jeff had never before opened up about his family, his roots, or the pain that had apparently remained in that farmhouse. I sat quietly for a few minutes.

"You know, sometimes we aren't OK, and it's all right. We just need to be sad. Being in that place helps us heal," I said. "Maybe your mom just needed to be where she was."

Jeff said nothing, and I said nothing more. We sat there, quietly. It felt nice to be getting to know this part of him.

All of a sudden, Jeff put his hand down the front of his pants. His sudden movement startled me and I gasped a little. Before I could ask what in the world he was doing, out came a little blue velvet box. I took a deep breath as he slowly moved from his rickety chair to the floor on one knee. "Uh oh," I said. I was shocked—but not that shocked—and scared, happy, and ecstatic all at once. He removed the simple, beautiful ring from where it was snuggled in the box and took my hand.

"Kimberly, will you..."

"Yes, yes, yes!" I cut him off midsentence then joined him on the floor and wrapped my arms around him as tightly as I could. "Be my wife?" he finished, laughing.

My hands framing his cute face, I replied, "I would be honored to be your wife." No one had ever proposed to me, even though I'd been married before. It was wonderfully cliché. "I have just one request," I said.

"Anything," Jeff replied, with a smile that went through me.

"You have to ask my father for my hand in marriage," I said. I wanted to do everything right this time. Everything.

"I absolutely will," he replied as he slipped the ring on my finger and gave me the sweetest kiss I'd ever had.

"Keegan was with me. We made it from scratch, picked out the setting, and the stones, the two of us. It's one of a kind. Just like you," he said, admiring the ring he had just put on my finger. It was the perfect proposal. The fact that Keegan had been included made the entire experience even more fantastic.

I regained my composure and just had to ask, "Why did you put the box down your pants, and how did you keep it there?" Jeff normally wore boxer shorts, not briefs, and this had me stumped.

"It wasn't easy," he laughed. "I knew you would see the bulk of the box in my pocket, because you don't miss anything," he said, with stress on anything. It's true; I'm naturally observant and notice the slightest little things. If someone is evading the truth, I always sense it. It sometimes gets me into trouble with boyfriends.

"I wanted it to be a surprise, so I had to wear tighty-whiteys to keep the box from falling out."

"You're wearing briefs? That in itself is a huge sacrifice!" I teased, and we both laughed. I then told him about the time Tyler began calling my father "Panty Man" because, like most dads, my father was a briefs kind of guy. Tyler had been wearing boxer shorts since he was potty trained, and one day he just decided to take notice of what his grandpa wore. I think my mother got a lot of mileage out of that one.

Since the moment we met, Jeff had showered me with little gifts and surprises. Godiva truffles flowed freely. I think I gained ten pounds in the first two months of our courtship from all the Godiva truffles. After our road trip to Utah, he sent me a first-aid kit that contained not Band-Aids and Neosporin, but chocolate truffles, each one wrapped in white paper with clever Sharpie-written labels that read things like "Hug Deprivation Antidote" and "Kiss Kit." I took the package to work to show Honey. She and the other girls in the office were making a big deal about how romantic it was. It was romantic. I'd never been courted in this way.

I was living something that resembled a dream, or a Lifetime movie. These things don't happen in real life. I thanked God continually and prayed I wouldn't wake up.

Jeff and I sat quietly in the loft of the barn as darkness consumed what was left of the sunset. Sipping our wine, I was dreaming of a long, happy life together.

Just as darkness fell, a golf cart came buzzing up to the barn. It was Jeff's sister Liz. Not having a clue as to what had just taken place, she parked the cart and looked up at us when Jeff called out her name. Surprised to see us in the loft, I think for a moment she thought she'd interrupted something.

We didn't say anything, as neither of us wanted to make her feel as though she'd hijacked the proposal. It was the perfect time to introduce me. Liz and Jeff were tight; I knew this from the way he'd talked about her. She told Jeff she was glad he was considering converting the barn into a home. I got the feeling that she was a tell-it-like-it-is kind of person, not a smile at your face and stab-you-in-the-back kind of person. I liked her.

Liz told us to come by for a glass of wine if we had time over the weekend. When we went over for that glass and Jeff told her and Folger, her husband, that he had proposed, she froze and said, "Is that what you were doing in the loft the other night?" Jeff chuckled and replied, "Yes, I'd just asked her, but she'd already said yes, so your timing was great." Liz rolled her eyes at herself then congratulated us, and I could tell she was sincerely happy for Jeff.

After coming back from the barn, we got in the car and drove about a half an hour north to Bradford. Jeff took me to a great little restaurant called Peyton Place. Perhaps it was the prelude to the meal, but food had never tasted better to me.

Saturday was spent with Keegan, and we were up and at it early. Jeff suggested we go to a rock-climbing wall nearby. Tyler was a rock-climbing enthusiast, but I'd never tried it. I couldn't help but wish he were there with us.

Jeff belayed Keegan; then I belayed Jeff. Neither of them made it to the top. When my turn came, I easily scaled the wall, reaching the top before I rappeled down. Jeff cheered, and before I knew it, I was carting Keegan around that evening, buying him baseball cards while Jeff played a few holes of golf. "Thanks for helping your dad pick out the ring," I casually mentioned. Being a little shy, he grinned, and without looking at me, asked, "Do you like it?"

"Keegan, I love it." I replied, grinning back at him.

# Ten

Back in Missouri in November, Jeff headed to California for second stage Q-school. A case of Joullian wine showed up on my doorstep that week. Jeff had seen a sign for the winery while driving to the course the first morning. He took time to make a visit and have a case sent to me. I was so flattered by Jeff's thoughtfulness, but I told him to focus on his game and get through second stage. And he did. After, he returned to Branson and continued working out and playing golf every day. Unlike snowy Vermont our golf courses remain open throughout the winter months, and that winter was warmer than usual, which guaranteed a full eighteen to thirty-six holes each day.

The final stage two weeks later was Jeff's next hurdle, and he approached the challenge with the mind-set that, regardless of the outcome, he was happier than he had ever been. I flew out to Palm Springs for the last two days. He was playing so well that on the last day he hit into the water twice on a par three for an eight, "a snowman" in golf lingo, and was still among the top twenty-five players when he finished his round. Other than the Utah Pro-Am, I'd never really watched him play an entire round of competitive golf. He made it look so easy. I recall thinking, "Wow, what's so difficult about this game?"

I snapped a photograph of Jeff immediately after he came out of the scoring tent. It's the most amazing moment I have ever had the pleasure of witnessing. A human being experiencing utter joy and accomplishment, following his dreams, grabbing hold of them. Something so very few of us do because some jerk of a school counselor or a parent with no sense told us we couldn't. Everyone watching must have had chills like me as we watched in awe.

After a few drinks in the clubhouse to celebrate, we went to dinner with Eric, Jeff's longtime friend, who had been caddying for him. I don't remember where we ate or what we ate. We were all in shock, I think. We stopped at the market on our way back to the hotel, where Jeff bought gerbera daisies for me and a bottle of champagne.

Eric joined us for champagne in the hot tub before turning in for the night. Jeff and I finished the bottle and went for a skinny dip in the pool. Even after all of that, Jeff was wide-awake. I don't think he slept at all that night.

On the flight home the following day, we upgraded to first class and ordered red wine. About a half an hour into the flight, we hit turbulence strong enough to take my breath away. Jeff and I looked at each other with more than a little concern as he grabbed hold of my hand and held it tight. Wouldn't that just suck? I thought. We find each other in this big world, and our plane goes down on the flight home after Jeff regains his eligibility to play on the PGA Tour. The plane leveled and became still again, and we both let out a nervous laugh before going back to enjoying our wine. That was the first time I felt it. Something tugged at me, as if saying, "Not yet, but soon."

During the flight we started planning our future, and I opened my mind to a move out East. Between traveling on tour and visits to Vermont to see Keegan, Jeff would have very little time to stop in Missouri. Originally Jeff had suggested we live in Missouri. He could head to Vermont once a month, and we could fly Keegan to us on holidays. I was once again puzzled by his desire to be far away from the place he called home. I knew how much he loved Keegan and couldn't understand what could be strong enough to push him away from Vermont and from his son.

We decided that the most logical approach would be for Tyler and me to move to Vermont. This way being together wouldn't be an issue. Moreover, having filed the restraining order against Ty's dad a few months before due to his drinking, I felt that getting Tyler away from that situation might be best for everyone. I had my attorney draw up a document that released him of all the back child support he owed me in exchange for his not fighting me on leaving the state. He signed it without hesitation, and we started packing.

I gave my resignation at the theater and began mentally preparing myself for giving up my world for Jeff's. Tyler was excited to be moving to a place that promised a ton of snowfall. I was excited about starting a new life in a new place; but I was also reluctant to surrender my independence, my friends and family, and my career. I knew it would be good for Tyler to experience a part of the country that was less conservative to foster open-mindedness and help him become a better-rounded young man. My parents were once again watching me leave Branson and were dreading being so far from us. This, of course, broke my heart.

Our first argument took place the day of the move, on December 19, 2000. Jeff was in charge of the U-Haul. He decided to rent a trailer so that we didn't have to ride in separate cars, which I thought was a great idea. The last time he was in Vermont, Jeff had driven his Chevy Tahoe back to Missouri. I had bought a brand new Ford Explorer six months earlier. Jeff felt that we should leave the Explorer in Missouri, so we asked my dad to store it and eventually sell it for us.

Jeff pulled up with a miniature trailer hitched to the back of the Tahoe. The trailer was so small that for a second, I thought it was a joke. It wasn't.

"Jeff, are you kidding me?" We were only moving a two-bedroom home, but we had way more to move than we'd be able to fit into that tiny trailer.

"Don't worry, it'll work fine." Jeff replied, nonchalantly. I was already in a delicate emotional state due to making some very big changes.

"Don't worry? Don't worry? I'm moving my entire life and you expect to cram it all into a four-by-eight cargo trailer? How?"

What with me on the verge of a nervous breakdown and his frustration over the realization that the trailer might indeed be too small, Jeff raised his voice to me. "I said, don't worry about it!" This was a first.

I started crying. Jeff walked over, reached out, gently grabbed me by the hips and pulled me in, wrapping his arms around me, at which point the tears flowed more freely. "You're going to be all right. I promise," he said in a calm, quiet voice, rocking me back and forth.

It wasn't that I was upset at the possibility of having to leave some of my things behind. It was that I was leaving so much of myself behind;

everything safe, everything simple. I was allowing him to lead, and I was scared.

Somehow, after four hours of playing Tetris, Jeff miraculously managed to fit into the trailer everything except my washer and dryer, my farm table from the kitchen, and Tyler's basketball hoop. I was amazed at what he did get into that little trailer. By the time we left, it was dark and beginning to snow heavily. We ended up driving twelve hours through a blizzard until we stopped in Ohio for the night. After an early start, we arrived in Vermont in time for dinner.

We stayed at the farmhouse for a few days while we completed our search for a place to live. Tyler would be flying in a few days after Christmas, and I was hoping to be settled in by then to ease his transition.

We found a condominium in White River Junction that was perfect. Two bedrooms, one bath, and a full basement we could use as an office and playroom. Jeff and I had everything in place before Tyler joined us. After the New Year, Tyler started school at Marion Cross in Norwich, where he easily adapted and quickly made new friends. His teacher was open to accommodating our travel schedule and agreed to send materials so I could home school Tyler while we were on the road. She said it would be a wonderful learning experience for him and asked that Tyler share all of his travels with the class.

# *Eleven*

We traveled to Arizona, then Hawaii for the first two tournaments. I was more at ease now that I wasn't leaving Tyler behind all of the time. I was able to relax a little more and enjoy myself, other than the newly added stress of being a caddy.

With plans to travel to Italy in the middle of February, Jeff decided we should get married in Italy and have a ceremony and party for family and friends once the weather warmed up, in June.

We wanted a quiet, private ceremony, so it was the perfect scenario. No one would get upset about not being included in a ceremony in Italy. After numerous phone calls, we realized what a pain it was to be married in a foreign country. All of the legal documentation would have to be translated (in writing), among other frivolous tasks. We could never get everything squared away before we left, so I assumed we'd just wait until after we returned.

My mother was arriving on Valentine's Day and would be staying with Tyler while we were in Italy. Jeff and I were running errands and tying up loose ends in preparation for our trip. One stop was Norwich City Hall, where we would get a "dump sticker" for discarding our rubbish. We walked in, down the steps, and up to the counter. "Hello, ladies," Jeff said. "We need a dump sticker." The clerk stood and approached the counter. "And a marriage license," Jeff continued. The clerk, the other girl behind the desk, and everyone else in earshot let out a little gasp as if they'd just witnessed a proposal. I didn't know what to do, so I stood there smiling, taking it all in.

Jeff then asked for a justice of the peace, and the clerk gave us a list of four names with phone numbers.

When choosing the venue for our ceremony, neither of us wanted to speak up. I was thinking his mom's graveside would be appropriate, since we had always felt she had brought us together, but I worried it would be too morbid. Jeff was thinking the same thing but worried I would hate the idea. Finally he went out on a limb: "Are you thinking what I am thinking?"

"Does it have to do with your mom by any chance?" I asked him, cautiously.

Jeff's eyes lit up. "Yes!" he yelled, relieved that yet again we were on the same wavelength.

Mr. Robert Huke was among the names the clerk gave us, and the one Jeff randomly decided to call. As it turned out, Mr. Huke had been a professor at Dartmouth and remembered having Jeff's father, Toby, as a pupil. When Jeff told him where we wanted to have the ceremony, he was a bit stumped. Jeff explained the story of how we met and the circumstances surrounding it, at which point he fell in love with the idea. We would be married the next day, February 15, at four o'clock in the afternoon.

We wanted to surprise my mom and the boys, so we left to run errands that morning and told my mom we'd be back that afternoon to pick up her, Tyler, and Keegan to deliver flowers to Jeff's mom's grave, followed by dinner in Quechee.

Once we were in the car, Jeff called his grandmother, Lena, better known as "Gram," and told her she would be dining with us that evening at Simon Pearce in Quechee, and he wouldn't take no for an answer. We went to the florist in Hanover and bought a large bouquet and nine white balloons.

While I was inside waiting for the flowers, Jeff stepped outside and called my father. He had yet to ask him for my hand in marriage. At this point Jeff was just being his wonderful self, and the conversation he and my father had was more for their benefit than anyone else's. Jeff and Dad had hit it off well, but after this they became the best of friends, which was awesome to witness. I'd finally found someone who, in my father's eyes, was good enough for me.

Jeff came back inside just as they were handing me the beautiful bouquet of lilies and white balloons. We placed everything in the back of the Tahoe under the cargo cover. Mom and the kids were ready and waiting when we arrived at the condo around three thirty. They piled into the back seat, all bundled up for our visit to Nancy's grave. "Dad, where are the flowers for Nana?" Keegan asked.

"They're in the back, Keeg. You'll see them as soon as we get there." Jeff looked at me and we both grinned.

We pulled into the cemetery to find a clear road from the entrance to the spot on the hill where we would soon be married. Over a foot of snow covered the ground. We didn't have any idea that Bob Huke had called the town and had the road plowed. We parked the car as another car was making its way up the hill. It was Bob and his precious wife, Ellie. They pulled up behind us as we were all getting out of the car. The boys, oblivious to their surroundings, played in the snow as we gathered the flowers and balloons. The Hukes got out of their car, and Jeff walked up to Bob and offered a handshake. My mother, assuming we had simply run into a couple we knew, politely stood nearby, smiling. Bob introduced Ellie to us. She was gripping her camera, ready to help us preserve the wonderful event about to take place. "Boys, get over here," Jeff called, corralling the kids while I introduced Bob and Ellie to my mother. The boys immediately stopped their horsing around and did as Jeff asked.

Jeff had made Bob aware of the fact that we weren't telling Mom or the kids beforehand.

"Keegan, Tyler, Mrs. Youngblood, do you know why we're here today?" Bob asked. Mother looked at me smiling but perplexed, and the boys looked at each other, brows furrowed. "Well," he continued, "it's a very special day because we are going to join your mom and your dad," he said, looking at Ty and then Keegan, "and your daughter and Jeff," he said, looking at my mom, "in marriage right here, right now."

The three of them had a moment of celebrating. "Oh, Kimberly, Jeffrey, this is just wonderful!" my mother said, clasping her hands together at her bosom. Tyler and Keegan looked at each other, then started whooping and hollering, cheering while grinning from ear to ear. We didn't expect such a joyous reaction from the kids. They were just little boys, and we didn't expect either of them to appreciate or even comprehend what was happening. To our surprise they clearly understood the significance of what was taking place, and, like us, they were relishing every moment.

Then we recited our vows. For better or for worse. In sickness and in health. Again, a tug of doom tried to ruin my joy. I pushed it back and ignored it.

We took pictures, and then the boys helped us free the balloons one at a time after using a red Sharpie to write one word on each: Happiness. Growth. Compassion. Patience. Joy. Connection. Goals. Commitment. Sacrifice.

# Twelve

Once we were back from Italy and out on tour again, Jeff was sure his game would improve. It was a known fact that players were usually hot after a life-changing event, such as a new baby or marriage. What we didn't know but soon would was that Jeff's game wasn't going to improve. It was only going to get worse, along with his overall health.

I recommended more time on the range, but he wasn't interested. In the first event following our honeymoon, the Honda Classic, a 7,268-yard, par 72 at Heron Bay, Jeff shot a 77, 75 on Thursday and Friday, missing the cut, which was at just a few under par.

Two months later we were in Atlanta for the Bellsouth Classic. The redbuds were in full bloom, their limbs bursting with pink flowers, and the dogwood trees would soon follow. My brother and his wife, Melissa, live in Atlanta, so my parents made the trip from Missouri so we could all be together.

That Friday after the round, we all stood in the parking lot in front of the clubhouse. Tyler was running around somewhere, probably in the clubhouse stealing chocolate chip cookies, the cookies that are so good, they're likely responsible for making all of the once-fit tour players not so fit. Jeff shot a 72 that day and the day before, missing the cut. This is when we would thank God for sponsors and endorsements.

The topic of discussion as we all stood there was not missing the cut, but Jeff's main concern in life, "What's for dinner?" It was one of those moments on which I would later look back. I was standing there looking at Jeff while he was running through the dinner venue options when I noticed a little saliva collecting in the corner of his mouth. The spit, stretching like spider webs with every word he spoke, gave me an urge to swallow.

The family dispersed with plans to meet at the Sundown Café, home of the world's best corn chowder, at seven p.m. After corralling Tyler we walked to the car.

"Hey, Jeff, do you feel that excess saliva in your mouth?" I blurted, wanting to ask before I forgot.

"Excess saliva?" Jeff replied, unconscious of what I asked because he was preoccupied with thoughts of dinner or perhaps his suffering game.

"Just swallow your spit more often," I said, shrugging my shoulders, then turned and yelled at Tyler, who, as usual, was lagging behind without a care in the world, "Come on, T. You're slower than molasses."

At dinner, we discussed the upcoming weekend celebration that we were planning for June 2, 3, and 4. My parents, Tim and Melissa, and my dearest friend, Honey, were all planning to attend. Friday would be golf, Saturday the ring ceremony and fireworks, and then a lobster bake on Sunday. I'd quickly learned that Jeff didn't do anything small. It was always a production.

Jeff missed the next several cuts, including the Shell Houston Open, the Greater Greensboro Classic, and the Compaq Classic in New Orleans, where on one hole a player who will remain nameless landed in the bunker on his approach to the green. After he hit it out, his caddy was busy raking. Using proper caddy etiquette, I offered to clean the player's ball after he marked it. I approached with an extended hand covered with Jeff's towel. Mr. Pro snatched the offered towel from my hand (already damp with fresh, clean spring water I might add), spat in the towel, and gave his ball a good shine before handing the towel back to me. Gross, I thought.

The grimace on my face must have revealed that under that caddy bib, I was a genuine girl. A few people in the gallery around the green, having witnessed this, groaned in support of my revulsion. I turned and walked back to my player, holding the towel with only my thumb and index finger. Jeff, focused on his game as he should be, missed the entire incident.

Jeff's performance continued to shock us. If he played well enough to make a cut, fatigue would get the best of him by the third and fourth rounds. Frustrated and worried about making a living, Jeff began contemplating a life without the PGA Tour, without competitive golf.

I tried to motivate him to push himself and not give up. "I hear Vijay is on the practice range for so long they have to turn the lights on for him," I said, hoping to motivate but getting no response. "How do you expect to keep your game at the level it must be without practicing every day?"

"I do practice," Jeff replied. But he didn't, really. One of the only times I had seen him practice was on our second date! "No, Jeff, you don't. You don't practice like a PGA Tour player practices. I'm sorry, honey, but I think you deserve my honesty here."

On a few occasions during the relentless New England winter before the season started, Jeff had hit balls on one of the holes at Hanover Country Club, a hole we could access from Route 5. We would park on the side of the road and walk down the hill to where a few evergreens stood, their branches drooping with heavy snow. Jeff would reach down, scoop up a handful of snow without lifting it off the ground, and squeeze it, sculpting it into the shape of a tee. He would do this again and again, hitting one ball after another into the hill from the patch of trees. After launching a dozen or so balls, Jeff would pause and the children would attempt to retrieve the little white balls engulfed in snow, under the direction of our yellow Lab, Max. It was a fun test of their memory skills, trying to keep track of where their dad had been aiming. Thanks to Max and his keen sense of smell, they would come back with a fair number of balls, which Jeff would again launch into the snow-covered hill.

In addition to prodding Jeff about practicing, I suggested a move to Florida so he could play every day of the year. There was a reason why he was the only Vermonter ever to make it to the big tour. Jeff was blessed with God-given talent. Fewer than two hundred men in the entire world were good enough to be on the PGA Tour, and, without practicing, he was one of them.

"Maybe we need to consider a move to Florida. If this is what you want, you have to find a way to hold on to it. Don't let go of your dreams, JJ. Take them and run."

"You know I hate Florida," Jeff retorted, trying to remain indifferent, despite my inspirational rant.

"Do you think the majority of the guys you play with every week live in Florida because they like it? It is astonishing that you play as well as you do without picking up a club for days."

I didn't convince him of a move to Florida, but it did at least spur contemplation. He knew I had a point. The question was would he act on it.

The June reception brought friends and family from near and far. Honey made the trip, my parents, Tim and Melissa. A friend of Jeff's came and brought a date he'd met on the Internet just for the occasion, which I thought was classless yet entertaining. We had a huge tent erected in the backyard at the farmhouse. On Friday after my family had arrived, Jeff took my dad, my brother, his dad, and few other guys over to Ragged Mountain, a course that Jeff had designed. Jeff's cousin Terri, her husband, Dave, and their little cutie, Ryan, were there, as well as Terri's mom, Chris, Jeff's favorite aunt, and her husband.

Saturday morning we all played golf at Woodstock Country Club. I had to sit out on golfing due to practically cutting a finger off while chopping basil the night before. All of the food was being catered on Saturday night, but Jeff and I would be providing the sauce for the pasta. Jeff prepared a red sauce, and I a pesto. Making the sauces ourselves was our little gift to our friends and family, and it gave the reception a personal touch.

We had bagpipes announcing the ring ceremony was about to take place. The booze was flowing, and even our wedding cake contained rum. When Jeff ordered the tiramisu cake from a wonderful Italian bakery, he'd requested extra rum. I swear, young children, including ours, were wasted after one small piece.

One of Jeff's sister's gave us the flowers as a gift, which was so thoughtful. Beautiful gerbera daisies, my favorite, decorated every table. Keegan and Tyler were bartenders, meaning they stood at the trough of beer on ice and handed them to whomever asked for one. They wore matching ties. God, were they cute. They made out with pretty good tips by the end of the night.

The Sunday brunch lobster bake was my favorite part of the weekend. All of our guests had left by three p.m., and we started changing gears to get back to work on tour.

Around this time, the head pro at Hanover Country Club, Bill Johnson, was retiring, and his position was up for grabs. Bill had held the position for decades. When Jeff heard word of this, he updated his resume and applied for the job. He was ready to give up competitive golf. I had mixed feelings about this. I didn't want him to lose sight of his dreams, but the idea of a job that would keep all of us at home in Vermont and near Keegan was appealing.

Not to mention that as exciting as it may seem, traveling on tour is just not that much fun: constantly lugging suitcases, living in a different place every week. It was wearing us both out. We'd both changed our minds and were seriously considering having a baby. One obstacle to having a child was the vasectomy Jeff had had not long after Keegan was born, but we'd talked about it and Jeff was willing to go through a reversal or whatever procedure was necessary. Also, Jeff knew traveling on tour with a newborn wasn't realistic, and the thought of traveling without me was not an option for him. We wanted a home with a white picket fence. We wanted to be a normal couple, living the normal, proverbial American dream.

Jeff set up an appointment with his urologist to discuss the possibility of a reversal and was told that success was likely. A world-renowned surgeon specializing in vasectomy reversal was going to be at Dartmouth Hitchcock within a few months, so Jeff scheduled a consultation for a date in November.

Around the same time, Jeff was called in to interview for the head pro position, and we were both certain he would get an offer. Jeff was a celebrity in the Upper Valley; he had played at Hanover Country Club for years, and many New Englanders had followed his career. Why wouldn't the position be offered to him?

It wasn't, and we were shocked. Jeff was left feeling deflated on all fronts and, in my opinion, slightly betrayed. Jeff had always internalized everything, and this situation wasn't the exception. He wasn't able to see Keegan as much as he wanted, his game was suffering—it had problems that needed answers—and his body was wearing out too easily. We received the news regarding the head pro job on a travel day while in an airport. God knows where. Ohio, I think. After processing the news for a few moments, he looked at me and, without warning, said, "Let's move to Missouri."

I had mixed feelings and didn't respond right away. I knew this was a reaction to Jeff's feeling cornered, as though he had no choice other than to make a move, even if it was an irrational one.

If he managed to keep his tour card, he said, traveling from Missouri would be less time consuming, and less costly. My parents could take Tyler when we had to be away. I could ask Yakov to welcome me back to work. We could fly Keegan to Missouri for holidays and vacations. Even though winters are cold and the snow does fall, the courses are open year-round. If Jeff failed to keep his card, he could easily find work in Missouri, an entirely different situation than the one in Vermont. Jeff also knew that guidance from my father would provide him with a backup plan. After analyzing the pros and cons, we decided to look for a house in July when we were in Branson on vacation with the kids.

# Thirteen

Jeff finally came to life at the Kemper Insurance Open near Washington, D.C., recording a 69 for the first round and a 66 for the second. Rain delays on Friday during the second round interrupted play several times, and they eventually postponed play until the following day. On Saturday the rain returned after two hours of play, which at least allowed them to finish what had been left of Friday's round before being sent home. This would force thirty-six holes on Sunday. Jeff not only made the cut, he was in the hunt and in first place, tied with Phil Mickelson.

Jeff was concerned about playing thirty-six holes in one day. He was playing well, but the fatigue issues he had been experiencing had him concerned about two back-to-back rounds in the same day. Being paired with Phil didn't help matters. From the moment he teed off, Jeff's ego got the best of him, and he started trying to outdrive Phil, one of the longest hitters on tour. After four holes I could no longer keep quiet. I told him to play his game and stop trying to hit the ball long, because that was Phil's specialty, not his.

He finished round three with a 76, cleared his head, and came back with a 70 for round four, ending up tied for thirty-seventh place. Phil ended up tied for third, and Frank Lickliter took the trophy. That's golf. A lot like life: Everything can change before you know it.

I wondered if Jeff's fatigue was connected to a horrible cough he had every morning upon waking. This had been going on for a while, but since it was only once a day, we had dismissed it. He would cough a couple of times as soon as he woke but not cough again until the next morning. He wasn't a smoker, so there was no logical explanation for it. Jeff had a lazy, New England drawl that concealed the fact that his speech had become slurred. We did not notice it, but others did. Some people even assumed that he had been drinking, we later learned, even if their conversation had taken place at eight o'clock in the morning.

We made an appointment with an ear, nose, and throat specialist at Dartmouth Hitchcock. We would be on the East Coast for two events in July just before our trip to Missouri making it easier to get to a scheduled appointment. We hoped they could shed light on this cough and perhaps find the culprit causing the fatigue.

By the time we visited the ENT at Dartmouth, the left side of Jeff's mouth was drooping, and noticeably so. The visit did not go well. The doctor tried inserting a tube through Jeff's nose to make it possible to look at his throat with the scope. Jeff's gag reflex was working overtime, and after ten minutes of trying, the doctor stopped and said, "I think I need to refer you to a neurologist. I'm scheduling you for a barium swallow, and a visit with Dr. Jeff Cohen." We were both utterly baffled. How did we go from fatigue and a persistent morning cough to the brain?

It was mid-July and we were between the Hartford and Milwaukee tournaments. With ten days off, we were able to get in at Dartmouth Hitchcock for the tests and then see Dr. Cohen to discuss the results. We showed up on that beautiful New England day, happy with our lives ahead of us, ready to find out what the culprit was, and left even more perplexed.

Dr. Cohen looked at Jeff's file containing the results from the nasty barium swallow. After performing a test called an EMT, where they hooked up little probes to different places on Jeff's body, even his tongue, he sat us down in his office and started scribbling notes. I suddenly felt as if we'd been sent to the principal's office and some form of punishment would be the only outcome.

He wrote at the top of a blank sheet of paper the word "Bulbar" and proceeded to say, "I want you to get a second opinion, but what I think we are dealing with is called Bulbar palsy." He began sketching illustrations like a cartoonist.

"So what is it?" I asked, trying to be nice. "Is it like Bell's palsy?" I'd heard of Bell's palsy and knew it made your face droop and was easily reversed.

"It involves the bulb-shaped brain stem that controls lower motor neurons needed for swallowing, speaking, chewing," Dr. Cohen continued, still sketching, while avoiding eye contact with either of us at all costs.

Something tugged at my heart, took hold of it, and started squeezing. Impending doom was present.

Jeff sat quietly, leaving me no choice but to interrogate the doctor on my own. "But what is it? And what do we do to make it go away?" I persisted.

"It's a cousin to Lou Gehrig's disease. And…in some cases…it has stopped progressing…but in most cases it doesn't," he continued calmly.

I'd heard of Lou Gehrig. Who hadn't? He was a Yankee, a first baseman. His nickname was "Iron Horse" because he played like a thousand games in a row, even when injured. He was strong and handsome. But wait, I thought, he died in the prime of his life. I guess I didn't know enough about Lou, and something told me not to learn any more about him or his cousin.

"Wait, wait, wait," I was becoming visibly irritated. I moved forward in my chair and held my hands up in front of me. "In most cases it doesn't? What exactly are you saying, Doctor?"

"It's a neurodegenerative disease that attacks the muscles. But I think what Jeff is experiencing are symptoms of something that's not as progressive."

"With all due respect, sir, am I going to be feeding my husband through a tube or what?" I asked, with angry sarcasm. I was fed up with this doctor and the elephant that was sitting on my chest.

"Hopefully not," he replied.

My heart sank.

We needed more information, but Dr. Cohen seemed to be withholding it, which was disconcerting; but what could we do? Hold him at gunpoint for an official diagnosis?

He recommended that we see a neurologist in St. Louis, Dr. Alan Pestronk at Washington University, for a second opinion. Since we would be traveling to Illinois for the next tournament, followed by two weeks in Missouri with the kids, a stop in St. Louis to see Dr. Pestronk was feasible.

When we left Cohen's office, I made Jeff promise me that he wouldn't worry about the potential outcome of what we were facing. We would wait to see the other doctor before looking into it and jumping to conclusions.

At the end of July, at the B.C. Open in New York, it finally dawned on me that whatever was happening was most definitely progressing. Jeff had made the cut and played fairly well, ending up turning in a 71, 69, and 72 for the first three rounds. The night before the final round, we were headed to dinner when one of Jeff's sisters called. She and the others had been bickering about their mother's land for months. Lizzy was demanding to be bought out to escape the drama, and Jeff was supporting that decision and even considering doing the same. Jeff had told them he didn't want to be involved in arguing, but they continuously tried to finagle him into it. A few minutes into the call Jeff became extremely upset. As the conversation continued, the slight slur in his speech became more and more defined. It sounded like batteries slowly running out of juice. I sat in the passenger seat listening, resisting the urge to snatch the phone from him and toss it out of the car window.

By the time he got off the phone, I could barely understand him at all.

I called Washington University and had no success in getting an appointment with Pestronk. I called my mother, and she went to work on getting Jeff scheduled for an MRI with a neurologist in Springfield during our vacation there.

In New York Jeff ended up tied for eighty-first place with a 78 for the final round. Jeff's dad, Toby, was at the event that week, and when I had a moment alone with him I expressed my concern. I told him that Jeff's condition must be stress related because of what I had heard when he was on the phone. I asked him to please talk to his children and persuade them to refrain from involving Jeff in their arguing over land and money from that point forward. He agreed with me and promised he would speak with them. I knew it was inevitable that if I took the role of protecting Jeff from his siblings, I would soon become the enemy, if I wasn't already. It was a risk I was willing to take.

Keegan joined us the following week in Moline, Illinois, for the John Deere event. Tyler was visiting his dad in nearby St Louis where we would pick him up on the way to Branson immediately following the tournament. Cutting off all outside contact to avoid distractions, including phone calls, Jeff made the cut. Jeff's birthday was that week, so Keegan and I spent some time shopping for his dad's presents. We found a Superman T-shirt and some boxers that read "I Love Dad" all over them. Keegan presented Jeff with his gifts and breakfast in bed on the morning of his fortieth birthday, which happened to be the last day of the tournament. Both father and son were beaming.

We had a wonderful visit in Missouri. The MRI came back clean, easing our minds. Jeff seemed shocked and relieved that the MRI was OK. I was overjoyed.

Jeff, however, had an altogether different reaction. "Kim, there were two guys that I played golf with at Hanover. They were both around my age, and they both ended up with brain tumors," Jeff said, almost in a whisper, as though he worried saying it too loud would make it true for him too. "I was positive we'd find a brain tumor today."

"What are you saying? You think it's environmental?"

"Yes, I do," he replied.

"What do you know that you're not telling me, Jeff?"

"I know that mercury was in the chemicals that were used to prevent snow mold on the greens," he answered, with a very serious look on his face, "I used to play barefoot in the rain on that course."

"Well, you don't have a brain tumor, so let's stop worrying about it." The thought of something as serious as brain cancer was horrifying. But when my thoughts returned to Lou Gehrig's cousin, I wondered which was worse, cancer or Lou's cousin? I also wondered if I was in denial about what we might be up against.

The kids had a blast riding go-carts, playing mini-golf, hanging out with Jeff in the pool, and being spoiled by my parents. Jeff and I were secretly searching for what would be our first real home together.

We found a modest, brick ranch within a one-minute walk of Mom and Dad. It wasn't on the golf course side, but that didn't seem to bother Jeff. We put an offer on it and started the process of applying for the loan,

which was a good diversion from the threat of the mystery disease that was
hovering.

We took the entire month of August off to make the move to Missouri.
The last week of the move we broke up the monotony of packing with a
daily trip to the Quechee club for a quick nine holes.

On Friday Jeff pulled up to the condominium in a huge moving truck.
I laughed, recalling the move to Vermont when he rented that dinky trailer,
forcing me to leave a few things behind.

"Honey, the only items we're moving this time that we didn't move last
time are the hutch we bought and your golf clubs. Is an additional twenty
feet necessary?" Jeff had come into our relationship with two cars, golf
clubs, and clothing. That was it. A touring golf professional didn't exactly
need anything else.

"No, but avoiding one of your conniption fits is absolutely necessary.
And, I'm trying to redeem myself." He was clearly proud of himself and
chuckled after I punched him.

"Hey, that trailer you rented last time was the size of a golf cart!"

"OK, let's get to work. I need you to run me back to U-Haul in White
River so I can pick up the Beetle and go get Keegan."

Friday night was awkward. The next day we would be leaving Keegan,
and although Jeff wasn't about to express it, he was having a difficult time
with it.

Liz came over on Saturday to help us load the last of the boxes. The
couch was the last thing to go into the truck. After we loaded it, Jeff and
Keegan sat on it for a long time, chatting. Jeff couldn't hold back his tears.
Leaving Vermont was easy, but leaving Keegan was extremely difficult.
Still, something was urging Jeff to leave. I was looking forward to recon-
necting with friends and family, sure, but I didn't care where we were as
long as we were together.

# Fourteen

Jeff, Tyler, and Max the Wonderdog rode in the truck with the Volkswagen Beetle in tow, while I followed closely behind in our SUV. The drive was long. We stopped for the night in Ohio at the same pet-friendly hotel we'd stopped at during the move out eight months earlier. We pulled into my parents' home late Sunday night, intending to stay until we closed on our house and were able to move in. Mom and Dad both helped. Mom and I talked and laughed while moving around in the kitchen, unpacking the boxes, strategically deciding where everything should go. I was lucky to have her there, sharing those moments with me, moments that I will never get back nor experience again.

The first two weeks in September would be spent in Canada. School was starting up for Tyler, so he and Max stayed with Mom and Dad. The Air Canada Championship in Ontario was first, followed by the Bell Canadian Open in Montreal. Every week seemed to present new travel challenges, and finding time to see Keegan made it even more of a logistical nightmare. Since we'd be in Montreal the second week of travel, September 3–6, we decided to drive to Vermont and go from there. It allowed more flexibility before and between tournaments for spending time with Keegan. We'd fly from Hartford, Connecticut, to Ontario, compete, fly back to Hartford, get our car, which would be where we left it at the Hartford airport, and try to see Keegan on our way to Montreal. It sounds confusing, and it was, but we managed to pull it off.

Ontario was full of great shopping and wonderful food; however, Jeff's game left much to be desired. Again he missed the cut.

The fans in Montreal the following week were fantastic. They cheered for all of the players, not just the top ten, which was refreshing. Jeff shot a 68 on Thursday and a 68 on Friday to make the cut. The fans were fascinated that I was caddying for him. After a birdie putt on one hole, he kissed me to get a rise out of everyone in the stands behind the green. The roar and applause was so loud that you would have thought Tiger was nearby. Jeff experienced fatigue on Saturday and Sunday, losing a strong place in the field; but he ended up finishing well enough to bring home $25,000. The Bell Canadian Open was the last time I witnessed Jeff play to his ability.

Heading back to the States, we waited at the border for what seemed like hours. I was exhausted from caddying all week, but Jeff was even more exhausted, so I offered to drive. Inching along in the queue eventually lulled me to sleep. My foot slipped off the brake and I tapped the car in front of us, jolting me from my slumber. Jeff looked at me, shocked and possibly a little angry. "Oh, my God, I can't believe I did that," I said. I was mortified. I put the car in park and got out, apologizing to the driver of the car in front of me, who was also getting out of his minivan. Our Chevy Tahoe was big and indestructible, and I was relieved to see that there was absolutely no sign of damage to the other vehicle. We laughed about it and returned to our cars. Jeff had moved to the driver's seat, so I walked around to the passenger's side and got in.

"You need a nap, my beloved," Jeff's anger had turned to concern.

"I'm so sorry. I totally fell asleep!" Then we both burst out laughing. "Stop it, stop it, I have to pee!" Wouldn't that be the perfect ending to an already frustrating day? I thought.

When we finally pulled up to the booth, the guard asked the usual questions. "Were you in Canada for business or pleasure?" As soon as Jeff answered the question, the guard asked us to pull over. The problem with Jeff's speech was a constant reminder of the mystery we had not yet solved. Explaining why his speech was impaired was difficult since we didn't even know.

We went inside and walked up to the counter. The supervisor who approached appeared rather bored and asked Jeff if he'd been drinking. "No, sir, I have not," Jeff replied, growing weary of being asked this question over and over again.

I was surprised Jeff didn't explain that he had to take the wheel because I rear-ended someone, and if anyone had been drinking, it was me. Jeff's speech had worsened after two long weeks of golf, hindering his sense of humor. I spoke up and explained that Jeff had a "neurological issue," but we had yet to receive an official diagnosis. Once I told him we had been in Montreal for the Bell Canadian because Jeff was a PGA Tour professional, he apologized for the inconvenience and let us on our way.

Unable to see Keegan due to a scheduling issue with his mom, we were anxious to get back home and finish settling in. So again we drove straight through the night. We arrived home on Monday afternoon and spent the day unpacking and doing laundry. We were considering skipping Tampa Bay the next week to focus on the house and relax but hadn't quite decided.

The next morning, rested and feeling energetic, we decided to hit the trails. In the car Jeff turned the radio on for some reason, interrupting the peace and quiet. It was a beautiful autumn day, not a cloud in the sky. We were almost there, and in my mind I was already hiking. I could feel the cool morning air enveloping me as I imagined descending toward the lake. I craved it; I craved God.

The news jolted me from my daydreaming. I don't recall what was said; I only remember Jeff making a U-turn in the middle of the road only a few yards from the entrance to the trailhead parking area. "Jeff, what are they talking about? A commercial plane flying off course and into a skyscraper?" I asked. "How is that possible?"

"I don't know, but something isn't right."

Five minutes later, without any thought or discussion, Jeff turned into my parents' driveway. Our safe haven.

We walked through the foyer and into the kitchen to find my mother and father sitting at the breakfast table staring at the television. We joined them at the table. Daddy and Jeff quietly discussed how unlikely it is that a pilot wouldn't be able to avoid a building such as the World Trade Center. My father had been flying, as a hobby, for years. A few moments later, as we watched the coverage, a second plane came into view and flew right into the other tower. Getting up from my chair, I moved toward Jeff and settled into his lap as he wiped a tear from my cheek, wrapped his arms around me, and kissed my shoulder. Concerned about what this meant, and what was yet to come, my father insisted that we take a few weeks off and stay close to home.

Close to home is the only place I wanted to be.

The PGA canceled the event to be held in Tampa Bay that week. A few weeks later, avoiding air travel, Jeff and I drove to the Marconi Pennsylvania Classic, an event that Arnold Palmer hosts every year. I didn't want to go. I had a sensation of homesickness that I couldn't shake. I wanted to stay close to my parents, my son, and our dog, where I felt safe. The season was winding down, and Jeff needed to play as much as possible to increase the odds of keeping his card. There was no way out of it.

The drive to Pennsylvania was long and tiring. Jeff drove while I stared at the roadside, my forehead against the window. Every tractor-trailer we passed had American flags flying, and every single one brought more tears. I had slipped into a deep depression, as the entire nation had. Our worries regarding Jeff's health were minor compared to what the families of those lost in 9/11 were dealing with, but I couldn't shake the feeling that things were only going to get worse.

We arrived in Marconi Tuesday night and were late for the Wednesday morning pro-am. When Jeff and I arrived, we found his group waiting on the second tee. Worried they would think he was drunk, he asked me to go along and explain. It was eight o'clock in the morning, but showing up late with slurred speech could easily be misunderstood. This situation made us realize that it was time to inform the officials; we didn't want Jeff's condition to reflect poorly on him or the PGA Tour.

He was playing with a good group of men. A group of doctors, ironically. During the round Jeff had explained the issues he was having. After the round while they sat together eating lunch, one of them looked at Jeff with concern and told him to get to a neurologist, and quickly.

Jeff had surprised me with my very own set of Callaway clubs for my birthday earlier that year. Since we had chosen to drive instead of fly that week, he had thrown my golf bag in the car along with his.

That evening after the pro-am, we found a small family-owned range near Latrobe. While Jeff was buying a bucket of balls for us, I came upon a little bulletin board that was nailed to the side of the building, with a photocopy of a picture at eye level. In the photo a man was sitting on a couch with a woman and three or four kids perched next to and around him. Under the photo was text explaining that he had just been diagnosed with a "rare disease called ALS, or Lou Gehrig's disease." His prognosis was "two to five years." There was "no cure" and "ALS progresses slowly, until every voluntary muscle in the body becomes paralyzed." How could this be? That's the cousin to what Jeff may have, I thought. Going against what I'd made Jeff promise—that we wouldn't research this Lou Gehrig's disease until we had received an official diagnosis—I continued to read.

The more I read, the sicker I became. I removed the tack that was holding the paper and walked up to the young man working there. Jeff had walked away with our bucket and was preoccupied with preparing to hit balls. I held the paper up and asked if he knew the man in the photo. He said he did and explained that his father was a good friend of the man.

I scribbled my name on a piece of paper with the name of our hotel and room number and handed it to the young man. "Can you please tell him to call me if he has a moment? I'd really like to speak with him." He assured me he would do so, and I thanked him and replaced the photo of the man and his beautiful family on the bulletin board. I then joined my husband, standing six foot three inches and the picture of health, already hitting balls, while patrons, abandoning their practice, stood watching him in awe.

I grabbed a nine iron and took my position on the tee behind Jeff, where he had placed balls for me, all the while hiding my worry, my fear, and my sadness for the man in the photo, his wife, and his young children. What did this mean for them? How would they go on without him?

Later that night at the hotel, we were getting ready for bed when the phone rang. I remember hesitating before picking it up, tempted to ignore the call and ignore whatever might be discovered. It's terrible, but I can't even remember his name. I could hear children making a ruckus in the background. I pictured him standing in the middle of a busy kitchen while kids came and went. Just hearing this made my heart ache. His family, so alive and real, was inevitably going to be without him in five years or less.

I told him I was very sorry to learn of his condition and mentioned we had been told Jeff possibly had something called Bulbar, a cousin to Lou Gehrig's disease. He explained there are two onsets of ALS, or Lou Gehrig's, bulbar and peripheral. "Bulbar is the more progressive form that starts in the speech and swallowing. Peripheral starts in the limbs." A lump formed in my throat. At that moment I succumbed to the fact that Jeff was going to be just like this person I was speaking to.

We talked a while longer; then I thanked him, and before hanging up said, "God bless you and your family."

Having mentioned the flyer I'd seen at the range and getting his permission to speak with the man, Jeff was curious to know about the side of the conversation that he didn't hear. Jeff looked at me for a report. "Let's not talk about it," I said to him, holding back tears. So we didn't. Jeff already knew his fate, as did I. We had simply been doing our best to ignore it.

I lay down next to him and snuggled up as close as I could. I wanted to stay there forever.

# Fifteen

The Texas Open at La Cantera and the Michelob Championship at Kingsmill were up next. Jeff missed both cuts, allowing us two full weekends of relaxing, drinking wine, and playing golf with our dear friends Toni and Andrew. Andrew had coincidentally missed both cuts, allowing us time together. That time with them gave us the most wonderful memories to reflect on.

Toni McLardy and I had immediately connected. She was not your typical "tour wife"; nor was I. The first time I saw Toni, she was sitting in the clubhouse reading a book. No makeup and beautiful without it. She was as natural as she was real. We both refused to wear our bitch pins, carrying them in a pocket until it was necessary to flash them. When I wasn't caddying, Toni and I would walk the course together while trying to keep track of both Jeff and Andrew. We lucked out once or twice when the boys ended up in the same group. Andrew and Jeff got along great, both easygoing, always ready and willing to enjoy time with friends and always ready to break the rules, as long as no one got hurt.

A couple of months before at the Westchester Buick Classic in New York we had hired a caddy so that I could have a week off. I believe it was during a practice round when Jeff and Drew walked into the private family area. Carrying two glasses and a bottle of red wine from the "public" bar area that they had either confiscated or charmed someone into giving them, they walked over to where Toni and I were lounging, passed the bottle and glasses off, said nothing, and walked out of the door. It was in the afternoon, of course, but alcohol was never allowed in the family dining area, so Toni and I kept the bottle under the table, giggling like little girls every time we discreetly filled our glasses, feeling quite proud of the rebellious spontaneity our guys had displayed. Innocent shenanigans. Good times.

The four of us didn't discuss the upcoming visit to Johns Hopkins during those two weeks leading up to it. But we all knew it was approaching, and I knew bad news was more than likely coming, but still I prayed it wouldn't.

The Kingsmill event was incredible. The tour stop there was one of my favorites. Kingsmill is home to Curtis Strange, who won the U.S. Open in 1988 and that same year became the first golfer to earn more than $1 million in a single season. Curtis's career includes seventeen PGA Tour wins, and he has played on five Ryder Cup teams. Needless to say the event is top notch, the locals are delightful and, oh my God, the spa located right there at the course is excellent! I spent some time there. All of the wives did. I had a facial and a body scrub that was so good Jeff commented afterward that my skin felt like a baby's.

On Saturday night, Curtis hosted a party, and the McLardys and the Julians were in attendance—and the last to leave. The party was on a large deck that extended out over the James River. A large round fire pit was surrounded by barstools in close proximity to a bar overflowing with libations. The setting was so inviting and unassuming that we didn't want to part with it. The four of us must have gone through seven bottles of wine that night. I don't remember any of our conversation, but I do remember laughing, feeling safe, secure, and thinking of nothing else. I had no thoughts of the upcoming visit to Johns Hopkins or Jeff missing the cut or Jeff keeping his card, none of that. We were all truly present. Living right then, right there, in the moment.

When we arrived that evening, Jeff and I found two tall chairs at a table near the entrance to wait for Toni and Andrew. It was a nice high table, close to the open bar. They walked in shortly after and joined us. Toni and I were discussing how wonderful the spa treatments we received earlier that day were, while the boys were carrying on about the day's round. I noticed another player walk past our table en route to the bar. I noticed him because I notice everything, and also because I saw who it was and recalled him making an ass of himself on the range the week prior at the La Cantera. The tee times had been moved back, but no one had told him before he made his way to the range, so he threw a hissy fit. That was the problem. If he had been a big boy, he would have been aware of the delay before he left the

GOLF WIDOW

clubhouse. And what is the big deal? The time was delayed, so now he'd have to go back to his cushy locker in the cushy locker room in the cushy clubhouse! What a whiner, I had thought.

Some tour players, Jeff and Andrew included, are accustomed to being coddled, and after several years of this, they suddenly can't wipe their own bums. Toni and I were in agreement that most of the guys on tour behaved like kindergartners, so Toni started referring to Jeff and Drew as "our ponies." That's what they were: baby horses. Toni and I were lucky because some players become helpless while maintaining their magnetic charm and demeanor, like Jeff and Drew, while others turn into real jerks.

Curtis Strange himself suddenly appeared at the entrance to the patio and asked the small crowd of early arrivals if we had everything we needed. This question seemed absurd because it was impossible to have needed anything more; he had provided a spread of food fit for kings and drinks of every variety, not to mention the ambiance! It was magical out there. Jeff, being a rascal held his gin and tonic up and pointing at it replied, "How about a topper?" Curtis grinned at Jeff and mouthed, "Smart ass," at which point they both laughed. Curtis told us to have a good time, then turned to leave.

As soon as Curtis was out of sight, the whiner turned around, abandoning the small crowd waiting for drinks, and grabbed onto the back of Jeff's chair as though he was falling down drunk and having difficulty standing. Then he mocked Jeff's comment to Curtis, obviously under the assumption that Jeff was drunk. It was a mistake anyone could have made. I held my tongue and tried to give him the benefit of the doubt. He didn't know Jeff was having a health issue that was affecting his speech; he simply thought he was drunk. The funny thing was I had never seen Jeff drunk. Spilling a circle around his feet with two gin and tonics and a huge grin on his face, yes; but I'd never really seen him drunk.

Our appointment at Hopkins was scheduled for the Monday following Kingsmill. We drove up Sunday, had a great dinner together, but slept very little that night. Earlier that week when Jeff was resting, I spent a few hours on the computer, looking deeper into the bulbar thing. I had to after my run-in with the flyer on the corkboard at the range in Pennsylvania.

I had found several resources, which surprised me, considering Dr. Cohen had referred to it as rare. What I found confirmed what I had been told, except that the disease was called ALS, or Lou Gehrig's disease, and there was no cousin, just two forms of onset. If symptoms are present in the speech or swallowing, it is considered "bulbar," affecting the lower motor neurons of the cranial nerves that isolate the symptoms to the head and neck. Isolate? I thought. Does this mean the disease stops once it has done the damage to the lower motor neurons? If symptoms are present in the limbs, it's a result of damage to the upper motor neurons. I read on: "Most of the morbidity and eventual mortality is primarily the result of the bulbar and respiratory involvement by the disease." And the best part, "ALS is the diagnosis that a neurologist most dreads giving." At this point I was hoping for anything: brain tumor, cancer, stroke. Anything to rule out this thing called bulbar ALS. The telephone conversation I'd had with the kind man in Pennsylvania was haunting my every thought. Jeff was going to be taken from me. And I'd just found him.

On October 8, 2001, we prepared to go to our appointment. Jeff was sitting quietly in a chair reading *USA Today*. It was silent in the room while I stood, ironing his shirt. I wanted to breathe him in, hide him away, and avoid the inevitable moment awaiting us. I knew in my heart that I would never feel the same again. I just wanted time to stop, to stand still. I knew that this could be it. This could be the day we get the news. Almost one month had passed since the horrific events of September 11, and I subconsciously accepted the fact that we were about to get news that would make us as sick as that day had. As we walked out of the safety of our hotel room, I had a sensation in my body that cannot be described. I felt weak and light, as if my body were leaving the room but my spirit had stayed behind. Jeff and I looked at each other and smiled, each of us trying to convince the other that everything was going to be all right.

# Sixteen

The hospital—what I remember of it—was massive. We had been scheduled with a neurologist who, I later discovered, worked closely with Jeff Rothstein. Rothstein, also a neurologist, was one of the most well-known ALS doctors in the country, my research had told me. The waiting room had a long, narrow seating area that extended along the wall. The long reception desk was located directly in front of the long row of seats. It reminded me of a bar in a pub, except no one was bellied up to it. No, they were waiting for something a lot less satisfying than an ice-cold beer.

We took our seats. The narrowness of the room was actually comforting. I examined those around us and caught a glimpse of a few people in wheelchairs but couldn't bear to really look at them. I wondered if any of them, like us, had come to meet Lou Gehrig's cousin, or if they already had.

We were called in almost as soon as we sat down. This impressed me, but I wondered if we would come out wishing we hadn't been called so promptly, as if a longer wait would prolong the verdict.

The examination room was the size of our walk-in closet. A work area and computer were situated in a corner. A little stool with wheels, two chairs without wheels, and an examination table also filled the room. A woman entered in a lab coat and introduced herself as Dr. Wagner. "I work closely with Dr. Rothstein, who heads up the ALS clinic here at Johns Hopkins," she said. "I understand that you're having some slurred speech?"

After we'd explained the fatigue, the slurred speech, and I came clean about my research, she asked Jeff to take his pants and shirt off and hop up on the table. He was too cute sitting there in his "I love Dad" boxers. I hadn't noticed until this moment, but Jeff's arms looked thinner. He was being his charming self and Dr. Wagner was falling in love with him just as everyone did. She thumped Jeff's knees, testing his reflexes.

Please, God, don't let it be ALS…anything but ALS…anything but ALS, I prayed over and over in my head. I had seen two other doctors perform the same simple tests, and those tests had pretty much ended up inconclusive, so I started gaining a little hope.

Dr. Wagner asked Jeff to lie back, and then she leaned over so her face was just a few inches from his chest. She stood there, just watching. It looked strange, and for a moment I started thinking, surely to God it can't be too complicated. I later learned she was watching Jeff's skin for fasciculations, also called misfiring—little twitches under the skin that are caused by the brain signaling the nerve to fire and move the muscle for no reason, another symptom of ALS. Eventually the nerve wears out, which is the cause of muscle death. When a muscle can't receive a signal to move, it atrophies.

After the exam Dr. Wagner told Jeff he could get dressed, and then left the room. I was surprised at her speedy departure, as I figured she would have needed more information before coming to a conclusion. If it were this thing called ALS, it would take more than instruments resembling Little Tykes toys and a close examination of chest hair.

Jeff pulled his pants on, followed by his shirt, and sat down in the chair without wheels next to mine. He put his arm around the back of my chair and crossed his legs, resting his left ankle on his right knee. We sat there in silence, smiling at each other as if our positive thinking would somehow influence the verdict. Would she give us life or death? This was a very awkward, surreal place to be.

Dr. Wagner reentered less than five minutes later, although it seemed more like twenty. She took a seat and wheeled her way to the computer, where she proceeded to type. Then suddenly, with abrupt grace, she swiveled around to face us, and without hesitation, as if she had to blurt it out or it wouldn't come out at all, she said it. She spoke those words that three out of every one hundred thousand people are ill fated enough to hear, those words that would change everything, forever: "This is ALS."

All of the air was instantly pulled from my body and the walls of the room closed in. I couldn't hear anything, couldn't speak a word. Jeff's arm, already around me, scooped me into him, like a mother cub protecting her young. I felt surprised and baffled by what I had just heard, even though I already knew the chances were good this would be the diagnosis.

Then Dr. Wagner spoke. "Do you need a minute?" she asked, still sitting on her squatty chair with wheels.

A minute? No, a lifetime, you stupid bitch, I thought, resisting the urge to verbalize it. Even though I knew it had to be difficult for her to hand us such a diagnosis and it was in no way her fault, still, I instantaneously hated the poor woman, a normal, psychological response, I would later learn.

Jeff said nothing, I said nothing, and Dr. Wagner left the room, quietly closing the door.

Jeff held my face in his strong, healthy hands, wiping each tear that fell, while looking at peace, as he always had, cool and content.

"This can't be happening," I mumbled, my throat thickened with phlegm that had gathered there.

Dr. Wagner returned a few moments later with a man in a white lab coat like hers. He had dark hair and looked as intelligent as his credentials. "Jeff, Kim, I'm Jeff Rothstein. Dr. Wagner tells me she has concluded that you are suffering from ALS, Jeff."

Dr. Rothstein offered his condolences and assured us that they weren't going to just give us a diagnosis and send us on our way to deal with it alone. "We're here for you," he said, then went into a sales pitch about a two-year, double-blind study of a drug called Celebrex to test its efficacy in ALS.

I was all for studies and advancing modern-day medicine. However, a double-blind study in ALS? How can these doctors give you a prognosis of "six months to five years, but more than likely two," and then in the next breath ask you to take a drug for two years that could end up being the cure, only to find out that you were on the placebo the whole time and it's too late? The fact that he even came in the room made me angry. However, he was just trying to help, and involving patients in the solution can often give them hope.

I recalled seeing ads for Celebrex. "Isn't Celebrex an FDA-approved arthritis drug?" I asked.

"Yes, it is," he replied kindly.

"It's a two-year study, and the drug is approved and available?"

We thanked Dr. Rothstein and informed him we would not take part in any blind study of Celebrex. I asked for a prescription and told him we'd be conducting our own study and would be happy to collaborate with him regarding the results.

They gave us a booklet with a purple cover and prescriptions for Celebrex as well as Rilutek, a drug that had supposedly been proven effective in extending an ALS patient's life by three months. It was the only drug available that had been proven to do anything at all, so of course the price was jacked up. We calculated it and found that the cost for one pill was over $50. And all it would give us was three additional months of being locked inside a totally incapacitated body. No thanks.

As we left Rothstein and Wagner, she gave us orders to stop and give a blood sample on our way out. "I'd like to rule out anything else," she said. This was just a ploy to give us hope and prevent us from having a nervous breakdown in the middle of the hospital, I thought. I'm OK with that, because it did give us hope, which is vital with this damn disease. That hope catapulted us right into denial, and being in denial was blissful.

The waiting area was buzzing with people. A nurse called us back and took the doctor's order. Her warm smile was comforting. I suddenly became keenly aware of how jaded I was feeling, so full of rage. I smiled back at her. She started preparing Jeff's arm to be poked. "They told us we have ALS," I offered. For some reason I needed to say it, as if she could make it go away or tell us it was all a sick joke.

"That's a tough one, guys, I'm sorry. But you know, some people do really well with it," she replied, remaining positive. The kindness in her response made me feel better, but I was on to her. We were totally screwed.

As soon as we reached the car, Jeff decided he was hungry. I'd been struggling as it was just to keep the phlegm in my throat from coming up. The thought of food called for an even more aggressive swallowing. "I want McDonald's," Jeff said with a grin. I had eliminated fast food from his diet shortly after we met. "I can eat McDonald's whenever I want, my beloved—ALS is killing me anyway," Jeff joked.

I didn't find it funny but agreed he should have whatever he so desired from that point forward. From then on we would never have another disagreement. I naïvely assumed that the normal dynamics of marriage would cease because I decided they would. I mean, how could I ever get upset with him? He was dying.

Jeff ate while driving as I flipped through the purple-covered booklet containing pictures of feeding tubes, shower seats, walkers, suction machines, wheelchairs, lifts, ventilators, and more. I'd never seen any of these contraptions. Each page represented another phase of decline. Looking at all of the equipment made me nauseous. It was as if I were reading a booklet about pregnancy. So, you're having a baby! Here is a step-by-step manual to help you prepare for your new little bundle of joy! You'll need a cradle and a crib for when he's too big for the cradle and you'll need to start that college fund.

I grew more and more furious. How dare they give us a death sentence followed by hitting us all at once with sketches of what we will be subjected to in the process! "No!" I screamed.

Jeff looked at me, "What? It's one Big Mac!"

Even in this moment of despair, he found a way to joke around. It didn't work. I was losing it.

"No! We're not going to do this! We're not going to be victims!" I yelled, throwing the booklet to the back of the car, as hard as I could throw it.

That was the beginning of our grief and all the bravery I could summon. I cried off and on throughout the remainder of the drive. I hadn't even eaten breakfast that morning, so Jeff made me eat at the airport. I agreed to try and stomach a veggie wrap. The first bite I took sent me scrambling for the closest ladies room.

I continued to break down off and on throughout the duration of the flight home to Missouri. Jeff was steady. It had not even fazed him, or maybe he was in complete shock. Feelings of hopelessness were hovering, leaving me feeling completely out of control. I hoped that our plane would go down and everyone on board would miraculously survive except for us.

We walked into the house, our home sweet home we had purchased and moved into just two months before, and found my parents sitting at our kitchen table. My mother had already put Tyler to bed. The house was so very quiet. Max, his tail wagging profusely, ran over to greet us. My dad stood up and looked at us as my mom met me in the doorway. Without saying anything she wrapped her arms around me and held me. I broke down. I didn't want them to go through what we were inevitably going to go through. I wanted to spare them the pain of losing Jeff. And they wanted to spare me the same. My dad shook Jeff's hand, holding on a little longer, making every attempt to avoid showing emotion. "We'll get through this. As a family we'll get through this," Daddy said, looking at Jeff. That was our one and only option; get through it. There was nothing more to say, nothing more to do. Dad offered to drive Tyler to school the next morning, and I accepted. I don't remember my parents leaving that night, nor do I recall going to bed.

As I woke the next morning, an overwhelming feeling of sadness came over me instantly, realizing the events of the day before were not a nightmare but a reality. I climbed out of bed quietly and walked through the kitchen to put the kettle on, then to Tyler's room. I quietly opened the door and stood there watching him sleep. He looked so peaceful. I wanted to lie down next to him and stay there forever. It had been just he and I on our own for so long. When I was single, I'd craved adult conversation and companionship, but Tyler and I were doing fine, just the two of us. Now look at the mess I had gotten us into. He loved Jeff like a father. I felt I had failed him. He would suffer right along with me, along with Jeff, and it would completely alter his childhood and forever change his life.

Tyler began to stir and opened his big blue eyes, followed by a grin when he saw that I was standing there. I sat down on the edge of the bed and smoothed his tousled hair. "Good morning, good morning, good morning, it's time to rise and shine. Good morning, good morning, good morning, I hope you're feeling fine. The sun is up, the day is new, and all your dreams are coming true, doodle de do, doodle de do, doodle de do," I sang. He was a sight for sore eyes, and for one second I forgot that Jeff was dying. Then I remembered.

I struggled to maintain my composure while we went through our morning routine getting ready for school. I kissed Tyler good-bye when my father pulled up in front of the house, then found myself back in Ty's room. It felt so safe there. I started making his bed, but that's all I can remember. The next thing I knew, Jeff was there, holding me. I had no visible injury but I felt such excruciating pain. I couldn't get a breath. Suddenly I realized I was screaming. I tried to stop, but I couldn't. I had no control of my body. My throat ached as all I had held in forced its way out of me. Jeff held me tightly but so lovingly. It felt as though my body would leave the universe if he let go. I would fly away if he let go.

Exhausted, I finally calmed enough to say, "Why you? Why? You have so much to contribute. All of the evil people in the world, why not one of them?" Jeff held me there on Ty's bed until we both drifted off to sleep.

That was the last time I questioned Jeff's diagnosis, the last time I asked why. He was one of three in one hundred thousand. Asking why is wishing this nightmare on someone else. Our lives had been turned upside down, and it was up to us how we would handle it. We took three weeks off to let everything sink in. We cried together many times and somehow found a way to begin ignoring it. I just kept telling myself, he is here now; don't think about tomorrow, think about today.

The afternoon following our return from Johns Hopkins, I was working in the kitchen and Tyler was sitting at the bar eating apples and nut butter, his favorite after-school snack, when he asked me how the doctor's appointment went. I hadn't mentioned it because I didn't quite know what I was going to tell him.

"Well, Dad has something that the doctors don't know how to fix," I said without hesitation.

"But he's going to be OK?" he asked, needing to hear me say it.

"Well, we don't know, because very little is known about this particular disease." He kept pressing the issue, his little nine-year-old mind desperately trying to grasp what was happening.

"But Dad will be OK? He will get better and be OK? Right?" he pleaded.

"Tyler, sweetie, I don't know. No one knows, but we'll do everything we can to make him better. We will get through this, one way or another, and you will be just fine, all right?" I reassured him.

"All right, Mom," he answered, finally accepting the unknown, the illogical.

The days that followed were quiet. Jeff played chess with Ty and entertained him with little things, like juggling onions in the kitchen while he prepared his famous French onion soup, or a frittata.

Tyler continued to ask an occasional question until I offered the complete truth. That the disease would indeed win, and nothing we could do would stop it. He had to accept that.

After school one day, I pulled into the garage, turned off the ignition, and started to get out of the car. Tyler just sat there quietly. "Mom, why is this happening to Dad? Why him and not someone who is bad? Jeff is good."

Realizing my son was asking the same question I had asked, I told him the truth. "Tyler, God doesn't make certain things happen, nor does God prevent certain things from happening, but God does give us strength to cope with whatever life throws our way. Because this happened to Jeff, there will be a new awareness of something that desperately needs it. Jeff will make an impact that no one else can come close to making. It's a difficult road ahead, dear one, and it won't be easy, but one thing is for certain, you will be a better person because of it. And one day you will do something amazing, something that you could not have accomplished without this experience. We must make good of it, as hard as it may be."

Three weeks later we returned for the final tour stop in Mississippi. I felt nauseous most of the time and couldn't bear to even speak to anyone. The tour had become aware of Jeff's diagnosis, and the media had caught word.

Jeff's dad, Toby, made the trip and stood behind us while Jeff hit practice shots on the range before teeing off on Thursday. I walked away momentarily to grab a bottle of water when a Golf Channel reporter came up and asked me if what she'd heard was true. "Yes," I replied, without emotion. She then offered her condolences, and I thanked her before finding water and returning to inside the ropes where Jeff was still hitting balls.

My head started spinning, and I was suddenly overcome with sadness. I sat down and lowered my body to the ground. Lying there on my back, I looked up to the heavens. Toby was concerned and asked me if I needed anything. I couldn't even speak. It was so comforting to have him there, and I felt so badly for what he must have been going through. I just couldn't express it because I was so overwhelmed by my own sadness. It felt as if Jeff and I were now on the outside looking in at a world we were no longer part of.

Jeff shot a 78 that day and hoped to recover with a 69 on Friday, but he still missed the cut. It made me so angry. Give him a break, I thought. Just one break!

The week had been more exhausting than I'd anticipated. Being in public, trying not to break down was almost impossible, and a smile was out of the question.

One day at a time I kept telling him—and myself.

We didn't know when we would have a chance to tell Keegan. We didn't want to tell him what Jeff had was terminal, but he needed to know there was an illness. Jeff didn't want to tell him anything over the phone, but he wanted it to come from him, of course. Unfortunately, before we had a chance to see Keegan, one of his classmates at school made him aware of the fact that his dad had some kind of incurable disease.

We left Mississippi knowing Jeff had more than likely played in his last event as an official PGA Tour cardholder. We began wondering what in the hell we were going to do. According to statistics, Jeff had less than five years to live. Now was not the time to lose his card, his dream.

# Seventeen

Days and nights that were once full of movement in our happy little home seemed to have come to a screeching halt. We did our best to ignore it, but it was always there in the back of our minds.

Tyler was chosen for the fifth-grade spelling bee. He never took things like this very seriously because he often overestimated his giftedness and passed off studying altogether. This time was different. He spent a couple of days scanning the list of over five hundred words they handed out as a guide. I sat in the middle school auditorium while Jeff stayed home, too weak to come along.

Being the only parent at your child's event gets old quick. I scanned the room to find other mothers sitting next to the father of their children, smiling, basking in that wonderful glow that is parenthood. Some I knew, some I did not.

I had finally found a partner, someone Tyler would look up to and count on. Tyler and Keegan had become like brothers.

An oblong cafeteria table was set up at the front left of the stage where three women were sitting with their backs to the audience. The vice principal and another teacher were standing in the wings. I spotted Tyler's teacher, Miss Anderson, sitting near the front. Mrs. Trimble, who ran the gifted program, was also sitting near the front. Mrs. Trimble had been my kindergarten teacher and ended up being my favorite throughout elementary school. Tyler was seated in the sixth seat from the end. Five kids went up to the microphone one by one. Tyler's friend Emily was among them. "Organize," "duplicate," "submission," "maintenance," and "encyclopedia" were all spelled correctly. Tyler's turn came, and he walked up to the microphone looking confident.

The pronouncer looked down at her sheet, and then up at Tyler. I was a little nervous for him but confident in his ability to do well. His vocabulary was as vast as an adult's. Then out of her mouth came the word: "incurable."

No way did she say what I think she said; it's all in my head, I thought. Tyler stood there for a moment, then asked her to repeat the word, as if he too was having a hard time believing his ears. "Incurable," the pronouncer repeated slowly. My heart fell to my stomach. I began spelling it in my head, hoping he'd hear me. I-N-C-U-R, drop the E, A-B-L-E. Drop the E, sweetie, drop the E.

Tyler took a breath, failed to drop the E, and was out in the first round.

Ellyn and Joe Lennon, sitting two rows in front of me, turned to me with a look of disbelief and pity. Joe was my chiropractor and had become Jeff's chiropractor and friend.

I just sat quietly smiling, while on the inside the pain ran through my body like the disease that was running through Jeff's. I wanted to confess how miserable I was, but I was afraid to, afraid of falling apart. My entire existence was a façade.

Once the first round was complete, my little guy came up behind me and quietly slid into the empty chair next to me. I gave him a wink and put my arm around him. We said nothing, because nothing could be said. I couldn't protect the man I loved from ALS any more than I could protect my son from the pain—or the words that cropped up to remind him. I could only go on.

I started focusing on Christmas, when my brother and his wife, Melissa, would be visiting. Jeff occupied his mind as best he could. Tyler slowly went from being inquisitive and caring to quiet and removed. He stayed in his room a lot more, and I could sense him pushing away from Jeff and Jeff pushing away from him. Jeff and I avoided looking at one another, because when our eyes did meet, we would both smile and immediately tear up. There was so much love there. But what did our future hold? My concern for Jeff's state of mind increased. I could sense him checking out, and I wasn't ready for that. We would have to concentrate on living one day at a time.

To get our minds off of death and make good of what we'd been dealt, Jeff and I, with the help of our family and friends, started the Jeff Julian ALS Foundation. This gave Jeff something to focus on while waiting for November's qualifying school. We set the date for the inaugural golf tournament that was first named "The Jeff Julian & Friends Golf Classic," and would later change to "The Julian," to take place in April of 2002. Jeff and I had a strong desire to do something more, something that would make a considerable difference in research and in the lives of present and future ALS patients worldwide.

Q-school was fast approaching. Jeff would again only be required to go through the second stage and, hopefully, finals. If Jeff made it through the second stage, we'd have a two-and-a-half week window before the finals, which would allow for a short trip to Vermont to see Keegan. While there we would go to Dartmouth Hitchcock for the appointment with that world-renowned urologist, who could help put Jeff back together again so we could make a baby. "I want a little girl just like you," Jeff had said. "Sassy, but sweet as can be."

Jeff had registered for the second stage qualifier being held at the Bayonet course at Seaside, California. We had spent a week in Monterey earlier in the year while Jeff played in the Pebble Beach Pro-Am and had fallen in love with the area. It had a quality about it that pulled us in and captured our hearts so much that we decided we would someday make Monterey our home and grow old together there.

We arrived in California on Saturday afternoon and moved into a little bungalow in Carmel, just like the one we'd stayed in earlier that year for Pebble. We went to bed early after a light dinner and spent the next two days practicing and avoiding any discussions regarding the future.

When Tuesday came it was cold, even for Monterey. Jeff, being from Vermont, typically played well in the cold and had an advantage in the field because he easily acclimated, unlike most golfers, who typically live in warm climates.

Jeff ended up with a 72 on Tuesday, a 77 on Wednesday, another 77 on Thursday, and a 74 on Friday, placing him at 12 over par when the cut line was at one under.

After returning to our bungalow, Jeff was feeling very deflated and hopeless. I wasn't sure how to help him. What could I possibly say? I sat quietly while holding his hand until he was ready to talk and finally spoke. "It's over. My career is over. I'll never compete again," he said, his mouth beginning to quiver. My heart ached for him. It was true. The disease was only going to progress. I wanted to support him, say something that would make everything better, but there was nothing, nothing I could say or do.

"It doesn't have to be," I replied, not sure of what I was going to say next. "Losing your card doesn't mean you can no longer play, Jeff. We live on a golf course! You can play every day. We'll go home, and we'll play all day, every day."

"It's not the same. You know that." My enthusiasm wasn't catching.

"Maybe you can qualify for Buy.com or a mini-tour." I realized Jeff's restlessness was going to be unbearable for him and began grasping at straws.

"Kimberly, it's even more difficult to make a cut on the Buy.com," Jeff replied. I said nothing, but I didn't have to. The look on my face made him aware of the pessimism he was dishing out. "I suppose I can try to Monday qualify for a few events," he said, a little color coming back to his face.

"How does that work?" I knew how it worked but wanted to get his wheels turning. He needed someone to kick him in the ass and I was trying to do just that, lovingly.

"Golf professionals can play in tournaments called qualifiers where they play a round to qualify for a spot in the field. They're similar to playing in a pro-am," Jeff answered.

"Oh, like the U.S. Open qualifier you played in?"

"Yep," Jeff replied. We sat quietly for a few minutes and I reached out to hold his hand. "I could also ask for exemptions from title sponsors," he continued.

"Exemptions?" I asked.

"It's basically an invitation extended by the event title sponsor. They can give an exemption to whomever they want. They typically go to players who, like me, have a story."

"Well, let's do it! We'll get you back out there playing and raise a little hell for ALS while we're at it. What do you say?"

Jeff looked at me and gave me a sweet, humbling grin. "I love you. That's what I say."

"I love you too, Jeffrey. And don't you forget we're in this together. I'm right here." Tears fell silently, and we held each other for a while.

We boarded a plane the next day and headed to Vermont to see Keegan. Jeff approached the diagnosis in the same way I had with Tyler. Keegan was the quiet one of the two boys and, unlike Tyler, rarely questioned what he was told. Jeff chose to talk to him alone, just as I had with Ty.

Keegan's reaction indicated he wasn't surprised. He responded by saying a classmate at school had told him. Of course he didn't realize the extent of this Lou Gehrig's disease his dad had been stricken with, and it was probably for the best. He didn't ask if there was a cure. I don't think kids think death is possible. Not for them or someone they love anyway, not until it actually happens.

On Monday, and still in Vermont, Jeff went to the follow-up at Dartmouth while I busied myself with shopping. The surgeon sat Jeff down and advised him to reconsider the vasectomy reversal. "In light of your recent diagnosis and prognosis," he had said.

"He told me you'd have enough on your plate caring for the two children we already have and eventually for me," Jeff said nonchalantly, as though he were suggesting we cancel dinner plans with friends because we were too busy.

"What?" I didn't want to hear what he was telling me.

"He said caring for a newborn while dealing with what lies ahead will be too much stress on you." I'd grown tired of doctors determining our fate, and this upset me. Yes, I was absolutely clueless as to the hard days ahead, but Jeff's diagnosis hadn't happened in my mind. I still wanted another child, now more than ever.

"Well, that's just great," I said, crossing my arms as tears rolled down my cheeks and every fiber of my being went numb.

"Hey," Jeff came close, eased me to the side of the bed, and kneeled down in front of me. "I think we need to take his advice, Kim. We don't know what we're up against here. Do you really want to raise another child alone? Are you going to sit here and tell me it's been easy raising Tyler by yourself?"

"Of course not, but you'll help me raise our child." I knew that our raising a child together was not going to happen, but I didn't want to admit it. I broke down and fell into Jeff's loving embrace and stayed there until my anger surrendered to the fact that I would never have a child with the man that I loved.

We returned to Missouri and went to work on letters to sponsors. We chose events that were scheduled during the first six months of the year to try and race the progression that would surely come. We sent out well over a dozen letters. The Pebble Beach Pro-Am request was the first one in the mail, and Ollie Nutt, the tournament director, was the first to call and extend Jeff an invitation. The event was scheduled for the week of January 31. Other invitations soon followed, and Jeff had a difficult time deciding in which events he most wanted to play. So much was happening in such a short amount of time. We ended up with a schedule that would allow us to be finished with tournaments by the end of June. After that the focus would be on Jeff's health.

# Eighteen

The pup was from a large litter that was born just in time to be ready to come home by Christmas. We found a hobby breeder in Springfield and visited his home where we met the puppy's parents, who were both a bit chubby and a little on the short side for Labs. The breeder led us into the garage where a huge cardboard box lined with fluffy towels and puppies was positioned next to a heat lamp. Tyler reached over the side of the box, which was almost as tall as he was, and pulled out a cute little squirming puppy, a little boy.

"Hey Ty, Max might not appreciate the competition of another male in the house," I suggested. And, my God, we did not need another Max.

Tyler ignored my question, then looked up at me with his big blue eyes. "He's cute, don't cha think, Mom?"

Every Max incident flashed through my mind. "Put him back! Now!" I commanded. Tyler gave the male pup a kiss on the head and slowly lowered him back into the box. "Buh-bye, little fella, don't worry, someone will take you home."

The second pup that Tyler pulled out was a tiny little girl, the runt for sure. She was quiet but not too quiet. Her eyes were lined with black, and she was the same color and had the same markings as Max, so light yellow she was almost white.

Determined to avoid ending up with another disobedient dog, we had actually prepared by doing a little reading. *Dogs for Dummies* had been loaned to me before we'd adopted Max, but regrettably I hadn't even opened the book. Finally I'd put it to good use. The book recommends you hold the puppy a few inches from the ground. If it wriggled and wriggled, that meant it would surely be a little rascal. Freezing immediately could mean the puppy was timid and skittish. If the pup fussed and wriggled for a few seconds and then became still, you were holding the perfect dog.

I took the puppy from Ty, leaned over the box where her brothers and sisters were frolicking, and held her there, a few inches between her little dangling paws and the bottom of the box. She gave a gentle squirm and moved her feet for a few seconds, then stopped. I looked up at Jeff. He stood there next to me, watching closely, and nodded at me.

"This is the one," I said as I stood up and pulled the puppy into the safety of my left shoulder. She nuzzled my neck and tucked her little head into my collarbone as an infant would. We bonded instantly.

"When is their birthday?" Tyler asked the breeder.

"October 27," he replied.

She had been born on the same day exactly one year after Jeff had proposed to me. We paid for our new addition to the family and left her with her mom, where she would spend the next two weeks until she was ready to come home. "We'll call her Peyton," Jeff suggested, naming her after the restaurant in Bradford, Vermont, where we had dined on that very memorable night, after Jeff's proposal in the barn..

We returned a week before Christmas to pick her up and take her home. We found and hired a trainer who would help us train Peyton and possibly work on Max too. I'd made the mistake of winging it with Max and was not about to do that again!

Having a new puppy around made the holidays a little brighter. Jeff, Ty, and I celebrated Christmas in Missouri with Tim and Melissa, my parents, my grandfather, and my aunt and uncle. Like many things in our lives, Christmas would never be the same. It seemed something would always be missing.

We did our best to live in the here and now, to enjoy Jeff while he was with us. Still, how disappointing it can be knowing time is short. In all honesty, Christmas sucked. New Year's Eve sucked even more. How do you wish someone a Happy New Year when a new year only represented time and progression and death drawing nearer? There was nothing happy about it. Of course, we went ahead and pretended we had plenty to be happy about.

Keegan spent Christmas with his mom in Vermont and then flew to Missouri for a week with us. Knowing we would be late getting home from the airport, we decided to save introducing the new puppy to Keegan until the next morning.

Jeff and I were awake, lounging in bed. I was holding Peyton like a baby, and Max, giving me the stink eye, had positioned himself between Jeff and me. Max was allowed to get on the bed in the morning for snuggling, when invited. I heard Keegan, who was always up at the crack of dawn, in the kitchen starting the kettle water. Max got up and ran out of the room. Peyton lifted her little head to see what all the excitement was about. I gently set her down on the floor and she took off after Max.

"Maxie, you bad boy," we heard Keegan say in a quiet voice. We naturally called him bad instead of good because he was always bad! "Oh, my gosh, where did you come from?" Peyton had introduced herself. Jeff and I walked into the living room where Keegan, sleepy eyed, lay on the floor with both dogs. Jeff and I stood there together, watching Peyton lick Keegan's face. He looked up at us. "We got a new puppy?" he asked, smiling behind Peyton's kisses.

"We did, indeed. Isn't she cute?" I asked, squatting down next to Keegan. "She was the runt of the litter, which is why she's such a punk," I added. From that moment Peyton was a.k.a. "The Punk" or "Punky."

The three weeks at home between Keegan's visit and the Pebble Beach Pro-Am were spent mostly ignoring what was happening to Jeff's body. We hired a trainer for the puppy since we were going to be traveling for the first half of the year. Time is of the essence when training a dog, and I didn't want to make the mistakes I'd made with Max. Jeff could no longer project his voice to yell, so we taught her hand commands as well as basic manners.

I wanted to grow old with my husband. I wanted it so badly. Dr. Cohen's first words often played in my head, "In some cases it stops progressing."

No noticeable signs of ALS were apparent except for his speech, which was becoming difficult even for those of us who were around him all of the time to comprehend. At this point his hands were unaffected. We bought a sign language book and video. The three of us watched it several times as a family. Signing was less tiring for Jeff and kind of fun, actually. I decided I could easily live with using our hands to communicate while growing old together. Eventually we'd develop arthritis, but after having lived a long, happy life together, we'd have less to say anyway and would at that point be reading each other's minds.

Meanwhile, Tyler was more than halfway through his fifth-grade year. Tyler loved school more than ever, especially his gifted class. They were preparing for their annual Live Wax Museum. The students were asked to write a report on someone famous who they admired. The parents would come to the presentation in the auditorium, where the children would be dressed like their chosen person, standing in front of booths they had erected and decorated with facts and hints as to who their person was. The parents walked around to all of the booths, and the objective was to present the person well enough that the parents would correctly guess who they were imitating. They worked on it for weeks. They also had to write a short essay about what they wanted to be when they were older.

For the live wax museum, Tyler picked Lou Gehrig. He dressed in a little Yankees uniform I had made for him and held a bat in his hand in front of his booth. It was an easy guess, especially for the parents who knew us.

At that point Tyler wanted to join the FBI, so his career essay explained the steps he would take in order to accomplish it. His plans involved a four-year degree followed by going to Quantico to train. It was very cute, but I couldn't help but think about how fast life was moving, and I couldn't bear the thought of him growing up and going off to college. It was coming, whether I had relished in his childhood or not.

Our search for a doctor was next on the list. Jeff refused to go back to the neurologist, which I wholeheartedly supported. Why would we want an EMG performed every three months to tell us how much more ALS had progressed? We assumed it would be self-explanatory. What we did want was a doctor who would look at how to help us make Jeff's quality of life the best it could possibly be.

Gail Scott, Honey's mom, referred us to Dr. Jeff Baker. Dr. Baker was a family doctor whose practice had transitioned from traditional medicine to an alternative approach, so he was exactly what we wanted. His office was located in Springdale, Arkansas, two hours from Branson.

Dr. Baker started with urine samples and blood work that confirmed the mercury in Jeff's system was "off the charts." It also showed us what Jeff's body was lacking, and what it needed to function at an optimal level. Our first plan of attack was intravenous chelation therapy to remove heavy metals from Jeff's system. We decided to wait until after the Pebble Beach event to hit the chelation hard. With no event for two months following Pebble, we had an opportunity to get into the groove of things. We did, however, begin a regimen that would require him to swallow numerous supplements throughout the day—so many that it would take an effort just to organize them. I found a compartmentalized box the size of a brief case. Each section was perfect for fifty to one hundred capsules. I labeled each section with the appropriate name and dosage.

I was a bit shocked to actually find Amyotrophic Lateral Sclerosis in a book I had referred to for years, *You Can Heal Your Life* by Louise Hay. Yakov had introduced me to it when I was working for him.

Basically the theory is that what we think about is what we manifest. We create our own "dis-ease" in our bodies. If I had a sore throat, it was due to holding back words that should be verbalized. Each ailment includes a mantra, a new thought process, that you can write down and post in various places to remind you of this new way of thinking. It was a brilliant book, as kooky as it may sound, and it had proved to be effective in my life, but I'd never put it to the test of an incurable disease.

I put the label maker to use and printed several of the suggested mantras, such as, "My children love and adore me," and, "I'm worthy of all that is good" and posted them all over the house: on the mirror over the vanity in our bathroom, in our office, in the kitchen above the sink, and in the briefcase-sized vitamin box.

Dr. Baker decided that intravenous vitamin C combined with the glutathione chelation therapy would help counteract any negative effects that could arise from heavy metal removal, which tended to drain Jeff of energy. Jeff did experience a noticeable energy increase after a two-hour drip of vitamin C, so it was added to the regimen.

We were still covered by Cigna health insurance through the tour, thankfully. However, Dr. Baker's treatments were considered "experimental medicine" and were not covered. Depending on the treatments Jeff would undergo in a month, we were shelling out anywhere from $5,000 to $10,000 per month.

Callaway offered to sponsor Jeff for the year, which meant we'd have money coming in regardless of his performance on the course. Jeff's strength would continue to decline, and the odds were against him making any cuts.

There were two reasons for playing in the events. The main was to keep Jeff going, to keep pushing him to do what he loved most; the other was to get the word out and raise awareness.

We were not at all prepared for what happened. Every event brought endless opportunities to speak about ALS.

The media frenzy created by the way in which Jeff was handling himself provided our sponsors with tremendous exposure. We spent hours with reporters. It was exhausting, but nothing compared to what an ALS patient must deal with every second of every day, which is what kept us going.

We were receiving so many requests for interviews that the PGA began holding press conferences at each event so we could accommodate all of them.

We went through the motions and avoided the disease at all costs, taking one day at a time, living in the present moment. Our attitude while in the public eye was a positive one. It wasn't a façade; we really did believe that being positive was the only way to be, but we were also denying the fact that we were miserable. At Muirfield, Ohio, during an ESPN interview, the reporter asked me if I felt we were in denial. I answered, "Absolutely. In denial is a good place to be."

Realizing how tiring it would be just to get to an event with all of the supplies we needed, we decided to hire a caddy. I was too busy focusing on Jeff to be worried about stepping in someone's line or raking a bunker improperly. I was his super wife now—no time for caddying. If he needed an interpreter to help someone understand him, I was right there. If he needed something that wasn't available at the tee, I would run to the clubhouse and retrieve it. If he needed me to walk inside the ropes and hold his hand, I jumped at the chance. Nothing could stop me. I was certain I could save him.

Taking my place on the bag was our good friend Jelly, who had been caddying for our dear friend Andrew for a few years. Drew and Toni happened to be in Europe competing on the European Tour in 2002, so Jelly needed a player. We were lucky enough to snag him for the first five events, until he got a gig working for Tim Petrovic.

Jelly has been a caddy on the Tour for years. His real name is Richard Hansberry, but everyone calls him Jelly, short for Jellyroll. His pear-shaped frame was well over six feet tall, and he always offered wisdom and pleasant conversation.

Jeff wasn't making any cuts, and without cuts a caddy gets only the weekly fee, which was around $1,000 at the time. When a player makes the cut, his caddy is paid 10 percent of that week's winnings. It was a lot to ask of a caddy, but Jelly came through for us. We lived off of our Callaway endorsement; thank God for Callaway. We didn't blame Jelly for leaving us to work with Tim, but we did miss him for those last few events. We were thrilled for Jelly when Tim ended up having a great year.

# Nineteen

Out of the seven events Jeff participated in during the first six months of 2002, I think Pebble is the one that stood out the most. First, it's simply magnificent. Jeff always said that Pebble Beach is the only golf course that looks as beautiful in person as it does on television. It has a magical quality about it. The fact that several of Hollywood's finest participate as well as pro athletes isn't what makes it magical. Something about Pebble feels less cumbersome. Less restricted.

The amateurs you meet are always unique individuals, and everyone has a great time. Jeff's playing partner, Pard Erdman, requested Jeff as his playing partner after following Jeff's story in the news. Pard and his wife, Betsy, owned a cattle ranch in Hawaii and split their time between their home there and their home that was situated right on the famous Cypress Point golf course near Pebble Beach. People like Pard and Betsy Erdman give life meaning and make it worth living. As good as gold right to their core, both of them.

Second, Pebble Beach stands out because it was the most emotional. The idea of ALS was still fresh, and we were seeing those who had been like family for the first time since the diagnosis.

My friend Selena spotted me just outside the player family area the first day of the pro-am and rushed over.

"Kim, oh my God, how are you guys holding up?" She looked as though she might cry.

"I don't know, Selena." For a moment I felt that I didn't need to remain positive, that it was all right to break down. "I don't know. We are taking it one day at a time. Being out here will be a good diversion, I guess."

She gave me a hug and said, "I just can't believe it. No one can. If you need anything, anything at all, please let us know, OK, love?"

"Thanks, Selena, I will. And tell Frank hello for us," I said, then turned and, not really knowing where I was headed, walked until I came upon a parking area that looked somewhat isolated, and I cried. I wanted to scream at God. I didn't want our friends to feel badly for us. I didn't want to see the pain in their eyes. It was just too much to bear. Our pain, Jeff's and mine, was causing everyone we loved pain.

At Pebble all kinds of people began surfacing. You would have thought we had won the lottery.

On the second or third hole, Mark Russell, a rules official, came over and handed me a note. It startled me. In all of our days on tour, I'd never before been handed a note in the middle of a round. I immediately feared something was wrong with a family member. I paused before I looked at it.

"Mary Ann (I forget her last name) will be arriving this afternoon." That was all it read. "Who?" I thought.

Then I remembered. Jeff had dated a Mary Ann in his college years. I think they lived together because I recalled him talking about a cat they had walked on a leash. I was confused as to why she was announcing her arrival. Jeff, periodically coming over to the ropes, read the note when I handed it to him.

"Mark handed it to me on the last hole,"

Jeff glanced down at the note. "And?" he said, in a sarcastic tone then chuckled.

"I don't know," I said, "stop the presses?" and smiled. Jeff leaned down and kissed me before walking back to the center of the fairway where his good friend and caddy, Scottie Peters, stood holding Jeff's bag.

Toward the end of the round, I noticed a couple walking along the path who hadn't been there before. The girl, right out of a Patagonia catalog except for the crutches she was on, had a stocky, athletic build and long, dark-blondish hair. The guy, skinny with dark hair, was wearing a backpack. They were a cute, crunchy couple.

Jeff soon came back to the ropes and pointed to the couple I'd noticed in the gallery. "That's Mary Ann," he said, in his slurry speech.

"Oh, I was noticing them earlier. They're cute. Very earthy and sporty. She probably injured her leg while rock climbing," I commented, watching her with admiration as she crutched along the grassy path.

"Nah, it's just a joke," Jeff corrected me as we walked along together to his next shot, which had landed in the fairway this time.

"A joke?" I asked.

"She thinks she's being funny," Jeff replied. "You know, because she broke her leg on our first date."

"Really?" I didn't quite know how to respond but felt that carrying on in this manner was somewhat presumptuous of her.

A group of about fifty people was following Jeff during his rounds at Pebble. Some were old friends, some family, and some were complete strangers who were so intrigued by Jeff's courage that they simply wanted to watch him swing a club. They were all there to see him play "one last time." It exhausted me emotionally and clearly irritated Jeff for the same reasons, though he was better than I at hiding his frustration. It's a quality that was both good and bad—bad because he held everything in and internalized it, something Louise Hay says creates dis-ease; and good because he was happy-go-lucky, non-confrontational Jeff.

I wanted to be grateful for all of these wonderful people who loved Jeff, but I didn't want to share what little time I had left with him. I didn't see the point in the sudden appearance of people who hadn't so much as entered Jeff's mind for years. It was intrusive, and it made Jeff's illness too realistic.

One man came up halfway through the round on the second day and introduced himself. I'd seen him in the gallery but didn't know him. His name was Brian. Brian and his girlfriend, Kitty, lived in Monterey. Brian was in New York on business when he saw the Golf Channel interview Jeff and I had given the day before. He cancelled all of his meetings and flew back. He said he just had to see Jeff play. Brian and Kitty became friends of ours. A year later Kitty, a talented artist, sent us a beautiful painting of the cypress that stands at the tip of Lovers Point in Pacific Grove. Another random act of kindness.

After the last putt on 18 the crowd of friends and family who were in the gallery gathered around the back of the green. Jeff was immediately enveloped by the mob.

I didn't want to witness it. There was a feeling of finality that I was not ready for. I walked down the hill to where our car happened to be parked and waited. After several photos were taken and every person had been greeted, Jeff felt my absence and escaped the scene to find me. I was feeling deflated, exhausted; it felt that I'd seen his last competitive round. He walked up with a look on his face that said, "What's the matter?" and opened his arms. I fell into his embrace but felt no relief. There would be no relief from what was now beginning to consume everything life had once been.

Jeff didn't make the cut that week, so Pard invited him to play at Cypress Point. Ask any golfer: this was one of those once-in-a-lifetime opportunities. Cypress Point has maybe two hundred members, Mr. Erdman being one of them, and possesses the most exquisite, breathtaking scenery one could imagine. The members don't even allow the course to be photographed, and although guests are allowed, they absolutely must be accompanied at all times by a member. Jeff and Pard played all eighteen holes while Betsy and I followed, chatting.

Betsy reminded me of my grandmother. She exuded elegance, was a sweet and dedicated wife, but would hold her own and speak her mind, and do so appropriately. Betsy made a tremendous impact on me that day. She gently helped me see the reality of our situation. After Jeff was gone, I would remain, and because of this we should get our affairs in order immediately, before Jeff started to progress and this topic became too close to home. She was right. We had purchased life insurance policies for both of us after we were married, but we had never talked about wills.

I spoke to Jeff about it later. He agreed to the advice Betsy had so kindly offered, and we made plans to visit an attorney as soon as we returned to Missouri. I knew it was best, but still, the thought of it was nauseating.

That evening we left the Erdmans before sunset. I grabbed the cell phone to call home. Tyler was already in bed but not yet asleep. "How was school, sweetie?" I missed him. I missed our dogs. I missed the smell of our home.

"It was good, Mom. How are you and Dad?"

"We are both doing well, honey; everything is fine. Did you see Max and Peyton today?"

"Yeah, Mom, Peyton is growing a lot!"

We'd asked a friend of ours to house and dog sit. Jared was just out of college and was an amazing golfer. His aunt and uncle lived at Pointe Royale, where we lived, so Jared played golf there, and he and Jeff had become buddies. Jared and his girlfriend, Kelly, lived with Jared's parents, so we knew that house sitting would give them time alone while also preventing Max and Peyton from being subjected to the kennel. It was a win-win situation, and when we approached them, they were thrilled with the idea. Tyler would walk over with Mom after school to play with the dogs and pick up anything he may need.

"You won't believe your eyes when you see her, Mom. When will you see her?" he asked.

"I will see Peyton tomorrow...and you...and that rotten Max too!" I replied.

As we drove up the windy road past Cypress Point, we saw Rob, a photographer we'd worked with on a *Sports Illustrated* article, sneakily climbing over the small wood fence bordering the course, his camera in hand. Jeff came to a complete stop, rolled the window down, and heckled him. "You're committing a crime, you know?" Jeff said laughing, trying his best to speak clearly.

Rob looked at us and held his finger up to his lip before clearing the fence and sneaking off into the trees. That was Jeff, always teasing, always happy.

The break from our travels allowed us to spend much-needed time with doctors and specialists regarding Jeff's care. A visit to a speech pathologist for an evaluation to determine a device to help Jeff better communicate was at the top of the list. It was becoming more and more difficult for even Tyler and me to understand and be Jeff's voice.

After we were back home, we decided that instead of delaying the chelation therapy for six months, we would drive to the six remaining events so we could take enough supplies with us to last a couple of weeks. Otherwise we'd be forced to delay the treatments until after the Hartford event in late June.

Dr. Baker suggested we have a surgical port placed which would allow us to start an IV anywhere at any time. It would eliminate the hassle of finding someone to access a vein and eliminate the possibility of having to put Jeff's regimen on hold until June.

The port could be placed with a simple outpatient procedure, and we had a few months before the next tournament.

In the recovery room after the procedure, the sight of the port upset both of us. It looked like a piece of Rollo candy trapped under Jeff's skin, just below his collarbone. It was the first surgery, the first surrender, and the first step down the road to progression. It was these facts that were probably the most upsetting; we just didn't realize it at the time.

ALS had slowly robbed Jeff of his voice and was now affecting his smile. Drinking liquids was almost impossible, which made swallowing the regimen of several pills a day a real challenge. I had started helping him eat because lifting the fork all the way up to his mouth several times exhausted him. It would take him an hour to eat even the smallest meal, and we were limited to pasta and soft foods.

It wasn't long before Dr. Baker also suggested a feeding tube, which triggered another round of resistance. Looking back now, it was better that we went through with the procedure when we did, before we had to. The healing time was longer and took more of a toll on Jeff's body than we'd expected.

As horrible as it sounded, the feeding tube proved to be convenient. The energy Jeff saved by omitting the task of swallowing all of those pills was reserved for eating. I would use our coffee grinder to grind the vitamins, mix them with juice, and then pour the mixture into the tube. Jeff could do it himself, because the tube only needed to be slightly above where it was placed, just above waist height. The thought of a feeding tube had once mortified me, but a few days after the procedure, it was a lot less scary. A case of the "foot in the door phenomenon": the feeding tube ended up being a blessing because by autumn Jeff would not be able to swallow anything without choking.

One day I walked into the kitchen to find Jeff at the sink with his back to me. All I could see was a wine bottle tipped upside down. As I got closer, I realized he had the syringe attached to his tube and was filling it with wine. My first reaction was to scold him. "Jeffrey! What are you doing? We can't put alcohol through that!" I was worried of what it might do to him. I was still learning about all of these changes and the rules that went along with them.

Jeff turned his head to the side and looked at me with a grin. "Honey, no need for Opus One. The cheap stuff'll be just fine." His extremely slurred words turned to a mousy cackle as his vocal cords struggled to amplify his laugh. Then I started laughing and couldn't stop.

"Oh, my God, you're right. You can get wasted in a matter of seconds— and cheaply!" We stood there in the kitchen, for the first time laughing at ALS straight in the face. We had surrendered to the progression that was going to come at us without mercy. Most importantly we'd learned that laughter would be necessary to get through it.

Speech pathologist Judith Peavey ran several tests on Jeff, then provided us with the document our insurance company required to cover the cost of an augmentative device. The device/computer would grow with the progression of ALS and allow Jeff to communicate with others when his speech was completely gone. She helped us choose the right one. It would have to be somewhat mobile and have the capability of speaking for Jeff, as well as functioning as a computer.

What we came up with was the size of an Etch A Sketch, with a touch screen. The software allowed Jeff to type, to save phrases, and to set fast keys so that one touch would speak an entire sentence he had programmed. He could also use the device with a mouse. The software offered several voices to choose from, men's and women's. They sounded less mechanical than most I had heard before. We had fun deciding which to use as the default voice and ended up choosing one named "Paul." We decided Paul sounded young but worldly, like Jeff. The maker of the software was a company called Gus Communications, located in Seattle. So we named Jeff's computer "Gus."

Gus entered our lives just in time. Not long after we received Gus, Jeff quit talking completely. We had gone from being able to talk all night, to deciphering what Jeff was trying to say to me and to others by reading lips and sign language, to not being able to talk at all. Then, I was doing everything else for him too. It was like having a six-foot-three-inch infant that weighed 170 pounds and possessed the intellect of an adult. He needed assistance in doing everything that he wanted to do, every single moment of every single day.

Gus had been created by Gordon Harris. Gordon had no idea what he was getting himself into when he told us to call him anytime we needed help troubleshooting.

Within a month we had received the little box that would provide Jeff a voice and be a source of entertainment for the rest of us. Jeff loved using Gus to curse like a little kid. The first phrase he programmed was, "That fucking sucks," for using with his cronies.

Another phrase that he used daily was, "Tyler, I love you, now get your ass in bed." Every now and then I would hear a sultry female voice come over the speakers that I'd set up throughout the house, say, "Kimberly, I love you," making me laugh hysterically. That's how we dealt with our reality. With dark humor. Jeff would type things like, "Honey, you're going to give the term 'golf widow' a whole new meaning," and I would occasionally ask him to do the impossible, like sing me to sleep or tell me a bedtime story.

We had Gordon install the same software on the PalmPilot so he could continue to carry it on the golf course. Gus opened up many doors for Jeff that had gradually been closing.

# Twenty

Knowing money was soon going to be tight, our friends Scott and Amy Peters began organizing a fundraiser to be held at the Quechee Club in Vermont, where Jeff once worked as assistant pro. The funds raised would help cover Jeff's medical expenses that weren't covered by insurance. It would also cover our living expenses after the Callaway sponsorship came to an end in June.

Jeff was able to apply for Social Security, which amounted to $1,400 per month. This helped but didn't begin until six months after Jeff stopped playing competitive golf. It seemed asinine to me that a person must be unable to work for half a year before receiving assistance that is rightfully his to receive—especially when the disease was in fact deadly and incurable. Upon researching this topic, I found that some ALS patients die before they become eligible to receive one payment.

Jeff's last competitive round was in June of 2002 in Cromwell, Connecticut, at the Canon Greater Hartford Open. Being only a few hours from Vermont, Scott and Amy strategically scheduled the Quechee fundraiser for the day following the GHO. The tour worked something out with Buick to allow the players to hang on to their courtesy vehicles for an extra day or two following the GHO to allow them to drive a few hours north and attend the event.

Knowing this was probably Jeff's last competitive event, family and friends were coming in droves. Dan Baker, a good friend and the GHO tournament director, took great care of us.

My parents drove their motor home to Connecticut with plans to continue north to Vermont following Jeff's final event to attend the event at Quechee. Resembling a bus it would require a large area to park, so Dan made arrangements for them to have a space in the player RV lot, which is set up at every event for a few of the players who travel in motor homes.

Jeff, Tyler, and I arrived on Wednesday morning and, just like every event, went directly to the course to register before checking into the hotel. We pulled into the small lot in front of the clubhouse and parked upon realizing that the valet had not yet arrived.

Suddenly a courtesy car (usually a Buick that is loaned to each player during the week of an event) with the music blaring pulled into the parking space next to us and came to a screeching halt as the front end tapped the makeshift fence that had been erected to border the parking area. As I looked over to see who I assumed would be an unkempt caddy, Jeff turned and said, "ErrGeeO" in his muffled voice as he raised his eyebrows. Translation: "It's just Sergio." And it was Sergio, in his sneakers, shorts, and a T-shirt, which are forbidden in the clubhouse and on event grounds.

The PGA enforces these rules solely for retaining the pretentiousness of the game, which I will admit I have to agree with. Golf wouldn't be golf without a little pretense. Sergio was at that time still considered one of the young guns. Everyone expected him to be a wild child, so his reckless driving and lack of trousers and a collared shirt were no surprise. I'm not sure whether he was seen and reprimanded that day. I would guess not. I never had an opportunity to hold a conversation with Sergio Garcia, but I do know he was simply too adorable to reproach, with or without the proper attire.

After registering and receiving the digital camera and binoculars Canon was giving to every player, we drove over to the hotel to check in and rest a little before returning to the course to practice.

It was getting dark by the time we finished walking the course and began our ritualistic putt-off to determine who would get to choose where we ate that night. Tyler was starving, so I sent him inside with some cash to get a snack. He came back with two chocolate chip cookies from the locker room. Jeff was still able to eat a little, then I would supplement with vitamins and smoothies through the feeding tube. Pasta was pretty much all he could physically eat, but we still enjoyed fighting over the dinner venue—like old times.

Jeff always wanted Italian, and I something on the lighter side. Jeff thought the putting contest was the perfect way to settle this ongoing dispute. Whoever made the first putt determined from where the other person had to putt, and the other person, nine times out of ten, was me. I had two chances to make the putt or I lost, and he chose what we ate for dinner. He almost always won, and tonight was no different. I would once again find myself at an Italian restaurant, searching the menu for something that would not result in my gaining five pounds. Tyler consoled me with a bite of his second cookie.

My parents rang as we were walking to the car. They had arrived and were parked and settling in. "You're just in time for dinner," I told my mother. "Jeff wants you to choose where we go," I said, sticking my tongue out at Jeff.

"OK, let's have Italian," my mother replied as I slumped forward. Seeing my reaction, Jeff knew exactly what she'd requested and started laughing. My mom was always looking out for Jeff, as if he were her own.

Dan directed us to where they were located, which was not easy to find. Not more than half of a mile from the course, yet somewhat hidden, we pulled into a drive and found four bus-sized RVs (my parents' RV being the size of a Greyhound but the smallest of the four) parked in a semicircle. I scanned the area for my parents and spotted John Daly, the bad boy of golf, sitting next to what I assumed he referred to as his "rig," in a lawn chair that looked as though it might at any moment buckle from the weight of his mass. Every few moments a blonde woman would emerge from inside as John sat there, oblivious. He was singing while playing his guitar and had obviously been into the sauce.

Mom was nowhere in sight, but to the right of the Dalys I spotted my dad standing with Davis Love III next to their house on wheels, chatting and tinkering with what looked like a large toy airplane lying in the underbelly. My mother then surfaced from the Blake abode. She and Marci were yapping away as Jay Don worked his way over to where my dad and Davis were standing. He was carrying a toy airplane similar to the one Davis and Dad were looking at.

The Blake and Love kids were running around behind the homes in what looked like someone's backyard. Tyler, in the back seat and unable to contain himself, jumped out of the car and joined in on the fun after stopping for a quick hug from my mother. Jeff made his way over to my mother first, then greeted John Daly with a handshake before joining the other boys in the toy airplane aisle. I waved hello to Marci as Mom embraced me while asking if I'd been eating and sleeping well. The boys suddenly disappeared, and Mom and went inside to have a glass of tea.

Life seemed so normal.

The Hartford event was bittersweet. Jeff, being Jeff, asked Dr. Baker to caddy for him, not knowing he didn't know the first thing about caddying. That's the way Jeff was; he wanted to offer himself to everyone around him and loved being able to invite others into his world, even though it often wasn't in his best interest. They got through two rounds, and Jeff ended his career with a 71 on Thursday and a 76 on Friday, missed the cut, and finished tied for 121$^{st}$.

On Thursday following the round, Jeff emerged from the locker room with a letter in his hand. The fan mail Jeff had received since Pebble was mind boggling, so this was no surprise. To this day I don't know who sent the facsimile, but the Tour office felt it was something they shouldn't ignore and placed it in Jeff's locker.

The fax was a copy of a New Yorker article about a young engineer named James Heywood, who, frustrated by the lack of research and awareness of a disease that was killing his younger brother, Stephen, founded an organization called the ALS Therapy Development Foundation. He had hired scientists and started a privately funded laboratory where research into ALS was being conducted every day. They were conducting three times the number of mouse studies on ALS that all other labs researching ALS were conducting combined.

We called ALS TDF as soon as Jeff was finished playing on Friday. A nice woman named Billie answered and invited us to come in some time to tour the facility. She also mentioned that Stephen's wife, Wendy, was from Branson. That's weird, I thought.

With our defenses up due to all of the crazies who were contacting us, we decided to take a closer look into ALS TDF and eventually go to Massachusetts to see for ourselves. If they were legitimate, we wanted to make them a recipient of the proceeds from the Jeff Julian ALS Foundation and any other fundraising we might get involved with. When Jeff and I finally talked about it, my comment to him was, "This dude is completely nuts, you know?" Jeff just looked at me with raised eyebrows, nodding in agreement, as if to say, "To cure this thing, it's going to take someone crazy enough to take it on." Jamie was the first person we had encountered who was thinking outside of the box, approaching it with the urgency needed to save his brother's life.

Those closest to my family also rallied in support of Jeff and traveled from Missouri to New England. The Redfords traveled up in their motor home and stayed in a campground near Quechee where my parents stayed. The Vintons, Kim and Chris, came with their little one, Olivia. My dad's golfing buddies, Loiuie Keener, Steve Redford, Gary Cox, and Jack Smith, made it along with their wives. Jack was the friend who my father was playing golf with that morning on the range at Branson Creek. So much had happened since then. So much in so little time.

The entire Upper Valley was at the Quechee event. It was a true testament of Jeff's kindness and generosity, and how much he was loved.

More than twenty tour players showed up to support Jeff. Including the auction and donations made by Jeff's golf mates, family, and friends, over $200,000 was raised.

After all of the craziness subsided—the media circus around the last golf events that Jeff would ever play in—I was wondering how I'd keep Jeff busy and eager to live life after he was no longer playing golf. My father was already on it and approached Jeff with an idea for a putting aide. My dad had watched Jeff practice on the putting green at tournaments, when he would use dental floss held in the ground by tees on both sides of the hole, to make a path from the hole back about six feet. Jeff said it helped him to later visualize a path to the hole throughout the round when he was putting. Dad suggested they work on a prototype and have it manufactured. Dad thought the invention was a great idea, but his main objective was to keep Jeff busy and focused on something. He feared that without golf Jeff would lose his purpose, and ALS would more quickly become victorious.

He was right. The Tru-path was the perfect way to keep Jeff's mind busy and his spirit fired up.

Daddy also involved Jeff in one of his favorite pastimes, buying and selling golf carts, something Jeff referred to as "horse-trading." Until Jeff could no longer go far without me, he would ride with Dad thirty or forty miles to pick up a golf cart they'd gotten for almost nothing. They'd then pimp it up, adding chrome, mirrors, headlights, and little reflectors on the back that looked like taillights, and then they'd resell it and make a killing. It was entertaining more than anything. Jeff loved listening to Dad wheel and deal. He'd stand next to him as if he were part of the whole thing, and then, after their buyer would leave, they'd be laughing and carrying on like two teenagers.

Jeff could eat so little by mouth that I was preparing him for the transition, when it would simply be too dangerous to attempt it. The thought of feeding Jeff liquid Ensure disgusted me. I started blending pasta in the blender we had at home, which worked fairly well, but pasta was not going to provide all the nutrients that Jeff needed. As I rebelled against what was usually an ALS patient's reality, I recalled using a Vitamix at Yakov's when babysitting his children. It was a Nazi of a blender. It could puree whole apples. If it could puree apples, why couldn't it puree something like a steak? I asked myself.

I went online, and $400 later we were the proud owners of a Vitamix. Within a few days, Jeff was eating every single thing that Tyler and I ate, and then some. I would prepare a filet mignon on the grill, throw it in the Vita-mix, add beef broth while pureeing it until it was the perfect consistency for the feeding tube, and pour it in. It wasn't long before we discovered that chasing the puree with carbonated water like San Pellegrino would produce a healthy belch, which, as gross as it sounds, allowed Jeff to taste the food he had taken in through the tube. It was pure heaven to him.

Simply put, our life was a perpetual adaptation.

# Twenty-One

I'm sure you've come across one of those inspirational networks where some babbling idiot is on stage armed with a microphone and big white teeth, screaming and hollering about Jesus and healing and repenting. Suddenly a man in a wheelchair appears, then stands up; and not only does he stand, but he starts cutting a rug right there on stage. "Praise the Lord!" Like me, you probably shake your head in disbelief and turn the channel to ESPN.

For years I passed judgment on people who attended these healing sessions, almost chuckling at them for even considering that they may be healed of their ailments if they could just get that evangelist's hand on their forehead; or if God would touch them through this person, they would surely be healed.

Well, the desperation of a terminal illness cannot be described. It compels one to believe in things that one would normally shrug off as bologna.

Jeff became that man in the chair, desperate to walk again. He was the man who arrived blind, certain he would leave with the ability to see. And I was right there with him.

We tried snake venom, chelation therapy (which, by the way, was effective and was never presented to us as a cure), stem cell infusions, resonators fastened around his waist, a device that a dentist somewhere in Illinois convinced us would cure him, and even a man who talked to Jeff's feet. He had healed others from spinal cord injuries by this method. One was a young girl that had no chance of recovering from paralysis that she suffered in a car accident.

So we saw this so-called doctor not once but on several occasions. And every visit Jeff would pay him a thousand dollars or more, and in exchange Jeff's feet would carry on a conversation with him or someone. We would

149

drive to different states to meet with him while he traveled around "heal-ing" people. Do you think we asked for a way to contact these patients whom he had cured, to make sure they were legitimate? No, and I'm now embarrassed that we didn't; however, at the time I was subconsciously afraid we would find that this method was not legitimate, and then our hope would be lost. We needed to believe something would work.

When you are desperate and want to believe in something bad enough, you will do almost anything to make it so, because to carry on, the one thing we cannot live without is hope. Our false hope was unfathomable. It wasn't just Jeff; I too believed he would be cured. We had to believe it; otherwise we would have lost our minds. All we had was hope, and hope is a powerful thing.

Perhaps I should be grateful for all of those who have claimed to have the cure. Perhaps they helped me get through another day. Regardless, we traveled all over the country seeking out these lunatics to give them money that we could have deposited in our boys' college funds or spent on traveling around the world. Anything would have been more sensible than spending thousands of dollars to cure a disease that had never, ever been successfully treated, let alone cured. I believe alternative therapies exist that definitely work and should be tried, but ALS is incurable. It's labeled "incurable" for a reason…because no one has ever been cured of it!

In December we traveled to Atlanta where we paid a clinic $25,000 for stem cell infusions. At least there was some scientific evidence that stem cells were effective in a few ALS cases. We knew it wouldn't be a cure; we just hoped it would slow the progression.

Being so close to Christmas, Mom and Dad traveled to Atlanta too, and with Keegan spending the holiday with his mom, we stayed following Jeff's infusions to spend the holiday with my side of the family. The stem cell infusions seemed promising. Other patients had experienced improve-ments, so we jumped at the chance. Jeff was one of only twenty-five patients that would undergo the infusions before the government shut the clinic down. Following Jeff's second round of infusions, we stopped for tea on our way back to our hotel room. Jeff took a sip and, to our surprise, didn't cough at all. Coughing was guaranteed after taking a drink of any liquid.

Realizing this at the same time, I looked wide-eyed at Jeff as he looked at me and then raised his finger to his lips. "Shhhh." As if to say, don't say anything, you might jinx it. Progression did seem to level off for about three months following the infusions but then quickly sped up again.

January of 2003 was a busy month. First, my friend Selena rang to tell me of yet another ALS diagnosis of a member of our PGA Tour family, but this time it was a caddy. Tom Watson's caddy, no less. "What? Oh, my God, Selena," I was shocked but not completely surprised. Jeff and I had predicted that someone else exposed to the same environment would eventually be diagnosed. "Does he have a family?" I asked.

"Yes, his wife, Marsha. I'm sure she will need someone to talk to."

"Yes, she will, but not until it sinks in. When was he diagnosed?" I asked.

"Just now, I think. Not long ago." I could hear the concern in Selena's voice.

"I will talk to her and be of any help I can; but Selena, she has to come to me. If I'm going to help her, she must view me as a friend, a confidante. If I approach her, I will be associated with the enemy camp, like one of the doctors determining their fate. She will come to me when she is ready. Just make sure she has access to my phone number and e-mail address, will you?"

"Certainly, Kim. How are you and Jeff holding up?"

"We're taking it one day at a time, my friend. Thanks for asking, and thanks for letting me know about Bruce and Marsha. I will be available when she decides to reach out."

In January we received a call from a representative of the ALS Association, congratulating us on being honored as the recipients of the 2003 Lou Gehrig/Catfish Hunter Humanitarian Award. We were asked to attend a gala in North Carolina that would be held in February to accept our award and to be keynote speakers. We agreed, viewing it as a kind gesture, knowing that we really were making a difference and people were noticing. The event was held on February 15, our second wedding anniversary. That day as we sat in the St. Louis airport waiting to leave for Raleigh-Durham, Jeff brought me a coffee and set down next to it a nip bottle of Bailey's Irish Cream. "Aw, just like our honeymoon. Thank you, my beloved."

Jeff leaned forward and kissed me. That evening at the Washington Duke Hotel, Jeff presented me with beautiful diamond earrings. I'd never cared about getting diamonds, but there was something about receiving them from him. It's not the diamond that makes the giver special. It's the giver that makes the diamond special.

These romantic gestures weren't as rampant as they'd been pre-ALS, but Jeff still had it in him. He had also planned a romantic getaway for when we returned to Eureka Springs, Arkansas.

Before the ceremony began, I was roaming around the silent auction and found a print of the photograph taken of Ben Hogan's famous one iron shot at the 1950 US Open. Jeff had told me that Ben Hogan was one of the players he most tried to emulate as far as his swing and style. While continuing to increase my bid as others wrote their bids down, I stood around the silent auction admiring another piece of art, a duplication of an original painting by Doug Phillipp, an ALS patient. He had finished it as he progressed by using his mouth. It was a depiction of a young girl at the end of apartheid called *The Wonders of Learning*. Something about the painting captured me. I wanted to bid on it, but the minimum was quite high and I was already spending too much if I ended up winning the bid on the Hogan print. I admired it until I had to leave and prepare for the ceremony.

Jeff and I both spoke after accepting our award. He was able to deliver his remarks, thanks to Gus, without my help. In the end I was not the winning bid on the Hogan photo, which saddened me. After the ceremony when we were at our table talking to several people who approached, a young woman came up to me, holding the painting I'd been staring at all evening. "I just want to say you and Jeff are an inspiration," she said, elegant in dress and speech.

"Thank you," I replied, not sure of her reason for being at the gala.

"So I saw you admiring this print. My husband painted the original, and I'd like you to have it."

"Oh, how thoughtful, but I can't accept such a gracious gift." Now I felt a little bad for admiring it.

"No, I insist."

"I will make a donation for it," I continued to resist.

"Mrs. Julian, what you and your husband have already given is enough. I'd like you to have the painting. I know Doug would too."

I accepted and was so proud of it. We talked for a while. She said that her husband was on a ventilator and couldn't come that night because of a malfunctioning backup battery, a necessity when leaving the house for an extended amount of time.

I took her name and address and sent her and her husband a letter after we returned home. The masterpiece, as I call it, has since adorned a wall or a mantle in every place we've resided. It's one of my treasures.

A few days after I sent that letter, we received a large box from the memorabilia company that supplied the auction items for the ALS Association. The note on the box read, "I heard you bid on one just like this and lost. This one is yours to keep." Inside, in a beautiful frame, was the same Hogan print I had bid on at the auction.

At moments like that, I caught a glimpse of just how kind and generous the human spirit is and could almost see a reason for what was happening to Jeff. He was touching people in ways they'd never been touched. They, in turn, were giving of themselves in an attempt to show gratitude for the wonderful love they'd felt because of his suffering.

We'd been back from North Carolina for a week or so when the phone rang.

"Kimberly?" a man's voice asked. Probably a reporter, I thought.

"Yes?" For months we'd been inundated with phone calls from old friends and the media reporters. I continued to answer, because every little bit helped spread the word about ALS; still, it could be rather exhausting.

"This is Len Shapiro from *The Washington Post*."

As I suspected, I thought. "Hi, Len, what can I do for you?" I was trying to be friendly but firm.

"I'm happy to inform you, Jeff is being honored with the Ben Hogan Award this April at the Golf Writers Association Awards."

"Oh, wonderful, Len. How about I give you a call back when Jeff is next to me so I can translate for the two of you?" I replied, completely oblivious to the prestige of this award. After having spent our anniversary accepting the ALSA award in North Carolina, I wanted nothing more to do with traveling to accept awards. We had traveled so much in just a few years, we were enjoying just being.

"That would be great. Please tell Jeff I said congratulations." Len gave me his contact information, probably thinking I was a complete bitch.

"I will, thank you." And I hung up.

Jeff had made his way into the office while I had been talking on the phone in the kitchen.

"That was Len Shapiro from *The Washington Post*. I told him we'd call him back. You won some Hogan award or something that they need you to accept at the Masters in April," I informed him nonchalantly.

Jeff's eyes got as big as silver dollars. "The Ben Hogan Award?" he said in moans, trying to sound as clear as possible.

"Yes, the Ben Hogan Award, that's what he said."

Jeff quickly moved to the computer to explain what the award meant and I felt like an idiot for my lack of enthusiasm when Len told me. The Golf Writers Association's Ben Hogan Award is given annually to an individual who has continued to be active in golf despite a physical handicap or serious illness. It's considered one of the most prestigious honors.

I immediately called Len back and translated for Jeff our appreciation and excitement, then started planning for our trip to Augusta.

In early March the phone rang. It was a private number but I picked up anyway.

"Kimberly? Tom Watson. How are you?" Tom sounded serious, and direct, but he managed to put me at ease with his friendly tone.

"Hi, Tom, I'm well, thank you." No, I wasn't, and he knew it. "Selena Nobilo told me about Bruce. I'm so sorry. How is he doing, and how can I help?"

"Well, he's doing OK. It's Marsha I'm worried about right now."

We talked for a while, and I was amazed at how much Tom already knew about ALS. He had become an expert overnight. He asked questions that I couldn't answer, and I had already been researching for over a year. I told him all I knew and mentioned Jamie Heywood and ALS TDF, and that Jeff and I felt they had potential.

Tom asked me to reach out to Marsha. I explained to him that I wanted to reach out to her the moment I found out but knew from experience that it takes a while before one can accept help, and I didn't want to call until I knew she was ready. Tom said he felt she really wanted to talk to me. I took her e-mail address and told him I would e-mail her and tell her to feel free to call me. I expressed the importance of her making that first step to reach out for help, but if I didn't hear from her within a few days I would make the first move. We ended our conversation with the kind of comments that soon became ordinary: let me know what I can do to help; hang in there; one day at a time; something has to give; keep the faith. I went into the office immediately and sent an e-mail to Marsha. I provided my contact information and told her to call me anytime, day or night.

What Tom did for Bruce throughout his illness and continues to do for the cause is not a façade. It is not something he does for publicity, like a lot of professional athletes do, or for any reason other than he wants to help. Not only is Tom an extraordinary golfer, he is an extraordinary human being, and in my opinion, after seeing him with fans, spectators, and ALS patients, he is by far the most gracious professional golfer to have ever played on the PGA Tour. And I've been around a few of them.

When Marsha rang me, I was getting in the car after an hour-long visit with a therapist I had just started seeing. Perfect timing, I thought. I sat there in my car in the parking lot, and we talked for what must have been an hour. We of course became friends immediately; how could we not? Our husbands were both dying of ALS. In the months that would follow, we were very lucky to have one another. Having someone we each could identify with was a blessing, making the situation seem almost endurable.

Bruce had let his health insurance lapse and wasn't covered. This was a problem, and I expressed that to Marsha. ALS is an expensive disease. Tom was helping him out, Marsha said. And I do know that Tom never stopped helping him out. He paid for all of Bruce's medical expenses.

After that initial conversation, Marsha and I were in contact several times each day through instant messaging online. We were soldiers, fighting side by side now, as our husbands became more and more frail. From the beginning I expressed how difficult and time consuming the trial of remedies had been, and she suggested we split the possible remedies between us. This was a brilliant idea, as it eliminated our wasting a ton of precious time.

Bruce tried one treatment called Henry's Remedy, and once he felt it could be promising, Jeff starting taking it too. Jeff was on a powdered formula created by a guy named Tim Cochran. We'd cleared it with Dr. Baker, and Jeff was certain he gained energy from it. He had been on it for three months when we met Marsha and Bruce, so Bruce went on it right away. If something didn't work, we collaborated, saving time and money.

Marsha and I were both very busy with our ill husbands and kids, but we wanted to do something that would make a significant impact for research. We wanted to do more than raise awareness and knew that it was quite possible using Tom's, Bruce's, and Jeff's celebrity. We put our heads together and came up with a concept: a funding vehicle that would generate donations through nationwide participation in organized golf events run by golf lovers, patients, and loved ones of patients wanting to help and get involved. Basically, we would do this by exploiting Jeff, Bruce, and Tom. Of course Tom's involvement was critical, as his name would attract the most attention. He required more convincing than the rest of us because he was associating his name with something not directly in his control. Our campaign would also spread ALS awareness throughout the golfing community. We would ask course professionals to host events as well as target individual donations and participation. The campaign would attract those with a connection to ALS as well as those with only a desire to play golf.

Having experienced it with our foundation, I knew obtaining tax-exempt status and creating a foundation would be more work than we wanted to sign up for at that time. I had no doubt that the laboratory in the faxed article, ALS TDF, was our best bet and would make good use of any funding we generated for it.

Marsha, Jeff, and I went to ALS Advocacy Week in Washington, D.C., where we met with the founder, Jamie Heywood, and a few of his colleagues. Jeff and I were already sold, but putting faces to names sealed the deal. Marsha was impressed with the organization and easily gave her vote of approval, so we set the wheels in motion. The ALS Therapy Development Foundation would be the recipient of all funds procured through our campaign, and we would filter everything through its 501(c)3 so that we would not have the headache of creating a foundation. TDF helped us create the name and logo, and once all six founders—Jeff and me, Marsha and Bruce, and Tom and Hilary—had approved the business plan and settled on a logo, we moved forward and made ALS TDF the exclusive recipient of the campaign we would call Driving 4 Life.

As we gradually accepted our reality, I went from being a mess to being strong, and Jeff went from being strong to being a mess. It was a sort of surrendering for both of us.

We were getting a routine down which involved several appointments each week, including regular visits to Dr. Baker, which were always an all-day event. Joe Lennon, brother of Janet and uncle of my ex, John, was our chiropractor and friend whom we visited once a week. It was as if the Lennon family was still my family and, by coming to our aid, had also become Jeff's.

Danny Macias, another uncle of John's and one of the most precious people I've ever known, was one of Jeff's massage therapists. Jeff had become a massage addict and eventually required more than one. He started out with one massage each week, then went to two, and then added cranial sacral massage. The other therapist was a sweet girl named Jill. Jeff loved Jill. If she hadn't been gay, I might have wondered if Jeff was having an illicit affair! I finally broke down and purchased a massage table to relieve me of driving him to an appointment every five minutes. Having regularly scheduled appointments kept Jeff busy and happy.

One day Jeff was missing in action, and after scouring every room, I found him in the garage. As I stepped into the laundry room, the door leading to the garage was open, and I could see him standing there, his back to me. I slowly walked over and faced him. Tears were running down his cheeks. I didn't speak; what could I say? I knew what was wrong. I reached out to offer the comfort of a hug, and he glanced down at his bicep, then back at me. His skin was rippling with fasciculations, the sign of muscles dying away, the sign of progression. For the first time, Jeff allowed himself to break down. We stood there in the garage holding each other up, not knowing what our future held other than paralysis and death.

This was the first time Jeff had really shown emotion and vulnerability since those first few weeks following the diagnosis. I was usually the one falling apart, but for some reason I had found my strength, possibly from the anger that was building up inside of me. It was as if he was surrendering to his fate. And I was reconstructing my wall, brick by brick, preparing for battle. My survival instincts were in full force.

I could hardly fulfill my role as a homemaker and caregiver and definitely wasn't fulfilling my role as a mother. Tyler was losing out in so many ways, and it was ripping my heart out. I felt so depleted most of the time keeping up with Jeff's every need. I never had a moment to just sit and be, let alone spend time being a good mother or taking care of myself. Due to the extensive traveling, I had missed my annual trip to the gynecologist. Doing anything for myself, even if it was simply going to the doctor, was just not possible. I started having abdominal pain from a cyst I'd been ignoring for a year. When it could be ignored no more, surgery was required to remove it.

Mom was always so helpful. She'd come over and hang out for an hour so I could get out and run an errand, or she'd pop in to dote over Jeff and do a load of laundry while she was there. Even with her help, I couldn't keep up. Finally Mom and my friend Kim suggested I hire some help, and before I knew it I was hiring Kim's housekeeper, Areseli, to come in for two hours on Monday, Wednesday, and Friday to cook, clean, and do laundry as needed. She was a blessing and took a lot of pressure off of me.

In April we set out for Augusta. Jeff worked on his speech for hours and Gus recorded the entire thing. He had perfected it with pauses and everything.

Getting there was crazy. We had Tyler too, so I was basically in charge of two kids, one overgrown. Lizzy was bringing Keegan all the way from Vermont, God bless her. I wondered if Jeff was sad that he was going to Augusta not to play but to take another step toward dying.

Jeff motioned that he would get the bags off the belt. In an attempt to let him continue to try to do things on his own, I thought it would be OK to let him try. What would be more emasculating, my doing it or not allowing him to at least try or failing at it? I told Tyler to assist his dad while I went to get the rental car, and when I returned they had the bags on a cart ready to go. "Look at you two," I remarked. "All packed and ready to go!" When we arrived at the hotel, I realized a bag was missing. I wanted to scream and curse Jeff for leaving it behind but couldn't because he was trying so hard. He was doing his best.

The one missing contained Tyler's clothes, so I had to take him to the nearest Gap to quickly get him something appropriate to wear. Then I had to be back in time to visit with Pard and Betsy Erdman, who were in town for the Masters. Somehow, by the grace of God, I made it.

I got Jeff dressed, and he gathered Gus and everything he needed while I was getting dressed. Jeff's arms were really limp due to the lack of muscle strength in his shoulders. He could still raise his hands to his mouth, but not easily. Five minutes before we were scheduled to leave, Gus wouldn't start up. Gus had never acted like this before.

Gus was on strike, and Jeff's pre-written speech was never heard. He would have to attempt to give it using his small communicator, typing with the stylus, one sentence at a time.

My parents and Jeff's dad were there. Liz and Keegan arrived in plenty of time. Keegan was dressed up so cute with a little blazer and tie. Jeff was so proud of him and of Tyler too. Tom, Bruce, and Marsha were at the next table, there to witness Jeff accept his award.

When Jeff finally got up there, he was incredible, and as difficult as it must have been to stand there and type, creating huge pauses while people waited anxiously, he did it. When he finally got tired, he waved me up. I resisted. I hadn't planned on being on stage, but I went, and we were able to complete his speech, with me verbalizing what he was saying to me in sign language. It was a very sad, touching, and beautiful evening.

While at Jeff's doctor one day, he asked me how I was doing healthwise. I hadn't been to my primary care doctor in ages and wasn't about to go unless I was sick because I didn't have a moment to spare. Obviously aware that I was neglecting my health, he asked Jeff to step out while he gave me a quick examination. Once we were alone, he asked me again how I was doing, and this time, instead of lying, I answered, "Honestly? Not well."

"Do you drink?" he asked.

"Yes, red wine with dinner."

He scribbled something on a prescription pad then handed it to me and said, "Drink more," with a kind smile as he made an attempt to empathize and make light of what I was going through. I actually laughed, smiled back at him, and left the room with the script. The prescription was for an antidepressant, which would go nicely with an extra glass of red. I was nothing special, though; he put Jeff on them too.

# Twenty-Two

During our travels we would buy coffee mugs or wine glasses in pairs, one for each of us. We had purchased these splendid green mugs from a Starbucks located in the Barnes & Noble in Holyoke on one of our trips between Bradley airport and Vermont. Green being my favorite color, we would always have our coffee in those green mugs every morning. Jeff wasn't speaking at all at that point, but he could still move his hands and legs. Each day was already so challenging, I would get stressed just thinking about what was ahead when he would become completely incapacitated. It was inevitable that it would happen, and how would I cope? How would I get through one day?

One morning, having no time to sit and enjoy my green mug of coffee, I brought it with me to the bathroom, where I was hoping to wash my face and perhaps even use the toilet. I placed it on the vanity, taking a sip here and there, until my elbow grazed it and knocked it off onto the marble tile floor. It shattered into five or six pieces. This wasn't the first of a pair I had broken. I had also broken two different wine glasses that were at one time a pair. This to me was symbolic of his departing. Of one of us breaking while the other tried desperately to pick up the pieces and avoid being left alone. I picked up the pieces, carried them into where Jeff sat at the computer, and had a meltdown. He wrapped his arms around me as best he could and comforted me. This was the last time I remember being comforted by him, because a few months later, he lost the ability to do so. Another moment of surrendering to the illness, the inevitable.

Later that day I walked into the kitchen to find the broken mug haphazardly glued together, and on one side it read: "Take a moment to sit with me; we'll talk and breathe and sip our tea." This was a profound wake-up call. I was so overwhelmed with the everyday routine that I had become unconscious to everything, even Jeff. He would remind me to hold his hand at least once a day, which I grew to love, because I would get so caught up in "doing" that I needed something to snap me back into reality and remind me that I had better enjoy him while I could.

Jeff was still walking but could not speak at all. He could still pour liquid into his feeding tube on his own and do anything else requiring no more than waist-high hand and arm mobility. We'd decided it was no longer safe for him to drive. He couldn't turn the ignition, and his arm strength had deteriorated to a point beyond being able to safely operate a car or anything else that could possibly hurt someone or himself.

Tyler and I could still understand him and would translate for others, but when we couldn't he would use the little bit of sign language we had learned or his handheld communicator.

The muscle atrophy in his mouth affected his ability to feel saliva in his mouth, so he would drool profusely. This required carrying a cloth napkin or washcloth constantly for wiping his mouth.

Jeff's jaw would slip out of socket, which caused two trips to the emergency room. The second ER doc taught me how to manipulate his jaw to get it back in. After that I would do it for him. Jeff became good at doing it himself—for when I wasn't around—by leaning against a hard surface. One day, when he was still able to drive, he'd gone downtown to the drugstore to pick up a prescription. Somewhere along the way he'd yawned, the main culprit for his jaw slipping out of its socket, so he parked and got out of the car. Leaning against the door to force it back in took a few minutes, and by the time he had successfully maneuvered it back into place, a policeman had responded to someone's concern about someone operating a vehicle under the influence. When the policeman approached Jeff, he of course couldn't speak, and as he started punching something in on his handheld communicator, the owner of the printing shop next to the pharmacy, who knew my family, noticed what was going on and came to Jeff's rescue. The policeman apologized and went on his way.

Even though it worked out, Jeff was somewhat humiliated by the incident. To prevent something like this from happening again, I ordered a medical alert tag for Jeff to wear around his neck that explained his condition and, in case of an emergency, would inform an EMT of his feeding tube and IV port and the fact that an ALS patient should never be given oxygen.

We visited with our doctor about the salivation, and he put Jeff on a drug whose side effect was a dry mouth. This made Jeff's mouth too dry, so we went to a radiologist to discuss killing the saliva glands with radiation, which would put an end to the drooling. We decided it wasn't an option and finally just continued to use washcloths and opted to take a very small dose of the drug. It was such a pain in the ass.

The immense isolation that came with every new day could not be explained, nor could another human being understand it, unless of course that human being was or had been in the same exact situation.

Marsha and I found sanctuary in sharing our frustrations with one another. We were both mothers, and we were both watching our husbands die while dedicating every moment of every day to caring for them. I could tell Marsha anything, and she would understand, and vice versa. Communicating throughout the day, we would share our innermost thoughts with never a worry of being judged. We were a true blessing to one another. If I could have just one wish, other than a cure for every terminal illness, I would wish that every caregiver had someone to talk to, just as Marsha and I had each other.

I could tell her how much I loved Jeff and, at times, how much I hated him. I could tell her that I didn't know how much longer I could go on, and she could tell me the same. I could tell her that I missed spending time with my son. That I felt I was neglecting him, making Jeff a priority over him. I had tremendous guilt regarding Tyler and simply felt very sad that I was missing so much of his life. I remembered when I was a child my mother constantly making comments about how fast Tim and I were growing up. It's true; you blink an eye and your little one is going off to college. I was missing those precious years of his life, and I was beginning to resent Jeff for it. I was also resenting him for leaving me, for being sick, for dying.

For the purposes of venting and letting go of the negativity that was stuck in my heart, I often expressed these feelings to Marsha. One morning in particular, she wasn't online, so I typed an e-mail and sent it. It went something like this: "I feel sorry for Tyler. He sits in his room alone most of the time. I wish I could take him away somewhere—just the two of us—for a few weeks to focus on him for a little while. I want to be a mother; I want to resume my role as a mother to my child; I am all he has...." The e-mail had nothing to do with Jeff and everything to do with Tyler. When Jeff read it, he felt differently. He felt I was horrible for having those feelings and needing to express them.

I later looked back on what occurred that day and realized that was the first sign of dementia, and patient-caregiver burnout, our tipping point.

It must have been around three o'clock when I returned from picking Tyler up from school. I pulled in the garage to find the SUV missing. My first thought was that my mother or father had decided to take Jeff somewhere, and Jeff must have insisted they take our car. When we walked into the mudroom, no wagging tails came to greet us. Why did they take the dogs with them? I thought.

"Hey, where are Max and Punk?" Tyler asked.

"They must have gone with Dad and Nannie and Papa, sweetheart."

"Where?"

"Don't worry, they'll be home before your bedtime. Why don't you sit at the bar and do homework while I make you apples and nut butter?"

Tyler carried his backpack into his room and then headed to the bathroom to wash his hands.

I entered the kitchen and on the counter found a copy of the e-mail I had sent to Marsha earlier that day. Below the text of the e-mail was a note from Jeff, written illegibly. It was this note, and the fact that he had felt so compelled to write it, that changed everything, because at that point I didn't know about dementia. I had been told all along that ALS doesn't affect the mind. Bullshit. It most definitely does.

I do not even remember his exact words, but in short he was upset over my e-mail to Marsha, the e-mail he obviously had found while snooping through my inbox, which didn't require a password. I didn't have anything password protected. If every e-mail I had written were posted on the bulletin board at the local market, I wouldn't care, and this particular e-mail to Marsha was no different. If Jeff had asked to read it, I would have offered it without hesitation, and never in my wildest dreams would I have anticipated the reaction and the drama it provoked.

I had never entertained the thought of poking around in his e-mail account. Not even after the e-mails he had received from ex-girlfriends and women he had casually slept with when he was a club pro. He told me about them because he didn't feel he should keep anything from me; nor did I keep anything from him. I resented the fact that replying to e-mails from people who were no longer a part of his life occupied a lot of time that we could have been spending together. I was selfish, and I had every right to be. Even then I didn't snoop, and I didn't ask to read them. I swallowed the hurt that it brought. I mean, he was dying; he had a right to every moment of my time, and he also had a right to be selfish and offer his time to whomever he chose, right?

I called Mom, who confirmed she had not seen or heard from Jeff all afternoon, and neither had Dad.

I sent several text messages, our only way of communicating when apart, and received no response. I didn't worry at first, assuming he would realize he was being ridiculous and come home. As time passed I began to worry that something had happened and abandoned texting his phone, instead calling it, hoping someone, anyone, would pick up and enlighten me. No answer. I called several times; still no answer. I was becoming more and more upset. Not only had he put himself and others in harm's way, but he had our dogs, the dogs that were like children to us.

I served Tyler dinner, fabricated some crazy story as to why Jeff and our dogs weren't home yet, and tucked him in for the night. I sat for a few moments wondering what I should do. Mom called, worried and wondering if he'd come home yet. "Should I just call the police, Mom?" I asked.

"I think maybe you should. I don't know what else we can do."

Once nine-thirty rolled around, I picked up the phone and called the non-emergency line at the police station. I explained my concerns and provided all of the information to the officer, who was being so comforting and helpful I wanted to cry on his shoulder. Just as he began searching for accidents on all roads in southwest Missouri, I heard the door in the mudroom open, and the two dogs barreled in as if they couldn't wait to tell me, through abundant wagging, of their day's adventure.

"Thank God. Sir, he just walked in. I apologize for the trouble."

"It's no trouble, ma'am, I'm just glad he made it home safe and sound. You take good care now."

"You too, thank you," I said, and hung up.

Jeff walked right past without even a glance as I stood there with fur-rowed brow. "Where on earth have you been?" I was so relieved that I wanted to hug him and not let go, and at the same time I wanted to slap him and tell him to grow up. He refused to even look at me, and after five minutes of this treatment, all of the frustration and anger I'd slowly col-lected every day, for months, disgorged.

"Pardon me, I think I deserve an explanation," I yelled as he continued to avoid eye contact.

"Jeff, you read an e-mail that wasn't addressed to you. Why? I don't mind you reading my e-mails, but if you do you can't get upset. What I wrote to Marsha is the truth, and I am sorry it upsets you. This is our reality. I am human too Jeff. I have needs just like you!" I raised my voice, and it felt damn good. "Does it surprise you to find that the world does not revolve around you and your needs, all the time? I give every second of every day to you and your needs while I disregard my own, and Tyler's, all without complaining! Nor does he complain. He sits in his room alone while I'm preoccupied with you. Marsha is the only person I can really talk to without feeling judged! Don't you want that for me?"

There was no response, no glance, and I was crying uncontrollably at this point and worried Tyler was now awake in bed hearing every word.

"You risked your life driving around all day and the lives of our dogs and everyone else on the road. You have become such a self-absorbed, nar-cissistic bastard, I can't stand it!" I'd lost it, clearly, as all that I'd held in for months forced its way out.

He had positioned himself in the living room with his communicator, so I was anticipating a response. But he sat there, looking at me with the lifeless face he'd been left with. The tears that fell down my flushed cheeks felt cool, and my body was trembling. I had reached the end, spiritually, mentally, and physically.

I walked out of the room feeling more hopeless than ever before. The guilt that typically occupied my head and heart when I lost patience with him was no longer tugging at me. Jeff was no longer capable of caring for anyone else, only himself, so why should I care? ALS had consumed him, our marriage, and our life together.

Twenty minutes passed while I called Mom to tell her Jeff was fine, warmed Jeff's dinner, used the coffee grinder to prepare evening meds, and then helped him pour all of it into his tube, one syringe at a time. Not a word was spoken. I was on autopilot.

By the time I finished with all of this, he had typed a few sentences for me. "I drove to Springfield. Just drove around. Highland Springs, Hickory Hills. I am a burden to you, to Tyler, to everyone."

"Yes, you are a burden! ALS is a burden! But what can we do about it? It is what it is, my beloved." A burden is defined as "that which is borne with difficulty; obligation; onus." In all honesty, no term better described what Jeff and I were facing. I was accepting that burden with love, compassion, and as much grace as I could muster. If it wasn't enough, I could do nothing more.

"Jeff, I am right here where I want to be. I'm doing my best, giving you my all. Please, please just understand that I sometimes need to talk to someone, complain, kick, and scream. I'm sorry my words hurt you. It was not intentional or even directed at you. Indirectly directed, I guess."

He apologized, but I told him an apology wasn't necessary. He was frustrated and I was frustrated.

I helped him get to bed and told him I loved him more than life itself. After cleaning up the kitchen and calling the dogs inside, like every night, I fell asleep next to Jeff.

Driving 4 Life was launched on June 23, 2003, during the second round of the U.S. Open. Bruce had severely slurred speech but could still be heard. Tom and Bruce graciously taped a public service announcement that was aired during the Open announcing the campaign. Tom was leading the Open when the PSA ran, and even though he ended up tied for twenty-eighth, all eyes were on him that weekend. It was a godsend. Within a few days, we had numerous calls from individuals wanting to host their own Driving 4 Life golf event to benefit ALS. Some were patients, some friends of patients, and some had no connection other than their love of the game. Driving 4 Life procured $500,000 for research in the first six months.

Jeff and I spoke to Jamie at TDF regularly regarding the campaign and the work it was funding. Jeff looked forward to the calls, and so did I. Stephen was five years into ALS by the time we met the Heywoods. It took Jamie, his parents, Stephen's wife, Wendy, and a nurse that stayed overnight to take care of Stephen. Jamie understood what I was going through to care for Jeff by myself, while at the same time coping with the fact that he was dying. Like Marsha, he became a great sounding board.

# Twenty-Three

I woke to a sensation on my foot and the sound of the alarm beeping. No telling how long Jeff had been nudging my foot. I got up quickly, wondering how I slept through it. I had to get going or Ty would be late for school. I woke him and then headed back to the kitchen to get coffee started. The smell of the brew filled the house.

I had become paranoid about leaving Jeff at home in the mornings, even though he was asleep in bed. He could at this point still walk but had trouble lifting up from a lying or sitting position. Plus, he had lost all use of his arms and hands, so his balance was not the best. I found myself struggling with the idea of not being able to drive Tyler to school. The fifteen-minute drive was the only quality time I had with Tyler every day, and I didn't want to give it up. I didn't really have any business being behind the wheel of a car. I was so exhausted, every day on the way back home I would nod off at least three or four times before I got back home. Still, that fifteen minutes was the highlight of my day. My mind was going in many ways. It had become impossible to carry on a conversation. It was as if my brain had atrophied. I would listen to messages on the answering machine at home and five minutes later have to play them again because I couldn't remember who had called.

I would arrive home from driving Ty to school, pull into the garage, turn off the ignition, and drop my forehead to the steering wheel for a few deep breaths. Then I'd go inside and take a quick peek at Jeff to make sure he was still sleeping soundly. I'd then feed the dogs, start a load of laundry, let the dogs outside, and finally, after pouring myself a cup of coffee, go into the office, where I would make a few calls and pay a few bills. Before I knew it, it would be almost ten o'clock, Jeff's waking hour. It was at this time every day that my day became the hectic, methodical routine that had to be strictly adhered to, to keep him happy.

First, I would attach the big syringe to his feeding tube and pour in a cup, maybe two, of coffee with cream and sugar, one syringe at a time. I would repeat this process until the coffee was gone, as well as the sleepy frown on Jeff's face. Then, I'd walk into our master bathroom, raise the toilet seat, then return to where Jeff still lay in bed to help him sit up and get out of bed. A big good morning hug was next; then I'd walk behind him to the bathroom in case he lost his balance. After that business I'd place a warm washcloth over his thin, weary face. I would then help him get dressed.

I prolonged Jeff's independence for as long as I could, but ALS is hard to keep up with. Sandy Vincent, a family friend and talented seamstress, had been my lifesaver when I needed alterations for Lady Liberty's costume when I worked for Yakov, so she was the first person I thought of when Jeff could no longer button his shirts. Sandy altered several of Jeff's shirts with Velcro so he could continue to dress himself for as long as possible. The Velcro worked perfectly. He was able to use the shirts for a few weeks before his hands progressed to the point that he could no longer lift his hands high enough to touch his collar. At this point he could hardly lift his arms at all. We would adapt one day and start all over again the next, facing new challenges.

We would then head to the office, where he would sit at the computer and read e-mails for an hour. The computer had become Jeff's connection to the outside, to family and friends. He could still peck at the keyboard with his index fingers, but due to the lack of movement in his hands, he had to rely on his arms to move over the keys. When it became difficult for him to bend his arms at the elbows and hold his hands over the keyboard, he panicked at the thought of losing that connection. Being stuck at home most of the day, Jeff became quite the online shopper. The UPS guy was at our door almost every day with a package addressed to Jeff, usually from Amazon.com, and every day I would answer the door—with Max at my heels hoping to bolt past me and jump on the cute guy dressed in brown.

One day I answered the door to receive a package that wasn't from Amazon but rather a scuba-diving shop.

"Honey, what did you order this time? Going snorkeling soon?"

Using his eyes, Jeff gestured me to open it, so I did and found a women's wetsuit top in size medium. It was black with purple and looked as though it would hit the lucky girl wearing it at about midriff.

I looked up at him without lifting my head, wondering if he had totally lost it, to find him laughing and turning to his keyboard. To make a long story short, he had ordered this for himself and had big plans for it. He asked me to call Sandy, who in Jeff's mind had become his personal seamstress, and Joe.

I made the calls, and that day Jeff consulted with Joe regarding the most effective positioning for rubber bands that would essentially be replacing muscles. Joe marked different spots on the neoprene where Sandy would later sew buttons. In less than a week, Jeff had created what we referred to as rubber band man, an apparatus that allowed Jeff to be positioned, arms held in place and bent, over the computer keyboard so he could peck with his index fingers. It was nuts but brilliant. He used it for over a month before it was no longer sufficient.

Back to the routine. I would grind his morning meds and give them to him with a protein shake through the feeding tube around eleven a.m. Our life became routine. I could have done it in my sleep.

At almost two years into it, Jeff had become someone that I didn't know 75 percent of the time. He was just not himself. Losing the ability to express himself with his voice was at the root of all of his frustration and anger as well as mine, but it wasn't until his body also began to give in to the progression that he became more of a stranger. He could no longer wrap his arms around me or make me laugh with his slapstick remarks. I couldn't bear to look at him, as all I could see was the cruel way in which he was suffering and slowly leaving me. He couldn't look at me, for all he could see was the way I was wearing down to nothing.

I couldn't and still can't imagine what it was like for him. He always made light of it and tried to make fun of what was happening. I can only tell of the way it felt from my perspective. Hearing the computer voice, Paul, say "I love you" just wasn't the same as hearing Jeff's voice.

My only strategy for making it through another day was remembering who Jeff once was, the Jeff that I'd fallen so madly in love with. I had changed too, however; I tried my best to remain positive, compassionate, and loving, but oftentimes I just couldn't hide my sadness and frustration.

From mid-July to mid-August 2003, we traveled back and forth to Vermont twice for extended stays. Being the only driver was, of course, exhausting. During our visits, we would stay at the Residence Inn located in Hanover. It allowed dogs, and we were quite comfortable there. We would spend time with Keegan in between his summer camps, and the rest of the time Jeff was focusing his energy on the cabin he was planning to build on the land his mother had left him. He wanted to build it, die there, then leave it to our boys to use when they one day would have families of their own. It would be his way of remaining present in their lives, in the lives that would one day be created, lives that he would otherwise never take part in.

We had met with our builder, a good friend of ours, Jim Howell. He and Jeff walked the land. Jeff was limping by now and had only enough movement in his arms to bend his elbow, but he would have to bend over slightly to meet his hand so he could wipe the drool that would constantly find its way out of the sides of his mouth. Lifting his arms even slightly was impossible. When we weren't with Keegan, the majority of our time was spent meeting with engineers, forestry consultants, surveyors, overseeing septic and perk tests, and much more, all in preparation for Jeff's cabin. The investment we had made thus far was substantial, but Jeff was adamant. He was nesting in preparation to die. He wanted to have the deed for the land signed over to him so they could start cutting the road up to the house site before we left to go back to Missouri, but there was a holdup: someone was refusing to sign the deed. More family dynamics. I didn't have the time or the energy to deal with anything more than what I was already dealing with.

Our departure in mid-August ended up with us in the ER again. Jeff couldn't clear secretions, even using the cough assist we had brought along on our journeys. It was a bulky machine and basically helped clear secretions by gradually applying a positive pressure to Jeff's airway, then rapidly shifting to a negative pressure, producing a high expiratory flow which would stimulate a natural cough, and, if effective, would pull secretions from Jeff's lungs.

I was worried about pneumonia setting in. We had been on the road for an hour when I turned around, worried about having to admit him to a hospital in an unfamiliar place. In spite of the secretions, his lungs looked good...no pneumonia present, and his oxygen level was 96 percent. The issues with our departure made me think Jeff didn't want to leave at all, concerned he wouldn't make it back to where he wanted to live out his last days, with his wife and children surrounding him.

We departed the following morning and drove for two days. I was at the wheel for the duration. We stopped in Ohio one night, and then stopped on our way through St. Louis to pick up Tyler after staying with his dad for a month. Tyler talked nonstop about the move back to Vermont. His excitement about going back and being with his old friends was a relief; however, neither of us was confident it would happen at all now, considering the issues with the deed which were delaying the process. If we didn't break ground in the next month and get the foundation poured, winter would be upon us and construction would be delayed until spring, and spring would likely be too late. Jeff would still want to die in Vermont, so this was a concern.

At home in Missouri, our family and friends were planning the second annual Jeff Julian & Friends Golf Classic, which would be held in September. I'd invited Tom, and Bruce and Marsha and the kids, and they were planning to attend. I was looking forward to familiar faces and a little deviation from a life that had become routine.

# Twenty-Four

Tom made the trip to Missouri, as did Bruce and Marsha. I was thrilled to have all of them as our guests. Marsha and Bruce flew in and drove down from Springfield a few days before the event, allowing us to be tourists with the kids and have a little fun. Bruce was all right alone, and Jeff was with my dad, preoccupied with the upcoming event. Jeff was always in charge of the putting contest, and the path along the green would have to be lined with twigs to imitate trees. He was busy delegating and supervising its construction, since he could no longer do it himself.

Tom flew into a private airstrip in Branson. I personally chauffeured him to and from the event, giving us time alone to talk. I confided in him about the issues in Vermont, Jeff's wishes to die there, and my anticipating a move back there even though I didn't want to go. Just as my own father would, he gave me the best advice I'd been offered in a very long time. I was surprised and relieved at his advice. He was one of the first people to remind me that I had a life, and that life involved another little person that I was responsible for. He reminded me that I had to do what was best for me and for Tyler. I've never told him just how profound our conversation was that day, but I think he knows anyway.

Needless to say the event was terrific, and everyone loved having Tom there, the gracious host. He stood on the last green for almost an hour signing photos taken during the round. I went up at one point to give him an out, and he looked at me and said, "It's OK, Kim. I don't mind," then stayed until every player had walked off the green, an autograph in hand.

When the leaves started to fall Jeff was still walking, but limping so badly that even a short distance would exhaust him. His arms hung lifeless at his sides, pulling his once broad shoulders forward. He still had movement in his fingers, enough to hold on to a handkerchief. He had fallen twice. Once was between the mudroom and the kitchen when Max, excited that we were home, ran in to greet us as usual and tripped Jeff, causing him to come crashing down on the tiled floor. The second time had happened in the living room, right in front of the fireplace. Jeff's head was two inches from the brick hearth when I ran in and helped him up. He could no longer stand up from a seated position without help. I was lifting him nonstop.

As Jeff's disease progressed, my whole family became more and more involved in caring for him. When you have no movement in your arms, it throws your balance off, and falling is the result. I wasn't the only one that was worried. My eighty-four-year-old grandfather bought one of those scooters called a Jazzy, pretending that he felt he needed it even though he was getting around as well as he had in his fifties. He pulled up one day in his truck, towing that scooter on his trailer. My dad arrived next, unloaded the scooter, and using mobile ramps at the front door, Grandpa rode it right into the house. He told Jeff he had bought it but didn't like it and thought he could use it. Jeff was like a kid in a candy store. Another example of the "foot in the door phenomenon." Jeff used Jazzy around the house constantly. He regained the freedom to get around when he wanted to instead of calling on me to help him stand up.

In September we visited a representative from Permobil, maker of the Cadillac of power wheelchairs. Four to six months later, Jeff would be the proud owner of a custom-fit chair, allowing him to remain mobile for as long as possible. The Permobil was so totally cool, it made buying a wheelchair just as much fun as buying a Vespa.

I left Jeff for the first time, to attend my friend Amy's wedding in Santa Barbara. I was going to be gone a total of three days.

We bought one of Jeff's sisters a roundtrip ticket and she came without hesitation. I worried about Jeff the entire time I was gone, so it wasn't in the least bit relaxing. It was as if I'd left my newborn baby in someone else's hands. Jeff's sister did a fabulous job of taking care of him. This made me realize that I and my parents weren't the only human beings capable of doing the job. Others could step up and help out too.

A few days before Keegan's arrival for Thanksgiving, Jeff asked me to come into the office because he wanted to talk about a few things.

"I want to reiterate my wishes so that you are clear as to what I want."

"Jeff, I can't talk about this."

"Kim, we must. It's going to be soon," Gus said.

Tears once again ran down my weary cheeks. I looked at him, and he seemed so much stronger than I felt. He wasn't emotional. He seemed confident and determined. That's what told me he was serious, and he was soon going to die.

"I want to see Keegan one more time. His visit is perfect timing."

"Jeffrey, as I've told you, if I'm faced with the decision, at this point in time, I don't think I can do it." There was still so much life in him, so much of him there, that I couldn't imagine having a "do not resuscitate" order (also called a DNR) hanging on the wall. Jeff had taken care of his living will and his wishes not to be kept alive artificially. I had durable power of attorney and would have to make any decision that Jeff was unable to make. I trusted God would take Jeff when he was meant to go, but I prayed it would be in his sleep, peacefully in his sleep. I didn't want him to suffer any more than he already had.

"I still want to be cremated, and I want you to give ashes to friends and family—anyone who wants some—to be spread wherever they see fit." Those were his final wishes, and I promised to do everything in my power to see that it was done.

A few days later, we drove four hours to St. Louis to drop Tyler off with his dad and pick Keegan up at Lambert airport. Tyler was going to be with his dad for Thanksgiving break, and Keegan was coming to see Jeff. It was unfortunate they were on opposite schedules and wouldn't see each other, and I worried about how I could entertain Keegan enough without Ty around when I was busy assisting Jeff with his every need. I wanted

Keegan's time with us to be as fun as possible, not boring and consumed with ALS.

It was after ten o'clock when we arrived back home, exhausted. We had been asleep for only an hour when I woke suddenly to the sound of Jeff gasping for air. I leaped out of bed, grabbed the phone, and called 9-1-1. The fear in Jeff's eyes made me feel sick to my stomach and completely alone. I helped him out of bed and onto the Jazzy hoping that sitting up straight would ease his breathing. We were ready and positioned in the living room near the front door when two ambulances pulled up to the house, followed by a fire engine. It was like the Christmas parade without the candy.

This part was so surreal. I assumed it would be like in the movies: they rush in, assess the condition of the patient, know exactly what to do, and do it at the speed of light. Perhaps things actually moved in slow motion because that is how I remember it. They slowly came in, looked at Jeff sitting there in the Jazzy, then to me for the assessment. I'm not saying the paramedics didn't respond correctly; they knew nothing about ALS or how to care for someone dying from it. Maybe they thought Jeff had just been out for a long run, sitting there craning his neck for every breath. He did appear to be healthy otherwise, just skinny, like a marathon runner. Recognizing the ignorance of the disease we were dealing with, I gave them strict orders: "No oxygen, only fresh air. I can't stress this enough; if you give him oxygen, you'll kill him." The diaphragm and respiratory muscles in an ALS patient weaken as the disease progresses, making inhaling, exhaling, and coughing impossible. When you can't exhale, carbon dioxide builds up in your lungs and your blood oxygen saturation drops. A level of 95 percent is normal, 85 percent, dangerous, and 75 percent, fatal.

I requested Cox South Hospital in Springfield, and they took off with lights flashing. I threw some clothes on, told Keegan to get dressed, and we took off shortly after. When we arrived Jeff was already in a room.

I don't remember much of the details. I don't even remember if Keegan was awake before they took Jeff in the ambulance. I think I left him sleeping peacefully until I had to wake him to leave, but I don't remember. It was difficult remembering that Keegan was not as acclimated to the situation as Tyler was after living with it. It was not easy remembering that what one child would see as normal, the other child would not. I don't remember the drive to the hospital, and I don't remember any details of those few moments that seemed like hours.

I had started carrying my journal with me everywhere I went because the desire to write would come out of nowhere. If not for the fact that I wrote most of it down, I don't think I could recall any of this at all. Life was moving along in a thick fog.

After what must have been two hours, a kind woman wearing scrubs and white clogs came out to where Keegan and I sat in the waiting area. I followed her into the room where Jeff was laying, with Keegan trailing behind, forgetting that he shouldn't see his dad as he was about to see him. Jeff was unconscious, hooked up to wires and tubes coming and going. They had performed a nasotracheal intubation, where a tube is inserted into a patient's lung through the nasal passages to provide air. This procedure would delay a more permanent procedure, called a tracheotomy, which was considered artificial sustaining of life. Jeff was now temporarily breathing via a respirator. It suddenly dawned on me that Keegan was with me. I looked over to find him sitting in a chair by the door, as white as a sheet. I rushed over and gently guided him out of the room, trying not to startle him, and led him to the bathroom. He threw up all over the floor just inside the bathroom door. I was a mess, and I needed to be strong for Keegan, but I was failing miserably. I wanted to stop time and hug him and tell him everything was going to be all right. I couldn't protect him or Tyler from the inevitable. It was all I could do just keeping myself from falling apart. I felt out of control and useless, as a mother, as a wife, and as a human being.

Mom and Dad were out of town, which made matters worse. I resisted the urge to call and wake them to ask that they return home immediately. I felt isolated, scared, and abandoned by everyone.

As the sedation began to wear off, Jeff's eyes opened wide. With the discomfort of the tube running through his nose and into his lungs, he became enraged and within seconds was having an anxiety attack. His legs were not yet completely paralyzed, so he used them often to express dissatisfaction. His legs kicking, and his body rolling so fiercely, I thought he was going to leave the bed. He naturally began trying to breathe against the tube that was providing him air, providing him life. He went into respiratory failure. His pulse oxygen saturation dropped to 80 percent, and his blood pressure went as high as 200/160. Doctors and nurses rushed into the room, sedated him again, and stabilized him. I knew exactly what was coming next.

We had already scheduled the surgery for a tracheotomy, but only for the purpose of suctioning and clearing Jeff's lungs. As the muscles were atrophying, he couldn't even cough. The cough assist was no longer doing the trick, so secretions were collecting in his lungs, and Jeff needed suctioning almost every hour. The tracheotomy would allow a deeper suction, and we hoped the procedure would result in a better night's sleep, for both of us.

The purpose of this tracheotomy, however, would be for life support. They would hook him up to a machine that would breathe for him, and as much as they tried to convince me that they would wean him off it within a few days, I knew better. If I ordered the tracheotomy, Jeff would be breathing via an artificial life-sustaining device...what we in the ALS world refer to as "on a vent." If I didn't he would stop breathing and leave me.

# Twenty-Five

The doctor looked over at me but didn't have to speak.

"He has a living will and doesn't want to be on a vent." I was at the point of sobbing. The doctor knew Jeff had a medical directive in his file indicating this; however, he also knew that I had medical durable power of attorney and could override anything stated in his living will in the event Jeff is incapacitated.

"Mrs. Julian, it's your call."

He was still so healthy and strong. I knew in my heart it was time for him to go. I was positive, as if God himself was whispering in my ear. His wishes were to die naturally, without being hooked up to machines. Our conversation in the office just a few days prior was playing over and over in my head. He told me that he knew it was going to be soon, that he wanted to see Keegan one more time. He did see Keegan, but had he meant simply lay eyes on him? Had he meant he just needed to "see" him? Keegan needed time with Jeff over Thanksgiving, and Jeff needed time with Keegan. I knew what I should do, but I couldn't. My last thought was, if he doesn't want to live on a ventilator, we have the legal right to later remove him from life support. I had forgotten something that Jamie had said to us: "It's easier to die than it is to choose to die." Of course I wouldn't remember this until it was too late.

"I can't do it. No, no way, trache him." I turned around to walk out of the room. "Oh my God!" I said as I covered my ears as if that would relieve what I was feeling, already struggling with my decision. I suddenly felt I was going to be sick, and I rushed down the corridor and outside into the fresh air. Daylight was breaking. I wanted to sprout wings and fly away, far away, to a place that didn't hurt so much. I wondered if Jeff would be angry. How would he react? It doesn't matter how prepared you think you are; when the time comes, you realize that for some things one can never be prepared. I couldn't let him go, but in the back of my mind, I knew that God was trying to take him home. It had been Jeff's time to go and I intervened.

As I stood outside, Jamie's advice echoed in my mind. My God, how long can I do this? Can I be the person that I have had to become, a caregiver, for months, even years? I was losing my mind to all of these horrible thoughts, second-guessing my decision.

I returned to the waiting area where I found Keegan watching television. "Hi, kiddo. You OK?"

"Yep." This was a typical response from Keegan. If you wanted something more, you had to ask an open-ended question. I knew that I had to help him understand what was happening, but I wasn't sure how to go about it.

"Keegan, I'm sorry. I'm sorry this is happening. It's not fair, but we can't change what is, so we have to press on. Your dad needs a ventilator now; that's a machine that will help him breathe. He'll not be able to go anywhere without it, but at least he'll be with us," I said, unsure of what I was telling him. "I'm here if you want to talk about it," I added.

"I know," he replied, without looking at me.

"We'll be able to see him after a while. I promise it won't be like it was in the emergency room. That was entirely my fault; I just wasn't thinking straight." I selfishly tried to redeem myself. "And Keegan, no matter what, you'll be all right. OK?" I added. I hoped he believed me.

"OK," he responded, giving me a quick glance. We sat there for a while; not another word was spoken. But even in the middle of all the chaos, it was a comfortable silence. Again I wondered if I would have a relationship with Keegan after Jeff was gone. I loved him like my own, but anticipating the inevitable I was still struggling with this tendency to keep him at arms length, preparing myself for losing him.

I called Mom and Dad. I called Jeff's father, Toby, and I called one of Jeff's siblings. Lastly, I called Jamie. His brother, Stephen, was back at home with his new ventilator that he'd been put on the week before.

Jamie told me exactly which ventilator to request, an LTV 900, and advised that I make certain they provide the same model for the backup vent. Insurance companies often attempt to save money at the expense of the patient. We'd be using the backup vent on the wheelchair, not just for emergency situations; therefore, it needed to be the same. The vent was the smallest available, not at all cumbersome, and one of the most expensive ventilators on the market.

I hadn't even considered all of this and didn't realize I could call the shots as to what equipment we were given. I was lucky to have Jamie's support and had no idea as to how much I would grow to depend on it.

Several hours later I entered the ICU, and one of the nurses looked up at me, smiled, and pointed to a room on the end close to the nurses' station. I walked up to the glass wall and looked in to find Jeff sleeping soundly. I stood there for a moment, wondering who he would be when he awoke. Did his spirit go to God in spite of the machine that was breathing for him? Is he still in there, or did his soul go ahead and take the trip? The breathing tube coming out of his throat was a little intimidating as was the machine attached to the tube. I walked in feeling slightly frightened and quickly took a seat in the chair next to his bed.

A large apparatus sat a few feet from the bed. A tube ran from it across Jeff's chest and disappeared into his throat, where it was covered with some bandaging.

Jeff looked so peaceful. He'd been pale for so long, but now his skin had its normal olive tone and his cheeks a pinkish tint. I couldn't stop looking at him, wondering if he would wake and be glad he was alive or upset that I hadn't allowed him to die. Then he slowly opened his eyes, bright and clear, and his face lit up when he saw me. My husband—the one I had not seen for so many months—was back. He looked like the Jeff I'd met on that memorable August night. His cheeks were rosy and full under his stubble. I gave him a smile and told him how good it was to see him. From the look on his face, he was glad to be seen. I told him I would fetch Gus and we'd somehow affix it to the foot of his bed so he could communicate.

The nursing staff insisted that I go home at night and get some sleep. "You'll need to be well rested for when he comes home." This worried me. I wasn't accustomed to getting sleep. For months Jeff had needed suctioning every one to two hours all through the night, every night. He couldn't do it himself, so he'd wake me and I'd get up and turn on the machine and clear the secretions that gathered in his throat.

I took their advice anyway. The drive was only forty-five minutes. I would drive to Springfield in the morning, usually stay until visiting hours were over, and then return the next morning. I was able to get a little sleep and catch up on a few things at home. Since Areseli no longer worked for us, my mother had taken over the cleaning. She would often have extra hands, thanks to a few ladies from her church who would show up to offer their help.

Jeff had many visitors during his two weeks in the hospital. His childhood friends, the Dunn brothers, lived just up the lane from Jeff's grandparents' home in Vermont, where Jeff spent every summer. Jeff would arrive and immediately head to the Dunns' home, where he would take up residence for the majority of his time there. Paul and Lance showed up on Thanksgiving, Paul from Houston, and Lance from Seattle, I believe. They were able to keep it together while at Jeff's side and long enough to get outdoors before breaking down. I watched this happening in many of our loved ones.

We had Thanksgiving dinner at the hospital, and a few days later, Mom and Dad delivered Keegan to St. Louis for us and grabbed Tyler before turning around and coming back. Keegan had been very strong throughout this ordeal. I was proud of him. I wasn't sure how Tyler would cope, but I would soon find out.

Jeff was as happy as can be on the vent—I guess breathing is underrated. Most of us don't even think about the fact that we're lucky to be breathing.

We had affixed Gus to the foot of his bed as promised and taped the mouse at the height of his left big toe. The nurses had never seen a device like Gus and thought it was wonderful. They explained that not knowing what a patient needs was a difficult position to be in.

Jeff felt great, but friends that came by couldn't hide their discomfort when they laid eyes on him and the vent humming next to him. My dear friend Kim stopped by and tried to hide it but stood there speechless. Jeff sensed it, of course, so he smiled at her and typed, "Kim V, I know this looks bad, but I'm in heaven." My idea of heaven didn't involve being held hostage by a wheelchair and ventilator, I thought. But I was happy Jeff was content, or at least I thought he was.

I had no idea that I too would soon be a prisoner right along with Jeff. I was too grateful that he was still with us to really understand the enormity of what was in store. The doctors had said he would be in the hospital for two to three weeks. A lot had to be done, including putting a rush on the power wheelchair we had ordered three months prior. I wanted everything to be perfect for Jeff when he came home.

During his time in the hospital, I would be required to stay overnight for at least two nights in a row so that the nursing staff could monitor me and be certain of my ability to care for Jeff and his vent on my own. After all, the ventilator was a complicated addition to Jeff's regimen, and they wanted to make certain I was comfortable with all that I had to manage as well as the new suctioning catheter. The catheter was a long and flexible tube attached on one end of the trachea tube and the other to a suction canister. A clear plastic sheath covered the catheter so it remained sterile. In a motion similar to threading a drawstring into a waistband, using a safety pin on the end, the catheter is inserted into the breathing tube and down into the airway to remove secretions and then slowly pulled back out. The nursing staff was quite impressed with my suctioning skills, and Jeff got to where he only wanted me suctioning him. He felt I was best at clearing all of the secretions. This made me feel good, of course. Even the caregiver needs validation every now and then.

Tyler was present for a lot of the technical teaching and would later be able to do almost everything I could do. He had quickly become numb to the sight of the vent. He had already seen so much that I wasn't sure anything would faze him.

One night while Jeff slept, I sat with his night shift nurse, who complimented my dedication to Jeff. She told me she had never before seen a patient's spouse as caring and involved as I was with Jeff's care. I had never thought about it in this way, as I was just doing what I had to do. Then she added, "You have what it takes to get through this. Some patients live a very long time on a ventilator." The length of life on the vent was not something I had considered. Oh God, what happens when he is totally incapacitated and completely locked in? What will we do? The vent stopped ALS from taking Jeff's air, but ALS was still progressing and would soon devour the rest of his voluntary movement, even the ability to blink.

Although the vent was quiet, light, and easy to transport, I knew Jeff would have to be confined to the wheelchair because the vent was now a permanent part of him. The thought of him carrying it on his back like camping gear came to mind. I knew that his legs were almost useless, and so did he. I would have been shocked if he'd been walking at all once he was released. I had prepared myself for the worst.

As the realization set in that saving Jeff's life represented mine being taken farther away from what I had always dreamed it would be, I began to feel cheated, tied down, and then guilt came over me for thinking about my needs. I wanted more children. I wanted to build a house in the country, find more dogs to love, have a pet goat that would graze in the yard, egg-laying hens, and maybe even a horse, because like every girl in America, I had wanted one since I was a little girl. I wanted to grow an organic garden. I wanted to watch in peace the sun rise and set. My tranquility had been gone for so long. I began getting accustomed to the fact that this was my life. This was it, all there was. Somehow this predicament began to exhaust me. I loved Jeff with all of my heart, but the disease was chipping away little by little, breaking my spirit a little more each day.

After all the bells and whistles, the power wheelchair cost $35,000. This disease was getting more and more expensive. Daydreaming, I pictured us homeless, me pushing a grocery cart containing all of our worldly possessions as Jeff strolled alongside in his power wheelchair.

I'm jolted from spacing out when the Permobil rep answers the phone. I explained the situation and he promised he'd do his best to expedite Jeff's chair. One week later he called to tell me the chair would be arriving the next day. This in itself was a miracle. I asked him if he could deliver it to the hospital at Cox South to surprise Jeff. Losing more movement in his legs every day, Jeff was growing concerned as to how he'd get around at all, let alone with a ventilator to carry. It was funny; we went from being nauseated at the sight of a wheelchair to being overjoyed at the thought of one. It happened that way: the dreadful becoming the relief.

When he brought the chair in, I met him out in the hallway then slipped back into Jeff's room, anxiously waiting his response. You'd have thought he'd made it through Q-school again. Relief…and pure joy.

# Twenty-Six

Our home was in need of adjustments to accommodate a wheelchair. I had replaced all of the doorknobs with handles several months before so that Jeff could more easily open and close doors. The wheelchair would require major renovations. I decided a ramp leading from the garage into the house would be less unsightly than one to the front door. Normally we didn't use the front door, so it made sense. I hired a guy to build the ramp as well as place a small one at the back of the house leading out to the porch. The lip was only four inches, but I worried the chair wouldn't maneuver over it without toppling.

Jeff spent a lot of time on the back porch, because it was screened and provided protection from the relentless mosquitoes and other bugs of southwest Missouri. I was determined to make life at home on the ventilator and in the wheelchair the same as life at home before the ventilator and wheelchair. Eight hundred dollars later, we were handicap accessible to the outside through the garage and out the back door to the porch. I considered a ramp from the porch to the backyard, but that left too much room for accidents. I had become a nervous worrywart as we adapted to so much so fast. Keeping Jeff from harm with all of these new apparatuses was going to be challenging.

The bathroom would be torn apart to accommodate the wheelchair, and the doorway into our bedroom had to be widened. The doorway into the master bathroom was wide enough, thankfully. A crew of guys from Mom's church offered to remodel the bathroom for absolutely nothing in return. Barry had already erected a basketball hoop in the driveway for Tyler. These precious souls just kept giving and giving and giving.

I purchased the lumber, tile, and new fixtures for the bathroom. The toilet was replaced with a taller one they called "handicapped" size, but it was perfect for a tall person and looked the same as the regular-sized ones. I wondered why anyone would ever install anything but a handicapped toilet. Our beautiful corner Jacuzzi tub was ripped out and replaced with a doorless tile shower, five feet by five feet, with six jets: a couple up high for me and four lower down for Jeff, as well as a hand-held sprayer for bathing the dogs. It saddened me to see the Jacuzzi go. We once relaxed in that Jacuzzi almost every night. I had not stepped into it since Jeff no longer could, and the new shower was pretty dope, or sick, as Tyler would say. I refused to allow ALS the satisfaction of preventing Jeff from enjoying a revitalizing shower: none of this sponge-bath-in-bed crap. Can you imagine never being able to stand in the shower and feel the water bouncing off your skin, replenishing your body?

When the renovations were finished, our handicap-accessible shower looked fabulous and not at all handicapped. Rick and Honey happened to be remodeling their house, including their master bath, so we gave them our beloved Jacuzzi, and it was a great pleasure because it would without a doubt be enjoyed by true love.

Needing to in some way compensate us, Rick arched both of the doorways in our bedroom and master bath, which really made a difference. Instead of just two gaping holes, they actually looked like they were meant to be doorless archways. The bathroom had a lovely Tuscan feel to it when it was done. The single-pedestal sink allowed plenty of room for the chair to turn completely around. I added the final touches: I installed a moveable screen that hung from a track on the ceiling and could be drawn in case one wanted privacy while using the toilet; I measured, purchased, and stained the baseboard molding; and just behind the sink I put in a splashguard of Italian tiles that Jeff and I picked out together. I was proud of my handiwork. The handrail next to the toilet was a complete eyesore, but oh well.

On homecoming day Jeff would, with our Permobil rep's assistance, ride in his new chair from his hospital room to the ambulance. Then the chair would be delivered to the house, where Jeff would then be moved from the stretcher to the chair and ride it into the garage, up the newly erected ramp, and inside. He was so spoiled.

The nurses were, as usual, doting over Jeff when I arrived at the hospital that day. They had grown very fond of Jeff and his charming wit. I was

in a very serious mood, anticipating the day ahead. As I stood there looking at Jeff and the ventilator inhaling and exhaling for him, I was already
dreading the moment I would see the respiratory therapist walk out of our
front door, leaving me all alone with the task at hand.

Once I signed all of the paperwork for the release and took all of the
instructions, I kissed Jeff on the forehead and told him I'd see him at home.
The respiratory therapist followed me to our house to start setting up the
home ventilators.

We'd been at the house for a few hours when the rep arrived with the
wheelchair. My parents came over, and my father took one look at the ramp
and said the grade was too steep. Sure enough, the chair wouldn't make it
up.

My dad called my uncle, who is a master craftsman and typically in
charge of projects such as this. Uncle Ron is the epitome of a handyman.
He was there in half an hour to make alterations. He took one look at
the ramp and laughed. "Well, Sissy, why didn't you just call me to begin
with?" he said, smiling and still chuckling. I didn't want to be a burden,
but now, feeling ashamed and frustrated about the waste of $800, I was
wishing that I had called him.

My family and our friends wanted to help. It made them feel good to
be contributing. However, I wanted to take care of it all by myself and
leave everyone alone for a change. I think it hurt my uncle's feelings that I
hadn't asked him. He grabbed me be the shoulders in his firm but gentle
way and looked right at me with raised eyebrows. "Hon, you could never
be a burden."

All we did was need, need, need. I have never been good at asking others for favors. I'd much rather be on the giving end. I am not sure why this
is, but it is. I understood that people wanted to help, wanted me to ask for
help, and expected me to ask for help, but it didn't make asking any easier.

Jeff arrived in the ambulance and was wheeled into the house on the
stretcher via the too-steep ramp. Dad and Uncle Ron ran to the lumberyard
and returned with materials to make the changes. By late afternoon they
had the ramp completely altered and Permobil ready. What started out as
five feet of steep ramp was nearly fifteen feet, extending from the entryway
of the mudroom all the way to the right-side garage door. Jeff would be

able to hit the opener in the doorway of the mudroom at the top of the ramp, and by the time he reached the end of the ramp in his wheelchair, the garage door would have opened completely, allowing him to wheel right out onto the cobblestone drive. I played this out in my head, trying to make sure we had thought of everything.

Jeff's homecoming was as big an event as it had been when I brought Tyler home from the hospital as a newborn. Everything was new, and everything required a procedure that I wasn't quite familiar with but was determined to conquer. I pictured Jeff lying in a tanning bed in the living room, sunglasses covering his eyes, like Tyler had been placed in that light box that was the size of a suitcase when he was jaundiced as a newborn, his little eyes covered by a soft blindfold that was being held in place by heart-shaped Velcro stickers affixed to his temples. I remembered crying when I had to leave him lying there when he began to wriggle and fuss; all I wanted to do was hold him. It was a helpless feeling, not being able to make his skin turn from jaundiced orange to creamy white.

I felt helpless now too. I couldn't help Jeff. Nothing I did would make it different. The outcome would still be the same. No matter how much I altered our home or how much I gave it my all, Jeff was still going to die, and my family and I would be subjected to seeing him becoming totally locked into his body until then, with no ability to communicate, move, smile, or blink. We were no longer in denial. This was our reality, and it was fast approaching.

We had gone over everything at the hospital and I was confident I had it down, but when the respiratory therapist left and there I was, solely responsible for making sure the vent was doing its job, I felt overwhelmed. It was different having a nursing staff within reach as my backup. Now I was alone. Jeff was trapped in a chair and permanently attached to a machine breathing for him.

Thanks to Jamie's advice, a vent sat by the bed, and another one just like it was strapped to the back of the wheelchair. We would switch back and forth accordingly. The first time I removed the tube to switch vents and move him from the chair to the bed, I was so freaked out I thought for sure I wouldn't be able to get it attached again, and that would be the end of it. It wasn't long before I could do it in my sleep.

The two weeks in the hospital were by far the last of the good days Jeff would have. Prior to the vent, he was slowly losing oxygen, irritable and restless. After the vent he was given a boost and felt so much better with all of the air he was getting again. Once confined to the chair after coming home, his attitude changed. We went on walks when it wasn't too cold, but he couldn't get in the car and go for a drive. Depression set in, and death was lurking. I could feel it. This time it was different. I could feel a void, and what filled the void felt not pure and simple but tainted and complicated.

The anger and frustration over what I was losing manifested into this eagerness to claim back what was mine and resist with all of my might what I knew deep in my heart was certain. I could handle anything that came our way, anything. I was no longer reserved and non-confrontational. If someone didn't treat me with respect, I didn't hesitate to stick up for myself. Life already sucked; I didn't need anyone trying to make it worse. I was fed up and I wasn't going to take shit from anyone. I wanted to attack anything and everything that threatened me or my family, especially Jeff. I didn't particularly enjoy being this person. I had become a total bitch.

I made certain that Jeff had everything he needed. I purchased a wireless doorbell so that Jeff could alert me when he needed something. I affixed the button to the left footrest of his chair nearest to the best functioning foot, and plugged the ringer into the living room wall outlet in the middle of the house. I turned the volume up as loud as it would go, and it could easily be heard in any room of the house. I connected computer speakers to the over-bed table I'd bought for Gus, allowing him to speak more loudly. The table could be raised and lowered. At night I raised it level with Jeff's toe at the foot of our bed just like in the hospital, and during the day I lowered it to be level with his chair. I would swap the mouse accordingly from the table to the footrest.

We went on walks when it wasn't too cold. I would bundle him up with blankets and arm him with the ambo bag. While keeping one hand and eye on Jeff and wrestling the dogs on leashes, we would stroll around in the neighborhood. A drive in the car was out because Jeff had no control over his body. He would need to remain strapped into his wheelchair. The purchase of a handicap-accessible vehicle would be the only way we would ever be able to leave the house. I felt a void, and what was attempting to fill the void felt very unfriendly. Like a perfect stranger.

At times I felt I was losing faith in God. At other times God was all I had faith in. We had so many wonderful people offering assistance, but still it was such a lonely existence. It's indescribable. I started reading my Bible for strength, and it worked most of the time.

Jeff had lost quite a bit of weight while in the hospital and continued to lose after he was home. His stomach had shrunk to nothing on the hospital diet, which consisted of Ensure morning, noon, and night. He was getting full quickly and often refused to eat. He also limited his water intake to avoid getting too full to take in food. Although almost completely incapacitated, Jeff was very much in charge of his care. What he couldn't communicate, I could sense. Using his left big toe to click the mouse, and a slight movement of his left hand to operate the wheelchair controls, he was mobile, vocal, and still in charge.

# Twenty-Seven

Christmas came and went, and I was reaching caregiver burnout. I had more and more difficulty being patient with Jeff's demands, especially when requesting several things at once. Every day was similar to the last but more difficult.

One evening he wanted a foot soak, and then he wouldn't put his feet in the water because his stomach began to feel sick from the ice cream I had just fed him, per his request. Then he wanted to pee but kept pointing to the couch (with his eyes) once I got him up with the urinal. He couldn't type unless he was sitting in his chair where the mouse was attached to the foot-rest, so it was impossible to decipher what exactly he needed. Oftentimes he didn't even know. It seemed he was losing it. Nothing he requested made sense, and we were both tired and frustrated. Remaining patient and struggling to do so, I gave up trying to figure out what he wanted and instead sat him back down and asked him to type what he needed. Instead of typing he had a fit, started going in circles with his chair, and bumped into the corner of the wall, leaving a huge gash in it. He was so careless and disrespectful at times I wanted to scream. But he too wanted to scream and couldn't. Acting out was the only way he could make any noise at all, the only way he could vent his anger.

People started coming often, just to help clean or bring food. One day, while attempting to thank two women from my mother's church for the dinner they had so kindly brought us, Jeff hit the wrong fast-key and instead announced, "That fucking sucks." I wanted to crawl under the sofa at first, then I couldn't help but laugh, so I attempted a recovery. "Oops! Wrong key! That one's for poker night with the boys." The kind ladies didn't flinch and perhaps they didn't even know what Gus had said. Jeff and

I got a good laugh out of it later. They brought vegetarian chili, cornbread, and Waldorf salad. I enjoyed it more than Jeff. He was a true blue carnivore, and loved the taste of those beefy belches. This made me feel special for a change. Like someone was thinking of me and what I'd like, instead of it being all about Jeff.

ALS was affecting my entire family, both mentally and physically. We hadn't seen Keegan since Thanksgiving. Jeff would speak to him, using the speakerphone and Gus, a few times every week. It had been his mom's year to have him at Christmas. Keegan was faced with having to be far away from his dad, while Tyler was in the thick of it, trying to be a normal eleven-year-old. He seemed happy when he was with his friends and he still had certain kids over to the house but not as often. Like me, he wished everyone could pretend that life at our house was normal. My parents were holding up, but I could tell Jeff's illness had taken a toll on them. For the first time, they looked older. Jeff's dad was also having a difficult time. He would visit occasionally but seemed removed at times. His dog, Gracie, died, and luckily, he quickly found a pup that needed a home.

Jeff was most definitely experiencing some cognitive issues. At first I wouldn't accept this, because Web sites will tell you that an ALS patient's mind is not affected; but how could it not be? If Jeff was feeling crabby and miserable, he wanted me to be miserable right along with him. Like a rebellious child, he knew the best way to get a rise out of me. If Gus was working properly, he would click and click until the system would freeze up, and then I would be on the phone with Gordon to troubleshoot the issue. The poor guy put up with so many calls from us, he deserved an award.

What is it about illness that causes everyone to think some kind of force can prevent all of the normal dynamics of marriage and life? Being sick doesn't give you a free pass to be an ass. If someone is being inconsiderate, it is what it is, regardless of his or her physical condition. I understood that Jeff was going through a tough time, but taking it out on me when I was already suffering was uncalled for.

On this particular occasion, my parents were coming over to watch the Super Bowl. The Patriots would be defeating the Panthers, and I was running around pretending I had a normal life, preparing food and beverages for our guests, which prevented me from giving Jeff undivided attention. Once again he fiddled around and pushed enough keys that Gus went into a coma. Just thirty minutes before, Jeff had brought my attention to the fact that Gus was not recalling all of his programmed phrases. After a failed attempt to troubleshoot the computer, I suggested that we not worry with it until after the game. The majority of the phrases he used were working, and he had the ability to use the easy-key program and type any word he wanted by clicking on each one (the method he used most of the time anyway). I did all but beg him to leave Gus alone and promised I would address the issue immediately following the game. A few moments later, I was in the living room straightening up and clearing room for snacks on the coffee table in preparation for Mom and Dad's visit to watch the game with us, when I noticed him still screwing around with the computer. I went over, looked him in the eyes, and calmly warned him again, for the last time, to leave it alone, because I was not going to call Gordon if he messed around with it until it wasn't working at all. "I just want to watch the game. Please Jeff, don't. Please?" I never sat down, and I hadn't watched TV in months. We'd watch movies together sometimes, but I was always up and down for the duration.

By the time my parents arrived, Gus had sure enough had a meltdown, and I couldn't get him started up again. My parents walked in, not having witnessed the events of the past hour, and looked at me with disgust as I was yelling, "Damn it, Jeffrey! Why must you ruin everything for me?" Jeff immediately played the guilt card and acted like a victim. I just wanted to watch the football game! I was making one simple request, and he couldn't honor it.

Mom went to Jeff's side to give him a peck on the cheek as she always did, and my father directed me into the kitchen, where my mom joined us a few moments later.

"What's going on here?" My father was clearly angered, giving me his authoritarian tone. He had no idea what it was like to be me, but he was reacting the way anyone would. From his perspective Jeff, who was dying and in a wheelchair, needed something that was being withheld by someone healthy and capable. Did they honestly think for a moment that I would ever deny Jeff anything? Yes, for that moment, they did. For some reason the person I was, their kind, generous, loving daughter, was forgotten and replaced with a horrible woman who was neglecting her patient for no reason whatsoever; and even if there was a reason, it was not good enough, because Jeff was dying.

Forget that I wasn't only losing Jeff; I was sleep deprived, mentally and physically exhausted, rarely left the house, and when I did it wasn't for more than an hour or so and was usually to go to the market or pharmacy. I hadn't worn underwear for six months because I wouldn't take the time to go buy any.

This is a perfect example of what it is like to be a caregiver. You lose track of yourself. Even those closest to you will lose sight of you, because the overabundance of sympathy overshadows you. There is no way to fully understand it unless you live it. And that goes for everything in life, not just ALS. A perfect example of why we should not judge, but if we have to, we shouldn't judge too quickly.

Even though he was taking ALS as best he could, Jeff wanted more. He wanted life. I wanted the same—life with him. Once I knew that was no longer a realistic option, I started feeling that in Jeff's illness, I was forgotten, left to serve him, to tend He Who Has Been Dealt a Raw Deal, the unlucky, helpless one. And I would be left with nothing when he was gone other than a never-ending ache in my heart, somewhat useful practical wisdom, financial debt, and a gap in my resume.

Even when Jeff was being unreasonable, it wasn't his fault. His needs took precedence because they had to, and I continued to neglect myself. My lower back was killing me, but lifting Jeff was necessary for the job. It seemed that everyone forgot about my needs, my dreams, and my desires right along with me. I couldn't voice these thoughts and feelings—and I felt tremendous guilt every time they entered my mind. *You're a horrible person*, I would tell myself.

It was a living hell.

It wasn't long before my best friend, Honey, and her hubby, Rick, proposed "Julian-Pickren night." They would come over for dinner once a week and we'd alternate dinner responsibilities. One week they'd bring carryout, the next I'd make a nice home-cooked meal or throw steaks on the grill. This provided us with some social interaction, and gave us something to look forward to every week.

They came over one evening right after I'd received the new bedding I'd ordered for the new Select Comfort bed we'd bought. Jeff had insisted on the two extra-long twin beds that fastened together, so that I, being a tummy-sleeper, could sleep flat, while he slept with the head of the bed on an incline to ease his breathing. I hated the idea of there being even a crack between us. It really bothered me. Jeff was adamant about it, making certain I slept comfortably, so I agreed to live with the crack between us on the condition that he wouldn't worry about me getting enough rest and suggest I sleep in a different room, not ever. "I will never sleep in the spare bedroom. I will only sleep by your side." He hesitated and then nodded his head in agreement. He knew I was serious and stubborn enough to stand my ground.

I'd ordered the new bedding from one of my favorite stores, hoping to make us forget we were now sleeping on somewhat of a geriatric bed. The quilt was colorful and happy, and Honey couldn't wait to see it, reminding me of such as soon as they arrived that night. I was in the kitchen preparing to put four big filet mignons on the grill. "Oh, right! Come with me," I said, setting the cookie sheet of filets down so we could walk back to the bedroom. We were gone less than two minutes, just long enough to take a quick peek at the new bedding. When I went to pick up the tray of filets, something was different. Instead of four filets, there were only three.

"Max!!!!" I yelled and turned to find the little bastard sitting right behind me, licking his chops. He then ran in to where Jeff and Rick were sitting in the living room, as if the guys had been in on the whole thing and would protect him.

On another Julian-Pickren night, Honey and I were sitting at the bar in the kitchen talking, and we always had a lot to talk about. Jeff was beckoning me to his side with the doorbell I had affixed to the foot of his wheelchair for exactly that purpose. Ten times in five minutes for absolutely nothing. Rick was sitting right next to him and happy to help, but he only wanted me. He asked me to scratch his nose, then wipe the drool from his mouth, followed by a dirty look because I wiped too firmly; then he needed to pee, and every request thereafter was not at all pressing, making it seem as though he just wanted to ask for something because he was bored, which was understandable but no less annoying for me. It was just never ending. I would always hop right up and take care of anything he needed.

Honey looked at me after doorbell number ten and took a slow, deep breath. "I would stick that doorbell so far up his ass he would never ring it again!" At last someone who gets it, I thought. We laughed until we cried.

Our dinner night with Honey and Rick was the highlight of my week. I looked forward to it. It was two hours a week that I could spend with Jeff and our friends and pretend life was normal. Jeff had simply become so restless that he could no longer allow me to enjoy those moments with friends.

Honey's comment gave me validation; something every human needs to thrive, and something that a caregiver rarely receives. She helped me realize that I was doing a great job caring for Jeff, and it was OK for me to have thoughts of frustration and anger—I wasn't a bad person or less of a wife to him because it was hard being a caregiver. I was attempting the most impossible task in the world: being a caregiver while continuing to be a wife. If I could go back, I would insist that Jeff allow me to hire in-home care for him right from the start.

Honey and Rick both loved Jeff and me so much that they were able to relate to us as they always had. They understood. They loved him enough to stick by him through thick and thin, and they loved and respected him enough to refuse to let him get away with behavior that didn't best serve us as a couple. We were still Jeff and Kim to them, not the poor patient and unkind caregiver. I don't know why others couldn't understand us the way they did.

It was their friendship and recalling that comment Honey made in the kitchen that helped me get over the guilt that would so often creep up on me.

# Twenty-Eight

Jeff had become very methodical and would easily get upset if something took place out of order. If I tried to wash his face before giving him all of his coffee, I was committing a cardinal sin. Doctors stress that ALS doesn't affect the mind, so I kept blowing it off. I didn't know for certain until one day when Honey came bearing gifts. She hated our shallow bowls and had found some cute cereal bowls she thought we had to have. After she gave them to me, I ran into the living room and included Jeff by showing them to him. He typed, "Nice. Thank you." Two days later I was eating a bowl of cereal out of one of them. Jeff was looking at me funny; then, with his left leg, signed "Where?" by moving it back and forth. Meaning, where did you get that? "The bowls? This is one of the four Honey gave us. They're nice, huh?"

He continued to look at me, brow furrowed with a confused expression on his face. "Jeffrey, don't tell me you don't remember me showing you these the other night. Honey brought them for us when she and Rick were over for dinner. It was just a few days ago!"

He had no idea—had never seen them before in his life. It was bizarre.

I did some research and found the symptoms to be exactly what I had witnessed. "Mood swings, often with brief periods of anger or rage, paranoia and suspiciousness, increased irritation due to change in routine." I talked to Marsha about it and she was certain she'd seen similar behavior in Bruce. Dementia is indeed part of ALS. My patient and Marsha's proved the theory correct.

Marsha called one morning while Jeff and I were still lying in bed talking—well, not talking, but clicking and typing. She was sobbing so uncontrollably I couldn't understand what she was saying and immediately assumed something was wrong with Bruce. Once I got her settled down, she expressed concern for what her future held.

Marsha had four children, two who were old enough to be on their own but weren't, and two young ones, ages seven and ten. They had a nice comfortable house, a nice car, and just about everything they needed, except an income, of course. But all of these possessions were Bruce's things, not Marsha's, leaving her with a lot of doubt and insecurity. She was in a state of panic, and my heart was breaking for her. I understood, because I had the same fears. What would happen to me after Jeff was gone? Would I be able to keep our home? Would I be able to make a living while grieving? It's a very scary position to be in, having no idea what your future holds. Marsha was older than me, already in her forties, even though she looked no older than thirty. As many divorcees experience, starting over at midlife is frightening.

A time comes when you must allow yourself to be crazy and just break down, and Marsha was there. After I hung up and explained the situation to Jeff, he started typing on his keyboard that was attached to his over-bed table at the foot of our bed. "Go. She needs you," Gus read, as Jeff looked at me with concern in his eyes. I admitted that I instinctually felt I should go and just check on her, but Jeff was on a ventilator and it was a little complicated. I called Marsha back right then and asked her if she needed me to come, and she said she really did.

Lizzy, who had been traveling from Vermont to Missouri visiting Jeff regularly, would be a great stand in. Jeff called her right away. She was in Germany buying a horse or something so he called another sibling, the same one who had come before, and she came to our rescue without hesitating.

We'd finally cleared it with our insurance company to hire a nurse to come in for four hours per day, allowing me to get things done around the house and go grocery shopping. I wasn't getting any rest, still getting up throughout the night to suction Jeff's lungs, but having the nurse gave me an occasional break to get a couple of things accomplished.

The first nurse was a large woman named Atina. I'd requested a non-smoker but soon found that my trash can smelled like ashes because she was putting cigarettes out on the back porch, then tossing the butts in the kitchen trash can. In addition to the smoke—I'm sorry—she smelled like a dirty person. It was disgusting. After she'd leave I'd remove and wash the covering on the cushion where she'd been sitting. Thank God they were removable, washable cotton.

I had only left Jeff once before, when I went to Amy's wedding in California. He wasn't even on a vent or in a wheelchair then, and I was a nervous wreck, pacing around my hotel room.

I was uneasy the entire four days I was in Florida, but I wouldn't trade that time I spent with Marsha and Bruce for anything. A very private person, Bruce spent most of his days in their bedroom with a computer and television, even though he was still able to move his limbs fairly well. Marsha was frustrated, understandably, because she felt he was giving up. During my visit they seemed to be all right, but I did sense tension; the same tension I was sensing in my own home.

A few days after I returned home from Florida, I noticed some yellowing around Jeff's trache and asked Atina to take a look at it. She later reported it wasn't anything to worry about. A few days later, Atina called and said she couldn't make it in because she was sick, so Mom came over so I could get some fresh air and run errands. Jeff had requested a movie. When I walked into the movie store, Atina was there with a man who I assumed was her husband, looking through the selection of movies. I stood and watched her for a moment. She didn't look sick at all. Then I said hello to her and she turned around, looking a little shocked.

I called the agency and asked for another nurse, requesting one who could come during the night hours so that I could sleep. I also mentioned I wanted an actual nonsmoker this time.

The new nurse accepted a midnight to six o'clock shift. Our insurance had a limited allotment on the in-home care hours we could have, and I was trying to use them sparingly. Christina was a pretty girl and had a sweet disposition and smelled good. A devout Christian, she was a little on the wacky spiritual side, but I liked her and that didn't bother me. Jeff seemed to like her too.

When Christina came in that first night, I asked her about the discoloring around Jeff's trache. She took one look and said, "That's a staph infection." She knew just by looking at it, and that other dumbass who had helped care for Jeff for two weeks didn't have a clue. Worried she'd wake me when suctioning and dealing with Jeff through the night, she told me

I should sleep in our guest room. I refused. Nothing was going to stop me from sleeping next to my husband. He had succeeded at getting the separated beds so we could have different sleep numbers and whatnot, but I wasn't going to budge on this one. I slept with one foot touching him, and that wasn't going to change. I did wake when she suctioned, but knowing he was being taken care of was comforting, and I'd go right back to sleep.

The next morning I called Dr. Baker about the infection. He called the agency and made arrangements to have a swab sent to the lab. He made a house call the next afternoon, and after seeing the infection, he was positive it was staph. The lab results a few days later confirmed it, and Jeff was prescribed a mega antibiotic.

Two months after starting to use the ventilator, Jeff's body had really started shutting down. He began wanting to stay in bed more and more. I hated seeing him in bed so often. I'd get him up and in the chair, and an hour later he'd want to return to bed.

Digestion was basically working, but the muscles needed to move his bowels were not, and they became impacted. A friend from my mother's church who was a nurse taught me how to insert a gloved finger into Jeff's rectum to gently dislodge the impacted feces. This was degrading for him, but Jeff being Jeff he made light of it for both of us, and after my first successful attempt at this, it provided him such relief that Gus exclaimed, "I didn't think it was possible, but I love you even more."

We never know what's around the corner and what we may end up doing for another human being, nor do we consider it possible that we will one day love someone to the extent that it is possible. I would have done anything for Jeff, and what a beautiful experience it was to love someone that much.

The Dunn brothers visited again in early March. While hanging out in our bedroom with Jeff, Lance suggested that looking out of the windows behind our bed would be uplifting and offered to turn it around. Jeff refused and typed something about having a bird's-eye view of the bathroom. He'd enjoyed watching me shower since it had become doorless, and that is what he was getting at. It wasn't often that his personality would come out, but I loved it when it did.

The Dunn brothers' visit was special to Jeff and crucial to his dying process. It was difficult for people, friends and family to face what was happening. Some stayed away because they couldn't bear to witness it. Others, as painful as it may have been, faced it with courage. Paul and Lance were definitely among the latter. Lance and Paul mentioned they could see substantial progression since their visit in November. It was almost as if Jeff's body was resisting the ventilator.

The last time Jeff would get into his wheelchair was on March 7. It was the night of *The Sopranos* season premiere on HBO. Jeff typically wouldn't have missed it for the world. We were James Gandolfini fans and loved the series. Paul and Lance helped me get him out of bed to watch the episode. We were making a big deal out of it, giving him something to look forward to. Five minutes later he was asking to go back to bed.

# Twenty-Nine

Once pneumonia had set into Jeff's lungs and signs of his body giving up the fight became apparent, Jeff asked me to let him go. He longed to die in Vermont.

"Let them take the burden for a while," he said, referring to his side of the family. "When Tyler goes to his dad's for the summer, you can join me, if I last that long," Gus said.

I understood his desire to die there as well as his need to remove the burden that had so long rested on my shoulders. He had watched me tirelessly dedicate every ounce of energy to him for so long, and it was becoming painful for him. Still, I felt betrayed. I am not sure how to describe it. I had stood by him in sickness and in health, and he was bailing on me, to die without me. It was as though I was not allowed to finish something I had started. I begged him to stay, to die there in Missouri.

"I know this is not home to you, but you are loved here, Jeff. Just stay here, please," I begged and pleaded.

"My beloved, you can't take anymore. You have gone above and beyond. Doesn't matter where I die. I'll always be with you in your heart," Gus said.

I finally agreed but insisted he wait until his doctors felt confident that he had very little time left. We began planning and preparing for his move to Vermont to die. My family invited Jeff's family to come to Branson for a few days so that we could have a family meeting, and they could all learn how to take care of Jeff.

When our doctors gave us a window of two weeks, we put the plan into action. On March 17, 2004, my father chartered an air ambulance, and Jeff and I flew to Vermont together, where he would live out the rest of his days. On the days leading up to his departure, I expected Jeff to say goodbye to Tyler. But he didn't, and Tyler didn't say goodbye to him. It was as if neither of them could cope with it, as if Jeff was suddenly in denial regarding his fate. I began to wonder if Jeff honestly believed he'd live until spring or summer when his doctor had predicted two weeks.

Tyler left for school that morning as if it was any other day. I didn't react to it but simply wondered if I was doing the right thing by not forcing them to gain closure. I thought about Keegan and how I'd pushed away from him, preparing myself for losing him completely because I feared that's what would happen once Jeff was gone. Still, I wondered why Jeff hadn't asked for Tyler so they could say, "I love you," one last time. Suddenly I realized that I resented him for not doing so.

I scrambled around trying to get everything together after the ambulance called saying the plane was ready and they were on their way. It made obvious the amount of equipment it took just to function. I couldn't really pack until the moment we were walking out of the door, since his basic survival required everything that needed packing. And part of me had avoided the packing, not wanting to accept that the move was going to happen. Jeff was very much in charge, so he and Gus were quite busy at conducting this process. I expected him to ask for a framed photo of us or something that was of sentimental value to him. All he was concerned with was his autographed Curt Schilling jersey. I resented that too. The longer the process dragged on, the more I felt abandoned.

The plane was tiny: enough room for Jeff on a stretcher, a nurse, me, and two pilots in the cockpit. We stopped halfway for fuel, and Jeff made the flight just fine, resting peacefully for the duration.

A large group of Jeff's friends was gathered on the runway of the small New Hampshire airport when we arrived. It was a wonderful homecoming for him. Most were shocked at his frailty. He resembled a cadaver because he was at the end, and that is what ALS does to one's body. No one wanted to accept this. It was too much to accept at once for most, because they had not slowly witnessed the progression like I had.

I had checked on hospice in Vermont and fortunately found that regardless of how long Jeff lived, they would help out until the end of his life. I knew it was in Jeff's best interest. The family resisted, but once Dr. Stadler who was assigned to Jeff came to the house to meet everyone, they changed their minds. What a wonderful man he was. Godsent.

Since Jeff loved his Select Comfort bed and the ability to change the firmness helped us avoid bedsores, we needed to get one in Vermont as soon as possible. He needed to be in the one at home until the moment we departed, so things got complicated.

I decided to order a new one and have it delivered. Well, the store in New Hampshire didn't provide home delivery to Vermont, nor did they ship the type of frame that would raise and lower the head and foot of the bed as well as vibrate. My mom called and ordered the mattress; one exactly the same as the one we had at home, and had it shipped to Vermont. I thought I'd found a solution when hospice said they could provide a frame for it. The mattress didn't fit the frame they provided perfectly, so it just wasn't good enough, and then things got really complicated.

I was trying my best to accommodate Jeff's needs even when he was in Vermont, but nothing I did was right or good enough. In addition no one wanted to contribute or foot the bill, but they had no problem making demands that were financially burdensome to me.

I stayed for one week to get him settled before returning home. I spent each night at Liz's house, a quarter of a mile down the lane, because I wanted the others to learn how to take care of Jeff without me there. If there I'd be accessible and also too tempted to take over. I couldn't leave him there unless completely confident that they could handle alone any situation that might arise.

I purchased all of the little necessities and did my best to make available there everything he'd had at home, without spending a fortune. I was keeping in mind that these items would only be needed for a few weeks. I bought a few perishables, Pellegrino water, broth for pureeing, and beef for the freezer. He was eating so little that the amount of food I bought should have lasted a month. Money was getting tight, and I wasn't sure how long it would be before I started bringing in a substantial income.

Lizzy would end up playing a vital role in Jeff's care. Like Jeff, I felt close to Liz where I didn't to the others. I knew I could depend on her. Before leaving I gave her a debit card linked directly to our checking account.

Hospice would be providing all of the medical supplies Jeff needed, all of the medicine, and all of the medical care, even massages and baths. The only expense would be food and toiletries. I told her to buy what Jeff needed and gave her the personal identification number. I stressed the fact that it was a debit card that pulls money directly from our bank account and, therefore, the importance of letting me know when she used it so I could transfer money as needed.

On the day before I left, I walked into the house after running errands and found our attorney, Steve Saunders, standing in the dining room. Steve had represented Jeff as he was attempting to get his one-sixth share of his mom's estate paid to him in the form of the land on Fox Hill. Steve had worked on it while Jeff still had enough in him to keep trying to get it resolved.

"Hi, Steve, what a nice surprise. What brings you out here?" I said, smiling at him. He was a good attorney and a good person, from what Jeff and I had experienced. Almost too nice for an attorney.

"Well, I was told that Jeff wanted to see me," he replied.

"Oh, Jeff didn't mention it to me. Have you gone back yet?" I asked.

"No, I was told to wait here," Steve said.

"That's nonsense, come on," I replied, and led him toward Jeff's makeshift bedroom.

"Honey, look who came to see you," I said, walking around to the front of Jeff's bed with Steve.

Jeff looked surprised to see Steve, leading Steve and me both to think that Jeff had not asked to see him at all. Jeff immediately started telling Gus what to say to properly greet Steve.

I walked over and closed the French doors that led into the hall.

"So, Steve, while you're here, I want you to draw up something that will state that I will have no interest in what Jeff's mother left to him. I don't want any bad feelings while Jeff is here. I know—after what we've been through—this house and the land is a touchy subject. That is why it was held up to begin with. They didn't want Jeff taking his one-sixth, knowing what was in store, and then see it left to me. They don't want that, and I don't either." I had this feeling in my gut that I just couldn't shake. I asked them to discuss the issue alone and left the room. I wanted Jeff to be able to talk openly about his wishes, without worrying about anyone else, especially me.

They were in there for a while before Steve called me back in.

"Jeff and I have talked at length. He insists that his one-sixth goes to you, Kim."

"I disagree. Jeff, why? Just leave it to Keegan. You know this is a sore subject after what Lizzy went through, after what you went through. Please, I don't want to be pulled into it."

"You build boys cabin. They go on weekends when older. Take friend's there. Be brothers there," Gus announced.

Jeff wanted his dream of a cabin on Fox Hill to come true, still. He wanted it to be a place that would keep Keegan and Tyler connected, where they could both go after they became grown men. Without each other they didn't have any siblings. They were both alone. Jeff wanted for them what he never had: a brother whom he could always count on.

"Jeff, I can create that for them somewhere else someday. I don't have a good feeling about this. You're making a mistake that I am going to have to deal with later on alone," I said, then left the room so he could finish his business with Steve.

I know Jeff was relieved to be near Keegan and looked forward to him visiting. I began wondering if I would feel a sense of relief when I returned home without Jeff. Would I find pleasure in being able to sleep through the night? Part of me thought so. Would I be glad that I was no longer chained to Jeff, or would I just feel empty?

After I returned to Missouri, I started shipping things north that I had forgotten to pack or couldn't pack. The Vita-Mix was one of them. Along with the Vita-Mix, I sent a compact disc of music I thought he'd like and a letter telling him I missed him. I also sent Jeff's tackle box to his friend Steve. I don't know why I felt it necessary; I just happened by it in the garage and knew Jeff would want Steve to have it for fishing that spring. It contained some lures, and rubber worms, a few of those ugly things with hooks in them, and the head of a Barbie doll attached to a hook which was a memento from a fishing trip with one of his buddies. Jeff told me the story but I don't recall it now. Something about finding the doll head in a parking lot before the trip and calling it a good luck piece and then the

same weekend he went on to win the Cape Cod Open or the Bangor Open;
I forget which.

Jeff associated fishing with Steve. Jeff loved telling a story about one
day when he was driving along Route 5, which runs parallel with the
Connecticut River. He spotted Steve out fishing on his pontoon boat and
pulled over, took his driver out of his golf bag that was, of course, in the
back of the car, and proceeded to hit several golf balls in the direction of
Steve's boat. I don't recall if he actually hit his target, but he came close
enough to get Steve's attention, golf balls landing around him like torpe-
does. Steve looked up to find Jeff across the river waving at him, holding
his driver in his hand. This tale so accurately describes the quintessential
Jeff. You can bet he was wearing his big grin the entire time too. I knew
Jeff would enjoy knowing Steve was using his tackle box.

I called to speak with Jeff a few times a day. Someone would answer and
put me on the speakerphone I'd set up next to Jeff's bed. Other than that
I had no connection or report from Jeff's new caregivers. It was as if I had
never been Jeff's wife. I was no longer needed.

Due to the tension, I immediately began communicating directly with
Dr. Stadler, who indicated that he was well aware of the family dynamics. He told me he'd be seeing Jeff regularly and to call him anytime for a
report. Thank God, I thought.

When Jeff had been there for two and a half weeks, I went to the ATM
to get cash and it wouldn't give me any. It was a Saturday afternoon, so
the bank was closed. I borrowed some cash from Mom and Dad to get me
through the weekend and used my credit card for groceries.

I had an interview set up at Carol Jones Realtors, a real estate brokerage
with a branch located just outside the gates of our housing development at
Pointe Royale. I had obtained my broker's license several years prior so that
I could assist my father with his business when he had to be out of town, and
I had kept it active. I thought I might as well put it to good use. A branch
office sat directly across the street from our bank, so I slipped in before my
interview to figure out what was going on with our account. I found that
in a little over a week, our debit card had been used at various places in

Vermont and New Hampshire, amounting to over $300. Liz hadn't called to tell me about any charges she'd made on the card, so not knowing what in the hell was going on and needing to get to my interview, I asked them to cancel the card. If it had been a credit card, perhaps I wouldn't have panicked, but this card accessed our primary checking account.

The interview went well and I was told the next orientation would be held beginning the week of April 18. I signed up and left feeling somewhat encouraged. It would take a while to begin bringing money in, considering I had to get out and network to build my clientele. It was a step in the right direction; however, my concern regarding our finances continued to escalate.

I received a call from Lizzy. She'd tried to use the card and found that the account had been closed. I didn't know it at the time, but most of the caregiving had been delegated to Liz. She was simply coming to grips with Jeff's dying and was probably experiencing caregiver burnout. I tried to make her understand that I was more than happy to pay for whatever Jeff needed. That is why I had left the card in the first place. However, I couldn't afford to pay overdraft fees resulting from a failure to communicate. In my opinion this was not an unreasonable request. I told her to send me receipts for anything she purchased for Jeff and I would reimburse her immediately. Not long after this conversation, Liz had a falling out with the others and resigned as a caregiver.

After only a few weeks, they had realized what it was like to be me. Three or more people were taking shifts to do what I had done alone for more than two years.

Despite all of the stress and worry over what was happening, Tyler and I were getting reacquainted and enjoying our time together. He was playing spring soccer and spending more and more time with his buddies—and less time with me, typical for his age. Jeff's absence was felt all around me. I felt lost not being at his beck and call.

Marsha and I were still talking every day, as Bruce's condition was worsening. He had refused any life-sustaining device, and even had a DNR, or "do not resuscitate" order, hanging in the bedroom. Bruce kept to himself and was spending the majority of his time in bed. For a few weeks he had been using a BiPAP machine, a breathing apparatus that helps get more air into the lungs and also helps to exhale without the muscular effort that is needed to do so. The BiPAP is where Bruce had drawn the line. Marsha had called in hospice to keep him comfortable. Bruce had been on morphine for a while, and Jeff too had been on it, ever since Bruce recommended it and felt it would help with the severe anxiety. It did help, tremendously, and in very small doses.

The Masters was beginning on April 8, and Bruce was being honored with the 2004 Ben Hogan Award the night before. Bruce and Marsha weren't able to make the trip, so Bruce's dad accepted the award for him. Bruce spoke to his father after the ceremony to ensure that all went well. Marsha called me early the next morning, the first day of the Masters. Bruce had passed away, and she was lying in bed next to his body. "He looks so at peace, Kimmy." I could hear relief and angst in her voice, all at the same time. "Marsha, I'm so sorry, honey. Do you need me to come today? If you do I'll be on the next flight." I wanted to be there for her.

"I think I'm OK. I really do. Just wait till the funeral," she replied.

"Call me when you know the details for the service so I can make flight reservations. And hang in there." I tried to act strong but I was a mess. How much courage did it take for Bruce to accept his illness and let go? A lot. I respected him for it. But he was gone, and I'd never get a chance to tell him.

That next morning I got a call from Marsha. No longer in shock, reality had set in. "Can you come today?" she asked.

"I can try, but if I can't get on a flight I will first thing tomorrow," I answered.

"Of course, just get here as soon as you can."

"I will. Hang tight."

I was on a plane from Kansas City to Jacksonville early the next morning. I felt guilt for leaving Tyler, but he understood that being a good friend often calls for sacrificing. When I arrived Marsha was clearly relieved to see me. I knew what she had been through. I had had to let Jeff go even though he was still alive in Vermont on life support. I settled into their bedroom. I slept on her side of the bed, and she slept on Bruce's, in the very spot he had been when I visited in February and massaged his atrophied hands. The very spot where he had died. Each night I was there, Marsha would wake up startled, and I would quietly tell her everything was all right. My heart ached for her.

On Sunday, the last day of the Masters, Mickelson was in the lead. Jeff and I for years had cheered Phil on to win the Masters, but he had never pulled it off. Wanting to share the moment with Jeff, I called. He and Scottie were watching the final round. With me on speakerphone, we all watched the winning putt drop. Finally Phil had won it. I think Jeff felt lucky to have witnessed it. In a sense this event and the Red Sox winning the World Series were at the top of his bucket list.

Marsha buried Bruce on that coming Tuesday. We spent hours just sitting quietly. She had become withdrawn, a natural response. I made sure she was eating and at least taking care of herself. I was worried about her being left alone after everyone was gone, so I stayed for two days following the funeral and finally left to go home at the end of the week. It was now the middle of April. I tried to feel guilty for being away and not being in Vermont with Jeff, and then I reminded myself that he made the choice to go. He was where he wanted to be, and I was fulfilling my role as a friend.

After I returned from Florida, I was looking forward to the orientation that was scheduled for the next week. I hadn't been able to reach Jeff, so it had been almost a week since we last spoke—the day Mickelson earned his first green jacket at the Masters. I couldn't get an answer at all when I'd call the farmhouse. Nor could my parents. I called Dr. Stadler on Friday and he said he hadn't been out to see Jeff in the last few days but expected to see him Monday or Tuesday of the next week.

Attempting to cope with Jeff being two thousand miles away was enough. Adding the challenge of going back to work, regaining normality with Tyler and being present for a change, and now not being in communication with Jeff, I was on the verge of a nervous breakdown.

I finally got a call on Saturday. It was Gus calling to tell me he wanted to live. After a twenty-second pause, Gus said, "Kimberly, can you please send my driver's license?"

"Why? You taking someone out on a date?" I joked, the way Jeff and I always had. "You need the car too?" I continued.

"I'd like to give it to Keegan," Gus said.

"OK, sure, I will find it and…" someone interrupted me and added that Jeff wanted his wheelchair too, then said they had to go because Jeff's massage therapist had just walked in and hung up before I could say goodbye.

I set the receiver down as a horrible feeling came over me. Something wasn't right. He was responding to my questions twice as fast as when I last saw him, meaning his left toe must have regained some movement. This was encouraging but provided me with no false hope of some miraculous recovery. I couldn't figure out why he'd want his wheelchair, since he had wanted nothing to do with it since the Dunn brothers' last visit in early March.

I called a freight company anyway to arrange for the chair to be shipped. I was shocked when I was told that the chair weighed five hundred pounds and would have to be crated by a freight company and then shipped. This would cost me a small fortune, and I didn't have money to throw away. If Jeff really needed the chair, the cost didn't matter, but I knew Jeff didn't need the chair, and even if he thought he wanted it, he wouldn't get in it and stay in it once it arrived. I had a feeling he was being convinced that he needed it and convinced that he was getting better. False hope.

I spoke with my parents, and we decided that it wouldn't make sense shipping it because, first, Jeff wasn't using it before he left, and, second, the old house was not wheelchair accessible. I wasn't even sure how they'd get it into the house; and if they did, the floors certainly would not support the weight of it. Having to make these decisions, even pondering them, was upsetting. I didn't know what to do, so I did nothing.

I was at a loss regarding how to handle the situation that Jeff had gotten us into. I told Mom and Dad that I felt that I should go check on Jeff, considering what was happening, but they were very uncomfortable with the idea. "I don't think it's a good idea, especially going alone. As a matter of fact, you absolutely shouldn't go alone if you go at all. Now we know Jeff is being cared for. He's their flesh and blood. You, however, are not, and I don't want you going." My father was having no part of it. He was telling me exactly what Tom had told me that past September. Live your life for a change. It's not all about him.

"I understand what you are saying, Dad, but I have a bad feeling that someone is reinforcing this fantasy of survival and giving him false hope. I don't think at this stage it's healthy," I replied.

"You need to be a mother to Tyler, Kim. That's going to require you focusing on yourself for a change. We will just do our best to keep in touch with Jeff." Dad had a furrowed brow, the same one I frequently saw as a teenager.

It was true. Jeff had wanted to go, Jeff had made the decision. Now he had to live with it. But I found a way to blame myself. Maybe his primary motivation for going was because he knew I was exhausted after caring for him for two and a half years. Somehow I was succeeding at making his decision my responsibility and beating myself up about it.

Later that day our mail carrier, Tammy, rang the doorbell.

"Hi, Tammy."

"Hi, Kim, sorry to bother you."

"No, no, it's quite all right. How are you?"

"I'm great, thanks. Um, I thought you should know that the postmaster received a power of attorney from someone in Norwich, Vermont. They want Mr. Julian's mail to be forwarded to a post office box up there."

I stood there in shock, not sure of what she was talking about. "OK, wait a second. I'm the only person with durable power of attorney."

"The postmaster also thought it was strange; that's why we thought you should know. Go by the office on Monday with your documents and straighten it out, OK? He's not allowing the forwarding until he speaks with you."

"I will. Listen, thank you for taking the time to let me know."

"No problem. You take care of yourself for a change, OK?"

Everybody kept saying that, I must have looked like shit, I thought, and closed the door.

Tyler had a soccer game, so I was busy getting him prepared for that while in somewhat of a daze, not knowing what to think of this news. I decided to forget about it until later so I could enjoy my kid's soccer game.

Monday and Tuesday were spent in Springfield at Carol Jones's main office. We finished by five o'clock both days, so Mom was on after-school

Tyler duty. Both nights Mom had dinner ready when I arrived at six, and we all ate together. "Mom, are you going to be working late every night?" Tyler asked, the second night at dinner.

"Of course not, and when I am at work, I'll be just outside the gate in those offices," I said, pointing out the kitchen window. "I can drop you off and pick you up from school just like I used to. Isn't that awesome?"

"OK, good. That is awesome," he replied, smiling.

Pulling into the garage that night, my cell phone rang. My caller ID told me it was our friend Jim Howell.

"Kimberly?"

"Yes?" I replied.

"Jim Howell here,"

"Yeah, Jim, how have you been?" I was so glad to be talking to someone who was within a fifty-mile radius of Jeff.

"Listen, um, I was just over to visit with Jeff today, and, I don't know, something's not right there. He looks bad, Kim, really bad. I mean, I know he isn't going to look good, but I think you better get up here." Jim sounded like he was shaking. "I showed up there unannounced today and they told me I couldn't see him and that I had to make an appointment or some bullshit. I told them I wasn't leaving until I saw him, and they finally let me go back there. Yeah, I think you should get up here."

"I've had a bad feeling since he's been there, Jim. Thanks for letting me know," I replied.

"You're welcome, and if you want a place to stay when you come up, we have plenty of room." Jim and his wife, Karen, lived in New London, New Hampshire, just half an hour from Norwich.

"I'll take you up on that, actually. I won't be able to fly out until tomorrow, but I will call you and Karen when I'm on my way and give you a heads up," I replied.

"OK, sounds good."

I called and made flight reservations for the following morning.

I then called and made arrangements with Mom for Tyler. I lied and told my parents that Jeff's cousin Terri, whom Jeff was close to and who had been supportive of me throughout, was going to drive up from Boston to go with me. Knowing that I'd be staying with the Howells, they felt better about my visit. The next morning I got on the first flight to Hartford, with the usual connection through Dallas, then I rented a car to drive two hours north to where Jeff lay incapacitated, at the mercy of those caring for him.

# Thirty

I pulled up the gravel driveway, parked the car, and walked around the garage to the back wing of the house. I walked in the side exterior door, then through the screen door leading into the room that was long and narrow with sage green walls. Jeff was lying in his bed next to the big sunlit window. One caregiver was on the couch asleep, and another one got up and left the room at the first sight of me. Jeff looked up and, unable to smile or show much expression, lifted his brows and smiled with his eyes. I was at his side holding his hand in under ten seconds after parking the car, so, yes, he was surprised, and he wasn't the only one.

"Hi, you," I whispered, as I felt a stinging sensation in my nose, and my eyes welled up with tears. Jeff had already started telling Gus what to say. "I wanted to surprise you—I hope that's OK," I added.

He had a week's worth of stubble, and his fingernails were longer than I'd ever seen them. His face was gaunt when I'd left him the month before, but now I could see where his jaw line met the gums of his teeth. His eyes had no sparkle. He was just skin and bones. His feet and head were raised a tad. The places where his body was lowest, like the bend of his elbows, his belly, and the tops of his thighs, were terribly swollen.

Waiting for his response, I looked around the room. I didn't see the original Gus, but a large monitor with speakers was positioned at the foot of the bed, displaying the text in a much larger font. There were several medicine bottles lying all over the side table along with a clipboard holding a chart that listed all of them, and the dosages.

"How about I give you a shave and trim your nails while you type on Gus." Jeff looked up and raised his eyebrows slightly, indicating he agreed with what I was proposing. I glanced at the screen. In a matter of five minutes, he'd only typed one small sentence. The scan speed was at the lowest setting, and even then, his toe was often missing the timing of the correct letters, so he'd erase the letter and try again. One thing he had not lost was his determination.

I placed a warm washcloth on his cheeks and held it there. His eyes rolled back in his head in relief. I shaved him and trimmed his nails as he continued to type. Occasionally, he paused to look up at me, as lovingly as his eyes would allow him while his arms and hands lay lifelessly next to his legs that had become as thin as my arms. When I was finished, he looked at me with such gratitude and then started crying. He missed the way I did things, I could tell. And I missed doing all of those things for him.

"Good u r here. I gain weight, u think?" Gus said. He was referring to the swelling that was visible to him, mistaking it for actual healthy weight gain. Jeff had not gained any weight. It was only fluids building up, as his body was shutting down. It was difficult to see him this way.

Tears ran down my cheeks, "No. Jeffrey, I will not lie to you or give you false hope. You have not gained weight," I replied. Already focused on typing again, tears continued running down his cheeks. His cries at that point consisted of only tears, and silence, as his mouth would open but no sound could be produced. Even his sorrow was locked in his body. I can't accurately convey in words just how utterly fucked up it was. It was just incomprehensible.

"U look good," Gus said, and maybe it was my imagination, but I thought his mouth made a movement that, if working properly, would have produced a smile. The smile I had not seen since that day in the ICU, when he woke hooked up to life support.

"I've got to look good, I'm your wife," I said, grinning at him.

"Orientation went well. Do you like the CD I sent you?"

He had no idea what I was talking about. "?" he typed.

I turned to look for signs of the photo on the mantel. It was nowhere to be found. "Well, I've sent you a couple of letters. I thought you'd received them, but I guess not. Jeff, I'm having trouble getting in touch with you when I call."

A caregiver entered the room and relieved one that I hadn't even noticed was there.

I carefully climbed up next to him on the twin bed. His body was so small and frail, I easily fit.

"Jeffrey, did you change your power of attorney?" I asked him. I wanted to know what was going on; however, I didn't want to upset him. I wanted his last days to be peaceful, not chaotic. He wanted to go to Vermont because he wanted to find peace there. The smells, the mountains, the childhood memories of hitting golf balls over the old stone wall.

Jeff began clicking the mouse with his toe. I typically wouldn't read what he was typing because it got on his nerves when I would finish a sentence for him, so I avoided looking at the screen, waiting for Gus to speak.

After five minutes Jeff looked at me with his eyes, then at the monitor, gesturing for me to look.

"Much drama," he had typed. Then he backspaced over the text I'd just read, instead of having Gus verbalizing it over the speakers.

I was at that moment informed that he would be getting a massage and a bath from the nurses who were scheduled to be there any moment, and they wanted to feed him some dinner first and administer meds.

"A massage and a bath, sounds nice, you lucky duck. Are they the ones in charge of shaving you too?" I asked Jeff.

"N" for no, Jeff typed.

"I was going to say, if they are, they're doing a lousy job," I said, loud enough that those who actually were responsible heard me loud and clear.

Jeff looked refreshed and content when I left him that evening with plans of going back the next morning before flying out in the afternoon.

Overall I felt very uneasy with the energy in the room and the rudeness I was being subjected to. It felt as if someone there had been passing out Kool-Aid. I expressed this to the Howells that night over a glass of wine. I was so glad to have them to go home to at the end of what had been an overwhelming day. An empty hotel room would have been the perfect environment for breaking down.

That next day, I spent the morning just sitting with Jeff while two or three caregivers came and went. I looked through the clipboard and copied the name and dosage of every medication listed, and I was questioned for doing so.

Between people coming in and out of the room, I told Jeff I didn't feel good about things that were happening. I told him I didn't understand why he would willingly change his power of attorney. I would have understood if he'd done so for medical power of attorney, but he had given two people equal durable power of attorney. They had the legal authority to do anything, which wasn't exactly in our best interest, and most definitely not in my best interest. "I don't like the decisions you're making. If you're making them with a clear understanding of what they are, then fine; but I don't think you are," I told him. I was trying not to get emotional. This was about me now, and Tyler, and our future. These decisions directly affected me, even more than they affected Jeff.

"Do you really want your chair?" I asked. Again he had no idea what I was talking about. Either he was completely losing it or something was very wrong and we were both being manipulated. "I suppose you didn't request your driver's license either." I was now just upset and disgusted at the whole scene.

I asked him to let me take him back home. "I'll call Dad. I bet we could have you home as early as tonight." Several minutes later, tears still rolling down Jeff's cheeks, Gus spoke: "won't make it."

He was right, he probably wouldn't.

I would go to Vermont only twice more before Jeff's death.

# Thirty-One

I paid a visit to the postmaster at the main branch downtown and he supplied me with a copy of the power of attorney he had received. I provided him with a copy of mine, which was indeed no longer valid. Upon inspection of the POA, it was signed with an "X." It was witnessed by the same attorney that had represented Jeff's siblings against Jeff in the process of his attempt to separate his inheritance from theirs, in the form of acreage on Fox Hill.

I spoke with Dr. Stadler upon my return and expressed my concern over not being able to remain in contact with Jeff. I also made contact with the therapist from hospice who was in charge of helping the family cope.

I was officially a broker for Carol Jones and could work as much as I wanted to, but I had found it difficult to communicate at work. It was as if I'd lost the ability to articulate anything. It was so bad that I withdrew and eventually wouldn't even go to the office. I didn't yet have any clients, nor was I trying to network and gain any. I called Yakov to see about the possibility of reclaiming my role as Lady Liberty. Dancing didn't require speaking. They had recently hired a new dancer that was working out well. I was somewhat glad, as I knew deep down I was just trying to find my way back to where I was before I met Jeff. Moving backwards was not the best route; I needed to move forward, and I knew it.

My friend and mentor at Carol Jones, Jim Strong, was the highest-selling agent within the company, and his office was at the Pointe Royale branch. He could see that I was struggling and took me under his wing. "Why don't you help me out, and I'll pay you," he asked me one day. He expressed that he could use the extra help and this would keep me in the loop at work but allow me to work more independently. I accepted and started working on projects for him, some from my desk at the office and some from home.

In addition, Jeff Walster, our club pro at Pointe Royale, had a new shipment of women's apparel coming in for summer and needed someone to merchandise it for him. Jeff Walster had been nothing but generous during Jeff's illness. He would drop everything and come to the house offering his help. He asked me if I would help him out for a little extra money. Visual merchandising is one of the few things I'm really good at so I jumped at the chance.

Tyler and I were both dealing with the loss of Jeff; however, he enjoyed having his mother back, and I enjoyed being a mother again.

The end of May came and school let out for the summer. Tyler was, for some reason, reluctant to go to his father's house. Typically he'd leave a few days after school let out, but this time he told me he wasn't ready.

"I'm not ready yet, Mom. I want to stay here for a few weeks and be with my friends," he had said.

I think he just wanted some extra time to acclimate to being home with a mother who was present and focused on him for the first time in three years. Or perhaps he knew Jeff was going to die soon and wanted to be close to me when the time came. I didn't question his motives or push him to go, because I wanted him to stay.

I sat down to pay bills one afternoon and noticed the balance was rather low and realized Jeff's Social Security check had obviously not been deposited. It was normally deposited on the last Wednesday of each month. I called, and they informed me that the check had been redirected to an account in Vermont.

Having a good understanding of what was now taking place, I called our broker and sold all of our stocks—at a significant loss—then moved what remained, which was a little over $7,000, from our joint account to a new account in only my name. It was obvious someone was exercising power of attorney not just medically but financially.

At first I was angry with Jeff, who, I had momentarily forgotten, was incapacitated and on morphine. I was feeling betrayed, wondering how he could do this to me; how he could put me in this position after everything we'd been through together, and after all I had done to care for him? How could he leave and disregard me as well as Tyler? Why would he put someone in control, knowing they would not do what was best for Tyler and me? I could not believe what was happening.

Without the monthly Social Security check of $1,400, I was barely able to meet our monthly bills. We didn't have health insurance. The Social Security check basically made paying the mortgage possible. It was then evident that we were going to lose our home. I figured I had a couple of months before the bank would take it, forcing us to move out. My parents offered to help, but I refused. This was my mess; why should they lose too? I felt hopeless and hurt.

I listed the house with plans to find a condominium rental nearby. Some of the older units were affordable. Renting would mean I would have to put my dogs up for adoption. I was starting from scratch: no savings, no investments, no retirement, and very little income.

One afternoon I pulled my car into the garage, hit the opener, and looked in the rearview mirror as the doors closed behind me. I sat there crying, the engine running, my head against the steering wheel. I didn't have the strength to go on. I wanted the pain to stop, and I was ready to give up.

I reclined the seat so I could lie back on the headrest and closed my eyes. Memories of Jeff came, of the wonderful times that we'd had. We were so happy. How could something so fantastic end up like this? Why did he abandon me? I had started believing something was wrong with me. That I had done something to deserve everything that was going on. I had always tried to be a good person and always wanted everyone around me to be happy and content, oftentimes at my own expense. I was convinced that I would be better off dead. I would no longer have to feel all of the pain I had then been feeling for almost three years.

I'm not sure why, but I opened my eyes and there was little Peyton peering in at me from the glass-paned door of the mudroom. She was barely big enough to stretch up and see out, greeting me as she always did any time we pulled into the garage. She would hear us, and while she made her way to the mudroom, Tyler and I would sometimes sit there waiting, just to see her pop up. A few times I even introduced her, as if she were going to come out and perform tricks. "Presenting..." I would say, and when she finally appeared, "...Punky!" It made Tyler giggle every time.

Oh, God, Tyler, I thought.

What would he do without me? Mom and Dad would take care of him, but his dad would want him. My parents would have to fight for custody and possibly even visitation. I couldn't abandon him like some kind of coward, I thought. I felt nauseated. I reached for my cell phone and dialed Honey's work number as I hit the garage door opener again and turned the car's engine off. I knew I wasn't in my right mind. I needed protection from myself. I needed the strength to do what was best for my child, not what in the moment seemed best for me.

"Taneycomo Projects," Honey answered. I was sobbing, and it was as if she immediately knew where my head was. "Don't give up now, Kim," Honey pleaded. "Not now. You've come so far. You've almost made it through this! You're so close, Kim!"

A minister, Harry, who was a good friend of Honey's family, was visiting from India and standing a few feet away chatting with Honey's father, a strange coincidence. He was a missionary and rarely in town. The next thing I knew, Harry was on the line praying for me, with me, asking God to give me the strength and courage to carry on. God had already given me what I needed to be strong and courageous twelve years before by blessing me with Tyler. I simply needed reminding. I'm not sure how long Harry sat there on the phone with me, but I suddenly felt at peace, and I knew what I had to do.

By mid-June, Jeff had been alienated from most of his visitors. Even Toby, Jeff's father, had been banned. They at least had the decency to allow Gram to visit. Terri's mom, Jeff's Aunt Chris, had taken her to see Jeff.

In the latter part of June, a friend of Terri's who lived up North, called Terri to tell her Jeff's condition was failing considerably and he wouldn't make it through the week. He was under the impression that the present caregivers weren't planning on calling anyone, not even his wife.

I got on a flight to Boston, and the next day Terri and I drove to Vermont. She had been incredibly helpful during the last few months, keeping in touch with me and offering moral support.

# Thirty-Two

Terri and I arrived at the Residence Inn in Hanover and settled into our room. Not knowing how long I'd be there, I had purchased a one-way ticket. The shock of everything that had taken place had finally worn off, and with Terri's support and advice I had come to the conclusion that Jeff, even with a lack of coherence, would never have made the decisions that had been made. Jeff was on morphine and totally incapacitated. For all I knew, he wasn't even aware of the financial mess I had been put in. I felt foolish for doubting him.

All I had ever wanted was for Jeff's last days to be peaceful. I blamed myself for allowing him to go to Vermont in the first place. I should have put my foot down. His getting whatever he wanted should have stopped there. I should have said no, you'll stay here with me and die here with me.

Terri and I had not made our visit known to anyone. Jeff did look more groomed this time, with stubble of only a few days. He was able to click one letter or two, at which point we would try to guess what he was communicating.

I stayed at Jeff's side for two days. I read stories from the journal that I was writing in when Jeff and I first met, starting at a few days prior to going to the party with Diane and continuing to well into our courtship and marriage. Jeff lay there with his eyes closed, listening. If I paused for too long, he'd peek at me and, by the look in his eyes, tell me to keep reading. I wanted Jeff to remember how great our life was together and how lucky we were just to have found each other. I needed reminding of the same.

By the third day, tension was at an all-time high. For some reason my visit had created even more fuss than was normal among Jeff's remaining caregivers. Terri and I talked and decided a longer stay wasn't an option.

Jeff was most definitely at the end, and our presence was only causing more chaos than already existed. Jeff was at their mercy, and we knew it was best that we go before the state they were in began to affect Jeff more than it already had.

I stood on the left side of Jeff's bed, facing the big window, trying my best to maintain my composure. I wanted to be strong for him, but how could I, knowing I was saying good-bye and would probably never see him again? I had already lost him. I'd gradually lost hearing his voice, feeling his arms around me, holding his strong hands, and feeling him kiss the nape of my neck as I stood at the kitchen sink. I'd lost all of him, everything but his soul. I stood there for several minutes, looking at his frail body and the ventilator that was pushing air into his lungs and pulling air out. I needed Jeff to go, so that I could begin mourning him.

Terri came up and put her hands on my shoulders. I moved aside so she could say good-bye. Maybe I could do it if she would first. After a few minutes crying quietly, Terri leaned down and whispered something in Jeff's ear. Jeff tried to lift his brow, his way of saying "yes" or "I agree." Terri leaned down and kissed Jeff. "It's time, sister," Terri looked at me and said. It was at that moment that Terri began fulfilling the promise she had just made to Jeff, to watch over me like a sister.

I placed a hand on both sides of where Jeff's hips rested and leaned in as close as I could until I was looking right at him. Tears that I could no longer hold back ran from both of my eyes and wouldn't stop. I'd never felt such pain. I struggled to take a deep breath and finally filled my lungs with air.

"Jeffrey. Terri and I are going to leave now, so that you can go. I wish you could have stayed here with me until we were old and gray." I smiled at him. "I know that you want to go home. It's OK to go, my beloved, I will be all right. I will miss you, but I will be all right because you'll always be in my heart," I said as I lifted his lifeless hand and pressed it against my chest. "I hope you know how proud of you I am."

Still having trouble breathing, I paused until I found a deep breath. "You've been so strong and so brave in this fight. I promise you I will keep fighting and I will do everything I can to continue what we started together." Jeff's mouth was opening and tears were streaming down his face. "It's time to lay down your armor and go home, Jeffrey. Your angels are waiting for you. I promise you they're waiting for you and they'll take you home." My tears were turning to sobs, and Terri was suddenly holding on to me. I told Jeff I loved him for the last time. Feeling faint and sick, Terri and I walked out of the house holding onto one another, together experiencing the most painful part of life.

Back at home almost a month later, on July 14, I was in the pro shop working on the finishing touches of the major floor move I'd started with the new spring golf apparel when my cell phone rang. Seeing that it was Jeff's doctor, I walked into the office for privacy. "Hello?"

"Kim, I wanted you to know, I was just over to see Jeff. He's totally locked in, Kim. He was very anxious and upset. I sedated him. Per his wishes I will begin the process of removing him from the ventilator first thing in the morning."

"I don't have time to get there. It'll take me a whole day even if I can get a flight out first thing in the morning." My first thought was that I should be there.

"Jeff won't be conscious again, Kim. He's heavily sedated to keep him calm. You've been through so much, and I know you had a good visit last time and were able to say goodbye. That's the most important thing," he replied.

In all honesty I didn't really want to see Jeff removed from life support, but for some reason I felt that everyone else would think I should.

"What remains now is not something you need to witness. Jeff knows how much you love him. And he loves you, very much. Gus has told me many times." He managed to bring a smile to my face.

"OK. Thank you for calling me. You don't know how grateful I am for you. I don't know what I would've done without you," I said as I started crying.

"Let me tell you exactly what will happen to help ease your mind. Jeff will be comfortable the entire time. He will not feel any pain. He'll be asleep, and I will slowly decrease the air being provided to him by the ventilator until he naturally lets go. I will decrease the air at a rate that is determined by how his body adjusts to each decrease. Sometimes the process takes only a short time, and sometimes it takes all day; it varies. I promise you, I will call you the moment it's over." Jeff's pain was finally going to be over and I would finally be able to let him go.

I thanked Dr. Stadler and hung up just as Jeff Walster came in and saw me crying. "You OK?"

"They're taking Jeff off the vent tomorrow morning. He's going to die tomorrow."

He didn't say anything but just walked toward me and opened his arms. As strong and independent as I was trying to be, I was grateful to have a friend there to hold me.

I finished my project and then stopped at Mom and Dad's to grab Tyler before going home. He was helping Mom pick okra from the garden. I told Mom about the call from Vermont, and she told me she would make dinner and to come back over around six o'clock, so we did. It was rather quiet at the dinner table: not a bad quiet, just a peaceful quiet.

I slept surprisingly well, and the next morning I delivered Tyler to school. By nine o'clock I was cleaning the house. In anticipation of what was taking place that day, I was busying myself with anything and everything.

I had an urge to listen to Sinatra, one of Jeff's favorites, so I went to the garage where I knew I could find the disc in the car. I found the disc, used the bathroom, and placed the disc in the player before I started vacuuming. I turned the volume up loud enough to hear it over the vacuum.

While vacuuming in the living room, the dogs suddenly ran toward the mudroom wagging, just as they always did anytime one of us came in the door. I assumed it was Mom or Dad coming into the house through the garage as they often did, so I turned the vacuum off but heard no one. "Momma?" I called out, walking toward the mudroom as the dogs came barreling back out and past me; but all I found there was the basket of laundry that needed folding.

I turned and watched Max and Peyton as they frolicked through the living room and out the open door to the back porch. For a moment I had a memory of the way Jeff would walk into the house coming back from the golf course. With the dogs at his heels the whole way, so excited he was home. He'd take them out to the backyard for one-on-one playtime while I was usually in the kitchen making dinner. We were able to enjoy our home for such a short time before he got sick and started progressing; it just didn't seem fair.

"You goofy mutts," I muttered at them, and went into the kitchen for a drink of water. At the sink I noticed the message light blinking on my cell phone sitting on the counter. It was Jeff's doctor.

I reluctantly picked it up, and listened to the voice mail. "Kim, I want to let you know Jeff passed away about three minutes ago, at 10:15 a.m." I looked at the clock. It was almost 9:20 central time. I had just missed his call, probably when I was running the vacuum. "I'm on the house phone so call me back at this number. I will hold on to the phone until you call me back, or for as long as I can."

I rang the doctor back immediately. "Thank you for letting me know, and for staying by the phone," I said.

"You're welcome. Jeff passed away very peacefully. I was surprised at how easily he let go, Kim. He was definitely ready. You can find comfort in that," he said.

"Thank you for everything," I replied. I couldn't possibly express how grateful I was for all he'd done for Jeff, and for me.

"You are very welcome. I'm so sorry for your loss. Please keep in touch and let us know how you're doing."

"I will. Take care now," I said, and hung up.

I walked out on the back porch to find Peyton and Max lying on either side of the Adirondack chair that Jeff always sat in. As tears came again, I sat down in my chair, right next to Jeff's. Taking a deep breath, I noticed it came easily.

"Welcome home, Jeffrey." I felt his presence, and I knew he was finally back home where he belonged, with his family.

# Thirty-Three

As I sat next to Honey viewing the film repeatedly, I felt overwhelmed with what a beautiful friend I was blessed with. She could have been doing something more enjoyable with her time, but instead she sat with me in a recording studio editing the film that would play during what we referred to as a "Celebration of Life." Since Jeff's body was cremated in Vermont, the film provided his loved ones in Missouri a way to connect with Jeff once more and say goodbye. We reserved the big dining area at Ledgestone Country Club, Jeff's favorite local course. I asked that dessert and tea be served, just as Jeff would have wanted. The club refused to take payment for anything.

Tyler sat next to me. My brother and Melissa were there, my parents, Honey and Rick, and so many others. I decided to wear the same thing I had worn on our first date. A bit morbid, I suppose, but I was trying to prove a point to myself. Just as our first date was the beginning of something beautiful, his death signified yet another beginning. It was the end of Jeff's pain and the beginning of a life without him.

Several people went up to the podium to talk about Jeff. After the eulogies the video lasted almost ten minutes, but it didn't seem that long. Everyone loved it. It brought more laughter than tears. Just the way Jeff would have wanted.

Afterward, everything seemed so quiet.

A few days later, Tyler asked me to take him to the mall. Tim and Melissa had gone back to Atlanta, and I was doing my best to act as though life would go on. I wondered why a twelve-year-old boy would volunteer himself for a trip to the mall, but I agreed without questioning his motives. I just wanted him to be happy and free of sorrow. I drove him to the mall, and he then asked me to stay in the car and wait for him. I didn't want to go in anyway; I just wasn't in the mood to talk, and I could never go anywhere without running into ten people I knew.

Tyler came back to the car and proceeded to tell me he wanted to give me a gift but was having trouble deciding which he liked best, so he wanted me to choose the one I liked the most. "You won't be able to wear it for a while, Mom," he warned. He was so adorable and so grown up but still a baby. No child that age should have to deal with such adult issues, but so many do.

I left the safety of the car, and we went into the store together, where I selected my favorite from the ones he had picked out for me. Sterling silver with larger links and an oval plate close to the clasp. I loved it. He paid for the bracelet with money that my brother, unbeknownst to me, had given him, and then asked me to drive him to the other mall because he needed to visit a store there too. So I did. I felt so proud of his sensitivity. He asked me to stay in the car again, left the car with the bracelet he had just bought, and returned ten minutes later, empty handed. "Can you bring me back here in a few days?" He asked, with a serious tone.

"Of course I can. What are you up to?" I asked.

"It's a surprise," he replied. It ended up being the first surprise that Tyler had ever successfully kept secret long enough for it to actually be a surprise.

Two days later I drove him back to the mall. This time he returned to the car carrying a box wrapped nicely, then jumped in the car and handed it to me. He was proud of himself and too anxious to wait another moment. "Open it!" he insisted.

I opened the box to find the lovely bracelet I had chosen a few days prior. It was so beautiful, especially because I knew it was from my little man, and as I picked it up, I realized there was an inscription on the oval plate. A closer inspection revealed a message from my son. "Remember the past...," it read on one side. I turned it over to find, "To live the future" inscribed on the other side.

Remember the past to live the future. "What a beautiful, thoughtful gift. Thank you, dear one, I love it," I said, and asked for assistance with the clasp. I admired the bracelet on my wrist while Tyler watched, smiling.

I hugged him tight. It felt as if I had not seen him, really seen him, in so long. "How did you become so wise at such a young age, huh?" I teased him.

About a week later I folded the clothes from the dryer to put in the bag that would accompany Tyler to his dad's for his summer visit. Stress from the last two weeks started creeping up on me, and the thought of Tyler going was making me feel sick. I had been able to give him undivided attention for the first time in what seemed like years. I had woken from a state of chaos and confusion. It literally felt as though I'd been in a coma or some sort of trance. I needed more time with him, wanted to keep him with me, but I knew it would be best for Tyler to be away while I dealt with preparing the house to be sold and the sadness that was hiding quietly in my heart, building a case for why I should break down, not be so strong. I had to let him go spend time with his dad, and he would be back in a month if not before.

My thoughts turned to Keegan. He would have been with us by then to spend a few weeks of his summer vacation with his dad. A few weeks before Jeff's death I had decided to reach out to Keegan's grandmother, Ann. I'd never been in contact with her before but knew that Jeff had stayed in touch with her by e-mail. I reached out, and she reached back. She eventually put me in touch with her daughter, and from that point forward, we would check in on each other occasionally. Ann had suffered from emphysema for years, and not long after playing a vital role in connecting Keegan's mother and me, she passed away.

Keegan remained in my life because his mom and I began a friendship and kept in touch. She was generous and gracious enough to allow me to have a relationship with Keegan.

Tyler kissed both dogs good-bye and we piled everything into the car. As I backed out of the garage, I sensed he needed to say something. I applied the brake and looked over at him. He looked back at me with his big, blue eyes so bright with innocence. "What is it, you OK?" I asked.

"Please just don't kill yourself or anything while I'm gone, OK, Mom?" he asked.

My heart shattered. "I will never leave you," I replied, and then immediately told God that he had better back me up on that.

Later I found myself in our closet, looking at Jeff's clothes hanging there. They looked so empty and lifeless. I had never looked at them like this before. They were just clothes, one of the necessities of everyday life, but I suddenly had feelings for the clothes, the shoes on the floor, and the belts hanging there, belts that once wrapped around his waist. The tuxedo he wore to the gala we attended around our second wedding anniversary was hanging there too. His watch was on the dresser, and his golf clubs were still sitting in the garage. Everything was so quiet. Anything he had ever touched was missing something now, and looking at those things made the hole in my soul so much bigger. Void of his body, it was now unbearable to be in the same room with his clothing. I had a desire to see movement in the clothes, but they just hung there motionless.

I could feel the lack of his body all around me and began wondering if I'd always noticed the presence of him all around me when he was here to the same extent that I was now feeling his absence. I thought of all those times someone older and wiser has said to me, "Live each day as if it were your last." Wouldn't it be wonderful if we could get a true understanding of this without having to experience it firsthand? That is one thing Jeff and I did—up until the diagnosis anyway. As Jeff once said, we lived a lifetime in one year.

Our closet must have represented a headstone in a graveyard, because I kept finding myself in there just looking at his clothes and waiting for movement, until one day I went into the kitchen, retrieved several trash bags, and began removing every article of clothing, every shoe, every belt. The orange tie we had purchased while in Italy—the only one he owned. I set aside a few shirts he had worn during memorable rounds—the one he wore when he played that round with Jack, the orange polo he was wearing when he made it through Q-school in 2001—and placed them in a box that I delivered to my parents' house for safekeeping. I wasn't ready to let all of him go; that was not the point. I simply needed to be free from the obsession of waiting for something to happen. I had to make it happen.

In no time I had emptied our closet of any remnants. I had removed any reminders from our garage, and my parents provided storage for everything I wanted to keep to one day give to the children, like watches, and coins dubbed as "good luck" because he'd used them as ball markers during particularly successful rounds.

The only keepsakes missing were my share of Jeff's ashes and his wedding bands, which never arrived—I assumed because they were never sent. I had given him two rings, a platinum wedding band and a sterling silver ring I presented to him as his "engagement ring," adorned with the inscription, "Ani ledodi vedodi li," Hebrew for, "I am my beloved's and my beloved is mine." I gave it to him during our hike one morning, after a hard rain the day before had lent water to the ledges where the trail comes to an end. It was the place we normally paused for a moment of quiet, maybe even a hug, before ascending back to the top. I told him he should have to wear something indicating he was spoken for, if I did, and he loved the idea.

That night, after the purging of the clothes, I woke suddenly, finding myself sitting straight up in a panic, wondering why I didn't hear the ventilator. He's not breathing, I thought. I quickly remembered there was no ventilator and there was no Jeff. It was just me, by myself. I began wondering what my life would now hold. Would I ever be the same person I once was? I got a glimpse of her on occasion, so I knew she was still in there. What would it take to get her completely back, and would it happen in time—in time to live a happy life? I wondered how much life I had left, how much time it would take to straighten this all out, to find myself lying under a huge catalpa watching its branches flutter in the breeze with a heart that is light and free, not heavy and anchored.

Then I realized that I was already living a happy life, that there was nothing to be straightened out; that we just have to embrace life as it is, and remember the past to live the future.

Made in the USA
Lexington, KY
26 August 2011